“The Million Dead, Too, Summ’d Up”

Iowa Whitman Series
Ed Folsom, series editor

"The Million Dead, Too, Summ'd Up"

Walt Whitman's Civil War Writings

Introduction and commentary by

Ed Folsom and Christopher Merrill

University of Iowa Press • Iowa City

University of Iowa Press, Iowa City 52242

www.uipress.uiowa.edu
Printed in the United States of America

Design by Omega Clay

Printed on acid-free paper

Library of Congress Cataloging-in-Publication Data
Names: Whitman, Walt, 1819–1892, author. | Folsom, Ed, 1947– writer of added commentary. | Merrill, Christopher, writer of added commentary.
Title: "The Million Dead, Too, Summ'd Up": Walt Whitman's Civil War Writings / by Ed Folsom and Christopher Merrill. | Description: Iowa City: University of Iowa Press, [2020] | Series: Iowa Whitman Series | Includes bibliographical references and index. |
Identifiers: LCCN 2020021087 (print) | LCCN 2020021088 (ebook) | ISBN 9781609387464 (paperback; acid-free paper) | ISBN 9781609387471 (ebook) Subjects: LCSH: Whitman, Walt, 1819–1892—Diaries. | United States—History—Civil War, 1861–1865—Poetry. | United States—History—Civil War, 1861–1865—Personal narratives. | United States—History—Civil War, 1861–1865—Literature and the war. | Civil War in literature. | Whitman, Walt, 1819–1892—Criticism and interpretation.
Classification: LCC PS3204.F64 2020 (print) | LCC PS3204 (ebook) | DDC 811/.3—dc23
LC record available at https://lccn.loc.gov/2020021087
LC ebook record available at https://lccn.loc.gov/2020021088

Contents

Acknowledgments

The commentaries that appear here originated with our work preparing for and teaching *Walt Whitman and the Civil War*, a Massive Open Online Course (MOOC) organized by the International Writing Program at the University of Iowa. The authors are grateful to Blake Bronson-Bartlett, Fatima Espiritu, Jake Fournier, Haley Larson, Jeffrey Lauber, Ethan Madore, Kristina Martino, and Timothy Orme, who served as our expert teaching assistants for the MOOC, monitoring, guiding, and actively involving themselves in the 24/7 international online discussions. Lauren Haldeman and Micah Bateman were creative and tireless technical guides and a continual source of support for all aspects of the course, and Matthew Arand and Andrew Jenkins offered valuable technical support as well. Susannah Shive and Natasa Durovicova oversaw the development of the online WhitmanWeb, which contained the materials for the course. The Bureau of Educational and Cultural Affairs at the U.S. Department of State provided key financial support; we are particularly grateful to Pen Agnew, David Benze, and Jill Staggs for their determination to bring Whitman's work to a global audience. We are also indebted to the Office of the Vice President for Research and Economic Development at the University of Iowa, especially Vice President Daniel Reed and Assistant Vice President Ann Ricketts, for their encouragement and support. Finally, the authors want to thank the more than 2,500 students who enrolled in the course for their dedication and involvement: their keen insights into Whitman's Civil War writings and their participation in our online discussion forums sharpened our own understanding of Whitman's inexhaustible work.

Acknowledgments

[illegible]

Introduction • How Whitman Wrote the Civil War

During his writing career, Walt Whitman produced six very different editions of *Leaves of Grass*, three published before the American Civil War and three after. His first three editions of *Leaves of Grass* (1855, 1856, and 1860–61) were increasingly dedicated to preventing a civil war that seemed to many Americans, in the uneasy decade of the 1850s, increasingly likely. Whitman's poetic project, from the start, had been committed to nurturing and creating a union of multiple parts, a nation that would learn to celebrate its variety and find growing strength in its diversity, a nation that would be proud to absorb its contradictory parts. The term "United States" was for him an almost mystical concept: each democratic citizen, after all, is an individual composed of many "states" of being and "states" of mind—we are all composites of those we have descended from, of those we have met during our lifetimes and come to know as "friends" or "enemies" or "family"; we are, as Whitman famously said, "large . . . [and] contain multitudes"—each of us experiencing joy and sorrow, attraction and repulsion, anger and love. Whitman was always imagining himself (and all democratic beings) as a single being of endlessly diverse (and equal) parts. As he wrote in his long 1855 poem that he eventually titled "Song of Myself": "Welcome is every organ and attribute of me, and of any man hearty and clean, / Not an inch nor a particle of an inch is vile, and none shall be less familiar than the rest":

I am of old and young, of the foolish as much as the wise,
Regardless of others, ever regardful of others,
Maternal as well as paternal, a child as well as a man,
Stuff'd with the stuff that is coarse and stuff'd with the stuff that is fine,
One of the Nation of many nations, the smallest the same and the largest the
    same,
A Southerner soon as a Northerner,
. . .
Of every hue and caste am I, of every rank and religion,
A farmer, mechanic, artist, gentleman, sailor, quaker,
Prisoner, fancy-man, rowdy, lawyer, physician, priest.

I resist any thing better than my own diversity,
Breathe the air but leave plenty after me,
And am not stuck up, and am in my place.

How, then, did Whitman deal with the failure of the American experiment that he had celebrated in the those first three editions of *Leaves of Grass*? How did he deal with a nation that ultimately could *not* maintain a union of its diverse parts? Soon after the 1860 *Leaves* appeared, South Carolina seceded from the Union, and a cascade of events began with the Confederate attack on Fort Sumter, leading to the four-year carnage of the Civil War, which caused more combat deaths than the combined total of all previous and subsequent American wars. This unprecedented fratricidal mass death demanded new forms of witnessing. Whitman's literary response to those events, in poetry and prose, is what Christopher Merrill and I set out to explore in the following pages. What Whitman described in his war poems in *Drum-Taps* and in the prose sketches included in *Memoranda During the War* offers us a darker, more nuanced understanding of his lifelong project, which was nothing less than to write the poem of these United States. "The proof of a poet," he wrote in the preface to the 1855 edition of *Leaves of Grass*, "is that his country absorbs him as affectionately as he has absorbed it." After the rupture of the War Between the States, there was an abundance of tragic material and shed blood to absorb, and Whitman, beginning in 1861, did just that.

The Civil War shattered the very principles that Whitman's book had been based on. If the United States could not remain united and instead broke in two in violent conflict, then *Leaves* itself seemed a lie, its faith in unity-in-diversity exposed as a sham. During the war, Whitman abandoned *Leaves of Grass* and began working on a new book that he would call *Drum-Taps*, a book responding directly to the conflict. In that book, eventually published just after the war ended, he worried about just how radically his poetry had to shift in tone and subject after the United States came apart at the Northern/Southern seam: "Must I change my triumphant songs? said I to myself; / Must I indeed learn to chant the cold dirges of the baffled? / And sullen hymns of defeat?"

After the war was over, however, as the shattered nation began the painful and fraught process of reconstructing and reuniting itself, Whitman decided to resume his *Leaves of Grass* project and to test just how resilient his notion of a country built on diversity could be. Initially, *Drum-Taps* seemed to him an entirely different project from *Leaves*; his all-encompassing "I" of the earlier book, an "I" that seemingly could absorb everyone in the country or perhaps even the world, was now broken into multiple personae, many of them soldiers that he talked to as he made his daily visits to the Civil War hospitals scattered throughout the nation's capital. Much of Whitman's postwar revision and expansion of *Leaves* involved his decision to open *Leaves* to the Civil War. When he compiled the 1867 edition of *Leaves,* he had the remaining unbound copies of *Drum-Taps* sewn into the book, and the table of contents listed it with separate pagination, as if its inclusion were an act of bibliographic suturing, of making a first effort to heal the violence by acknowledging that the four years of national fratricide were now forever a vital part of the country's identity and had to be contained in the book that probed how an American democratic identity could still be formed out of the mass death it had experienced. For the final two editions of *Leaves,* appearing at the beginning of the 1870s and the beginning of the 1880s, Whitman worked to bleed his Civil War poems into the very fabric of *Leaves,* forming them into new "clusters" within the book and scattering some of the war poems throughout (and revising other poems to include references to the war). By the end of his life, Whitman could not imagine *Leaves of Grass* without the Civil War at the very heart of it: "Without those three or four years and the experiences they gave, 'Leaves of Grass' would not now be existing," he wrote in "A Backward Glance o'er Travel'd Roads," acknowledging that, although he had "made a start" on *Leaves* before the war, it was "only from the strong flare and provocation of that war's sights and scenes [that] the final reasons-for-being of an autochthonic and passionate song definitely came forth."

* * *

In this book, Christopher Merrill and I have set out to take readers back to the actual period of the war, when Whitman was first experiencing the horrific results of battle and was learning how to write his war experiences. His experiences led him to view the war not as battlefield-centered but as hospital-centered: "America," he wrote, has been "brought to Hospital in her fair youth," and he would demonstrate the power of viewing the war from the vantage point of those places of death and amputation. We examine his war writings as they appeared during those years when he had abandoned *Leaves of Grass* as the new song of democratic unity, when he was reeling from day to day from the endless streams of mutilated soldiers that were being hauled to the Washington, D.C., hospitals that he made it his habit to visit virtually every day after he relocated to the nation's capital at the beginning of 1863. And, while we present and examine in this book many poems from *Drum-Taps* and its follow-up pamphlet *Sequel to Drum-Taps,* we also include Whitman's wartime prose and read it with the same kind of care we devote to the poetry. All of Whitman's Civil War texts in this volume are printed just as he published them in the original editions of his work, instead of in their more familiar later revisions, so that we can examine the work as it was forged directly from the cauldron of his war experiences. When Whitman later revised his Civil War works, he sometimes added or changed the titles; to help readers identify these passages, we occasionally refer to his more familiar final titles.

* * *

We think of Walt Whitman as a poet, and certainly he is best known for his lifelong work of poetry, *Leaves of Grass.* And yet he wrote far more prose during his life than poetry. He was a journalist before turning to poetry, and he in fact continued publishing journalism his whole life, along with essays on a wide range of topics—from Shakespeare's works, to the nature (and importance) of slang, to the "democratic vistas" of America's future—and an autobiography, titled *Specimen Days.* He also wrote a prose book about his experiences during the Civil War, much of it gathered from his wartime notebooks and from his wartime journalism published in newspapers like the *New York Times.* The resultant book—a kind of collage of informal notebook entries and more formal newspaper articles—was published in a very limited edition in 1875–76 as *Memoranda During the War.* Whitman ultimately simply included *Memoranda,* in a revised form, in his autobiography, which was much more widely distributed and better known, and so this is where most readers today encounter the material. Whitman, however, soon after publishing *Memoranda* as a separate book, included it in his little-known book titled *Two Rivulets* (1875–76), which was itself a kind of experiment in exploring the boundaries between poetry and prose. *Two Rivulets* begins with a typographical and stylistic experiment that positions both poetry and prose on each page—"two rivulets" of words running next to each other, the poetry at the top and the prose at the bottom, with an implicit challenge to the reader to decide just how one is supposed to deal with this unexpected and unsettling juxtaposition.

Whitman experimented throughout his whole career with this kind of melding of prose and poetry. The first edition of *Leaves* opens with a long prose preface before breaking into poetry, and both his poetry and prose in that volume challenge typographical conventions by discarding normal punctuation and instead using ellipses of various numbers of dots to pace the reading of both genres in identical ways. The final "deathbed" edition of *Leaves* concludes with a long prose essay where Whitman takes a "backward glance" over his writing career. Throughout his career, then, but especially during the Civil War, Whitman juxtaposed poetry and prose and moved back and forth between them daily. His prose influenced his poetry, just as his poetry influenced his prose. He sometimes repurposed language he originally wrote in prose for use in his poetry, and vice versa.

Here, for example, are three different descriptions of Whitman's experiences caring for wounded and dying soldiers in the Washington, D.C., Civil War hospitals. Each is in a different genre. The first, a passage from *Memoranda During the War,* is written in Whitman's distinctive prose nonfiction voice:

In one of the Hospitals I find Thomas Haley, Co. M, Fourth New York Cavalry—a regular Irish boy, a fine specimen of youthful physical manliness—shot through the lungs—inevitably dying—came over to this country from Ireland to enlist—has not a single friend or acquaintance here—is sleeping soundly at this moment, (but it is the sleep of death)—has a bullet-hole straight through the lung.......I saw Tom when first brought here, three days since, and didn't suppose he could live twelve hours—(yet he looks well enough in the face to a casual observer.) He lies there with his frame exposed above the waist, all naked, for coolness, a fine built man, the tan not yet bleach'd from his cheeks and neck. It is useless to talk to him, as with his sad hurt, and the stimulants they give him, and the utter strangeness of every object, face, furniture, &c., the poor fellow, even when awake, is like a frighten'd, shy animal. Much of the time he sleeps, or half sleeps. (Sometimes I thought he knew more than he show'd.) I often come and sit by him in perfect silence; he will breathe for ten minutes as softly and evenly as a young babe asleep. Poor youth, so handsome, athletic, with profuse beautiful shining hair. One time as I sat looking at him while he lay asleep, he suddenly, without the least start, awaken'd, open'd his eyes, gave me a long, long steady look, turning his face very slightly to gaze easier—one long, clear silent look—a slight sigh—then turn'd back and went into his doze again. Little he knew, poor death-stricken boy, the heart of the stranger that hover'd near.

Here is another hospital scene as Whitman described it in a letter to his mother:

One poor boy (this is a sample of one case out of the 600) he seemed to me quite young, he was quite small, (I looked at his body afterwards)—he groaned some as the stretcher-bearers were carrying him along—& again as they carried him through the hospital gate, they set down the stretcher & examined him, & the poor boy was dead—they took him into the ward, & the doctor came immediately, but it was all of no use—the worst of it is too that he is entirely unknown—there was nothing on his clothes, or any one with him, to identify him—& he is altogether unknown—Mother, it is enough to rack one's heart, such things—very likely his folks will never know in the world what has become of him—poor poor child, for he appeared as though he could be but 18—

Finally, here is a similar scene, this time in poetry, from his 1865 *Drum-Taps*:

The crush'd head I dress, (poor crazed hand, tear not the bandage away;)
The neck of the cavalry-man, with the bullet through and through, I examine;
Hard the breathing rattles, quite glazed already the eye, yet life struggles hard;
Come, sweet death! be persuaded, O beautiful death!
In mercy come quickly.)

From the stump of the arm, the amputated hand,
I undo the clotted lint, remove the slough, wash off the matter and blood;
Back on his pillow the soldier bends, with curv'd neck, and side-falling head;
His eyes are closed, his face is pale, he dares not look on the bloody stump,
And has not yet looked on it.

I dress a wound in the side, deep, deep;
But a day or two more—for see, the frame all wasted and sinking,
And the yellow-blue countenance see.

I dress the perforated shoulder, the foot with the bullet wound,
Cleanse the one with a gnawing and putrid gangrene, so sickening, so offensive,
While the attendant stands behind aside me, holding the tray and pail.

I am faithful, I do not give out;
The fractur'd thigh, the knee, the wound in the abdomen,
These and more I dress with impassive hand—(yet deep in my breast a fire, a
    burning flame.)

Which of these passages is most affecting? Which best captures the immediacy of the experience? Which piece(s) of writing influenced the other(s)? Do Whitman's distinctive parenthetical statements have a different effect in poetry than they do in prose? Every reader will have a different set of responses and reactions to these passages, and each reader will discover distinct ways to talk about the differences between the passages and about just how much those differences are the result of the genres in which they appear. Merrill and I have chosen to arrange our selections in such a way that the mix of genres is highlighted. Merrill is himself a poet and a nonfiction prose writer who has also published experiments in correspondence with other writers; I have taught Whitman's poetry and prose for a number of decades, and I'm currently editing his correspondence for the *Walt Whitman Archive*, so both of us have a particular interest in examining the remarkably wide and diverse range of Whitman's war writings and thinking about the ways the poetry, nonfiction, and correspondence nurture each other.

* * *

When Christopher Merrill and I decided in 2016 to offer a massive open online course (MOOC) focusing on Whitman's Civil War writings, students from around the world enrolled and joined us for the journey, reading Whitman's work and writing their own responses to the issues that his war writings raised. War was the subject, but, as we moved through the course, peace and reconciliation gradually became key themes as well, and they revealed themselves to be just as challenging as war to write about. The works in this book are arranged in a roughly chronological order, though we begin at the end, with Whitman's remarkable one-sentence attempt to sum up and summon up the "million dead" in the war. Then we go back to Whitman's 1855 *Leaves* to see what he had to say about war before he had experienced it himself. We work through his pro-war writings as the Civil War broke out, then follow him to the Fredericksburg, Virginia, battlefield where he had traveled to find his wounded soldier-brother George, then to his extended residence in Washington, D.C., where he worked as a government clerk by day and spent his evenings and often long nights in the capital's many makeshift hospitals, talking to and comforting wounded, sick, and dying soldiers. We follow him a little beyond the war, as he offers some troubling thoughts on the new challenges of building a biracial reconstructed nation, and we end by examining Whitman's own questioning about whether *anyone* could capture the war in words: "The real war," he concluded, "will never get in the books."

Over the years, there have been numerous critical and biographical works that deal with Whitman's Civil War writings, though not as many as we might expect, since most critics have argued that the Civil War period marked the beginning of a decline in the power and originality of Whitman's poetry. That view, however, has recently begun to be challenged, and the bibliography at the back of this book tracks the shift in perceptions, pointing to some of the most significant work on Whitman and the war. But Whitman's Civil War poems seldom have received sustained and detailed readings, nor have his Civil War prose works. Christopher Merrill and I have set out to accomplish just that.

What follows, then, are forty selections from Whitman's war poetry, prose, and correspondence, each followed by my detailed critical commentary, then a writer's response by Merrill. My critical responses emerge from decades of reading, reading about, and teaching these works; Merrill's afterwords are impressions written after rereading each section, often while on the road in various locales around the world as the director of the University of Iowa's International Writing Program, and often accompanied by memories of his own experiences in countries ravaged by their own civil wars: he reported from Sarajevo, Bosnia and Herzegovina, during the siege of that city in the Yugoslav wars, and he has recently traveled extensively in Afghanistan and Iraq. My commentaries tend to closely examine the language of each selection, while Merrill's often radiate out from the piece to view it in an international context or to examine it in relation to other poets who have in fascinating ways responded to Whitman's language. As was the case with Merrill's and my previous collaboration, a dual commentary on Whitman's "Song of Myself," our commentaries here are intended to evoke (and provoke) a reader's (*your*) active response, to invite a reading of each work and then to encourage a deeper and richer rereading after encountering the commentaries. Whitman was in some sense the inventor of "reader response" criticism, the poet who first articulated how one major challenge to the creation of a democratic society was the need to change the nation's reading habits, to move the country from a citizenry that accepted "authors" as "authorities" (the word itself has in its etymological roots the sense of "leader" or "master") to a populace that instead wrestled with writers on equal terms. The "process of reading," Whitman wrote in *Democratic Vistas* (1871), is "an exercise, a gymnast's struggle," and the democratic reader "must himself or herself construct indeed the poem, argument, history, metaphysical essay—the text furnishing the hints, the clue, the start or frame-work," because what is needed for democracy to flourish is "a nation of supple and athletic minds." This book is dedicated to more supple and athletic readers of one of America's greatest and most challenging writers, writing during one of America's darkest and most challenging times. As Christopher Merrill and I finish this book, in the summer of 2020, the nation is going through another dark and challenging period. It is a perfect time, then, to engage in a "gymnast's struggle" with Whitman's Civil War work, to discover if we—like him—can wrest a future out of a period of major civil unrest and mass death.

Ed Folsom
Iowa City, Iowa

1

"The Million Dead, Too, Summ'd Up — The Unknown"

The Million Dead, too, summ'd up—The Unknown.—The Dead in this War—there they lie, strewing the fields and woods and valleys and battle-fields of the South —Virginia, the Peninsula—Malvern Hill and Fair Oaks—the banks of the Chickahominy—the terraces of Fredericksburgh—Antietam bridge—the grisly ravines of Manassas—the bloody promenade of the Wilderness—the varieties of the *strayed* dead, (the estimate of the War Department is 25,000 National soldiers kill'd in battle and never buried at all, 5,000 drown'd—15,000 inhumed by strangers or on the march in haste, in hitherto unfound localities—2,000 graves cover'd by sand and mud, by Mississippi freshets, 3,000 carried away by caving-in of banks, &c.,)—Gettysburgh, the West, Southwest—Vicksburg—Chattanooga—the trenches of Petersburgh—the numberless battles, camps, Hospitals everywhere—the crop reap'd by the mighty reapers, Typhoid, Dysentery, Inflammations—and blackest and loathesomest of all, the dead and living burial-pits, the Prison-Pens of Andersonville, Salisbury, Belle-Isle, &c., (not Dante's pictured Hell and all its woes, its degradations, filthy torments, excell'd those Prisons)—the dead, the dead, the dead—our dead—or South or North, ours all, (all, all, all, finally dear to me)—or East or West—Atlantic Coast or Mississippi Valley—Some where they crawl'd to die, alone, in bushes, low gulleys, or on the sides of hills—(there, in secluded spots, their skeletons, bleach'd bones, tufts of hair, buttons, fragments of clothing, are occasionally found, yet)—our young men once so handsome and so joyous, taken from us—the son from the mother, the husband from the wife, the dear friend from the dear friend—the clusters of camp graves, in Georgia, the Carolinas, and in Tennessee—the single graves in the woods or by the road-side, (hundreds, thousands, obliterated)—the corpses floated down the rivers, and caught and lodged, (dozens, scores, floated down the Upper Potomac, after the cavalry engagements, the pursuit of Lee, following Gettysburgh)—some lie at the bottom of the sea—the general Million, and the special Cemeteries in almost all the States—the Infinite Dead—(the land entire is saturated, perfumed with their impalpable ashes' exhalation in Nature's chemistry distill'd, and shall be so forever, and every grain of wheat and ear of corn, and every flower that grows, and every breath we draw,)—not only Northern dead leavening Southern soil—thousands, aye many tens of thousands, of Southerners, crumble to-day in Northern earth.

And everywhere among these countless graves—everywhere in the many Soldiers Cemeteries of the Nation, (there are over seventy of them)—as at the time in the vast trenches, the depositories of slain, Northern and Southern, after the great battles—not only where the scathing trail pass'd those years, but radiating since in all the peaceful quarters of the land—we see, and see, and ages yet may see, on monuments and gravestones, singly or in masses, to thousands or tens of thousands, the significant word

UNKNOWN.

(In some of the Cemeteries nearly all the dead are Unknown. At Salisbury, N. C., for instance, the known are only 85, while the Unknown are 12,027, and 11,700 of these are buried in trenches. A National Monument has been put up here, by order of Congress, to mark the spot—but what visible, material monument can ever fittingly commemorate that spot?)

As I write this conclusion—in the open air, latter part of June, 1875, a delicious forenoon, everything rich and fresh from last night's copious rain—ten years and more have pass'd away since that War, and its wholesale deaths, burials, graves. (*They* make indeed the true Memoranda of the War—mute, subtle, immortal.) From ten years' rain and snow, in their seasons—grass, clover, pine trees, orchards, forests—from all the noiseless miracles of soil and sun and running streams—how peaceful and how beautiful appear to-day even the Battle-Trenches, and the many hundred thousand Cemetery mounds! Even at Andersonville, to-day, innocence and a smile. (A late account says, "The stockade has fallen to decay, is grown upon, and a season more will efface it entirely, except from our hearts and memories. The *dead line*, over which so many brave soldiers pass'd to the freedom of eternity rather than endure the misery of life, can only be traced here and there, for most of the old marks the last ten years have obliterated. The thirty-five wells, which the prisoners dug with cups and spoons, remain just as they were left. And the wonderful spring which was discover'd one morning, after a thunder storm, flowing down the hillside, still yields its sweet, pure water as freely now as then. The Cemetery, with its thirteen thousand graves, is on the slope of a beautiful hill. Over the quiet spot already trees give the cool shade which would have been so gratefully sought by the poor fellows whose lives were ended under the scorching sun.")

And now, to thought of these—on these graves of the dead of the War, as on an altar—to memory of these, or North or South, I close and dedicate my book.

Folsom Commentary

Let's begin our examination of Whitman's war writings at the end—the end of the Civil War and the end of Walt Whitman's book of prose recollections called *Memoranda During the War,* where he writes the longest sentence he would ever compose. It was a sentence so vast that he initially wrote it out as a poem, using his long catalog-lines to tally the dead. Instead of using those long lines to absorb an ameliorative, evolving, progressive, expanding self and nation and cosmos into his affirmative song, as he had done in his prewar editions of *Leaves of Grass,* he now catalogs mass death. We can find pieces of this catalog throughout Whitman's wartime poetry, but perhaps never so effectively as in this sentence, where he invented a syntax of mass death, an undiagrammable utterance that wanders the ruined nation to gather up "the infinite dead," pausing again and again to absorb the horror, the details, the unimaginable numbers of dead young men whose bodies eluded the grave and were composted back into the landscape itself. The sentence buries seven parenthetical insertions among its thirty-some dashes, creating a jagged syntactical field sliced with phrasal trenches. And this astonishing catalog of a sentence ends up, after its nearly four hundred words, being a sentence *fragment.* There is no way, Whitman discovered, to predicate *this* subject: "The dead in this war." These numberless dead are of course beyond animation, themselves now fragments of bodies, amputated selves, irretrievable, that have so "saturated" America's land that we the living are now all fated to reap forevermore a harvest of death, with blood in every grain we eat.

Whitman titled this section of his *Memoranda* "The Million Dead, Too, Summ'd Up," using his characteristic contraction-apostrophe, which here creates a haunting ambiguity, because the sentence with all its embedded statistics, its death-data, does give us the Civil War dead *summed up,* but the contraction also invites us to fill in a few more missing letters, as we realize this death sentence literally summons up the dead, reminding us of their actual physical presence throughout the landscape, north and south, and insisting on their physical emergence in everything that grows from the soil they dissolved into. It's the million dead *summoned* up. (Whitman is reminding us here of the opening words of *Memoranda,* where he tells of the technique he has used to write his book: "Each line, each scrawl, each memorandum, has its history.... Out of them arise active and breathing forms. They *summon up,* even in this silent and vacant room as I write, not only the sinewy regiments and brigades, marching or in camp, but the countless phantoms of those who fell and were hastily buried....") Whitman's catalog, then, is a summing and a summoning, and the summons is not just *of* the dead but also *of* the living, who are being summoned to witness this mass death and, grotesque as it may seem, *ingest* it, live off it, make a future out of it.

The apostrophe in "summ'd" is a slippery one, where one missing letter suddenly morphs into three missing letters: once the absence begins to take away what should be there, the absence seems to demand a right to more. That *three*-letter absence, we suddenly realize, turns out to form the word "one" ("summ[one]d"). This elided and silenced "one" is precisely what has been lost in Whitman's relentless summing up of the dead, where individual identity is subsumed by mass anonymity: "we see . . . on monuments and gravestones, singly or in masses, to thousands or tens of thousands, the significant word *Unknown*." Whatever summoning up of the dead the chemistry of nature may now do, what the wheat and flowers will never produce in their composting magic, is the *one* who is lost, the one with a name and identity that is compounded into the "infinite dead"—an infinity of elided "ones." We can sum up the ones into the million, but we can never summon up any *one* of the million. This is the loss that Whitman now has to confront in his postwar writing as he tries to reconstruct a nation.

Merrill Commentary

The root meaning of "memorandum" is to be remembered. It may take the form of a short note, a record or written statement, a diplomatic communication, a summary of the terms of a transaction, or a page in a publication honoring the memory of someone who has died. Whitman's *Memoranda During the War* employs all of these ways of remembering, and its final entry, "The Million Dead, Too, Summ'd Up—The Unknown," is a long sentence fragment that bears witness to the scale of the carnage caused by the Civil War, the blood-stained horror of the battlefields in Gettysburg, Vicksburg, Chattanooga, Petersburg, Antietam, Manassas, the Wilderness, and beyond, the stench of field camps and hospitals, the piles of amputated limbs, the men dying of typhoid and dysentery, the silence of the burial pits—"the dead, the dead, the dead—our dead—or North or South, ours all, (all, all, all, finally dear to me)"—all leading to military cemeteries and countless graves bearing "the significant word: *UNKNOWN*." For in the face of the greatest American tragedy, the effects of which still shape our body politic and bearing in the world, Whitman summons the dead lying in the earth, not to name them, since that is impossible, but to honor them, remembering the role they played in the conflict that will forever mark this soil, this nation.

His brother's name on a casualty list from Fredericksburg, in December 1862, was what inspired Whitman to travel to Falmouth, Virginia, to find him. Relieved to learn that his brother's wound to the cheek was slight, Whitman discovered in the Army of the Potomac's winter camp that he had entered a new world of "deep things," as he wrote to Ralph Waldo Emerson, "unrecked by current print or speech." Accordingly, he began to take notes, "memoranda of names, items, &c," in order to remember what he was seeing and experiencing. "This thing I will record—it belongs to the time, and to all the States—(and perhaps it belongs to me.)" From the camp he moved to Washington, D.C., where in the coming years he would spend his free time ministering to the wounded and the dying—writing letters for the young men, bringing them gifts, holding their hands, giving them a last kiss, staying with them until the end.

Much else remained unknown during the war: how Whitman would reconcile his prewar anthem to possibility, "Song of Myself," with the anonymity of mass death; how the Emancipation Proclamation would alter the American experiment in liberty; how to come to terms with Lincoln's assassination—a man the poet was accustomed to seeing on his daily rounds about the city; how to reconstruct his own soul and the soul of his nation. From forty notebooks Whitman filled in the hospitals or after work at the Bureau of Indian Affairs he fashioned "a special history of those years," which culminates in this hymn to the unknown: the compass for his darker, and deeper, journey into the heart of this vast, unknowable country.

2

"Song of Myself," Sections 33–37

33

. . . I am the hounded slave, I wince at the bite of the dogs,
Hell and despair are upon me, crack and again crack the marksmen,
I clutch the rails of the fence, my gore dribs, thinn'd with the ooze of my skin,
I fall on the weeds and stones,
The riders spur their unwilling horses, haul close,
Taunt my dizzy ears and beat me violently over the head with whip-stocks.

Agonies are one of my changes of garments,
I do not ask the wounded person how he feels, I myself become the wounded person,
My hurts turn livid upon me as I lean on a cane and observe.

I am the mash'd fireman with breast-bone broken,
Tumbling walls buried me in their debris,
Heat and smoke I inspired, I heard the yelling shouts of my comrades,
I heard the distant click of their picks and shovels,
They have clear'd the beams away, they tenderly lift me forth.

I lie in the night air in my red shirt, the pervading hush is for my sake,
Painless after all I lie exhausted but not so unhappy,
White and beautiful are the faces around me, the heads are bared of their fire-caps,
The kneeling crowd fades with the light of the torches.

Distant and dead resuscitate,
They show as the dial or move as the hands of me, I am the clock myself.

I am an old artillerist, I tell of my fort's bombardment,
I am there again.

Again the long roll of the drummers,

Again the attacking cannon, mortars,
Again to my listening ears the cannon responsive.

I take part, I see and hear the whole,
The cries, curses, roar, the plaudits for well-aim'd shots,
The ambulanza slowly passing trailing its red drip,
Workmen searching after damages, making indispensable repairs,
The fall of grenades through the rent roof, the fan-shaped explosion,
The whizz of limbs, heads, stone, wood, iron, high in the air.

Again gurgles the mouth of my dying general, he furiously waves with his hand,
He gasps through the clot *Mind not me—mind—the entrenchments.*

34

Now I tell what I knew in Texas in my early youth,
(I tell not the fall of Alamo,
Not one escaped to tell the fall of Alamo,
The hundred and fifty are dumb yet at Alamo,)
'Tis the tale of the murder in cold blood of four hundred and twelve young men.

Retreating they had form'd in a hollow square with their baggage for breastworks,
Nine hundred lives out of the surrounding enemy's, nine times their number, was
    the price they took in advance,
Their colonel was wounded and their ammunition gone,
They treated for an honorable capitulation, receiv'd writing and
    seal, gave up their arms and march'd back prisoners of war.

They were the glory of the race of rangers,
Matchless with horse, rifle, song, supper, courtship,
Large, turbulent, generous, handsome, proud, and affectionate,
Bearded, sunburnt, drest in the free costume of hunters,
Not a single one over thirty years of age.

The second First-day morning they were brought out in squads
    and massacred, it was beautiful early summer,
The work commenced about five o'clock and was over by eight.

None obey'd the command to kneel,
Some made a mad and helpless rush, some stood stark and straight,

A few fell at once, shot in the temple or heart, the living and dead lay together,
The maim'd and mangled dug in the dirt, the new-comers saw them there,
Some half-kill'd attempted to crawl away,
These were despatch'd with bayonets or batter'd with the blunts of muskets,
A youth not seventeen years old seiz'd his assassin till two more came to release him,
The three were all torn and cover'd with the boy's blood.

At eleven o'clock began the burning of the bodies;
That is the tale of the murder of the four hundred and twelve young men.

35

Would you hear of an old-time sea-fight?
Would you learn who won by the light of the moon and stars?
List to the yarn, as my grandmother's father the sailor told it to me.

Our foe was no skulk in his ship I tell you, (said he,)
His was the surly English pluck, and there is no tougher or truer,
    and never was, and never will be;
Along the lower'd eve he came horribly raking us.

We closed with him, the yards entangled, the cannon touch'd,
My captain lash'd fast with his own hands.

We had receiv'd some eighteen pound shots under the water,
On our lower-gun-deck two large pieces had burst at the first fire,
    killing all around and blowing up overhead.

Fighting at sun-down, fighting at dark,
Ten o'clock at night, the full moon well up, our leaks on the gain,
    and five feet of water reported,
The master-at-arms loosing the prisoners confined in the after-hold
    to give them a chance for themselves.

The transit to and from the magazine is now stopt by the sentinels,
They see so many strange faces they do not know whom to trust.

Our frigate takes fire,
The other asks if we demand quarter?
If our colors are struck and the fighting done?

Now I laugh content, for I hear the voice of my little captain,
We have not struck, he composedly cries, *we have just begun our part of the fighting.*

Only three guns are in use,
One is directed by the captain himself against the enemy's main-mast,
Two well serv'd with grape and canister silence his musketry and clear his decks.

The tops alone second the fire of this little battery, especially the main-top,
They hold out bravely during the whole of the action.

Not a moment's cease,
The leaks gain fast on the pumps, the fire eats toward the powder-magazine.

One of the pumps has been shot away, it is generally thought we are sinking.

Serene stands the little captain,
He is not hurried, his voice is neither high nor low,
His eyes give more light to us than our battle-lanterns.

Toward twelve there in the beams of the moon they surrender to us.

36

Stretch'd and still lies the midnight,
Two great hulls motionless on the breast of the darkness,
Our vessel riddled and slowly sinking, preparations to pass to the
 one we have conquer'd,
The captain on the quarter-deck coldly giving his orders through
 a countenance white as a sheet,
Near by the corpse of the child that serv'd in the cabin,
The dead face of an old salt with long white hair and carefully curl'd whiskers,
The flames spite of all that can be done flickering aloft and below,
The husky voices of the two or three officers yet fit for duty,
Formless stacks of bodies and bodies by themselves, dabs of flesh
 upon the masts and spars,
Cut of cordage, dangle of rigging, slight shock of the soothe of waves,
Black and impassive guns, litter of powder-parcels, strong scent,
A few large stars overhead, silent and mournful shining,
Delicate sniffs of sea-breeze, smells of sedgy grass and fields by the
 shore, death-messages given in charge to survivors,

The hiss of the surgeon's knife, the gnawing teeth of his saw,
Wheeze, cluck, swash of falling blood, short wild scream, and long,
dull, tapering groan,
These so, these irretrievable.

37

You laggards there on guard! look to your arms!
In at the conquer'd doors they crowd! I am possess'd!
Embody all presences outlaw'd or suffering,
See myself in prison shaped like another man,
And feel the dull unintermitted pain.

For me the keepers of convicts shoulder their carbines and keep watch,
It is I let out in the morning and barr'd at night.

Not a mutineer walks handcuff'd to jail but I am handcuff'd to
him and walk by his side,
(I am less the jolly one there, and more the silent one with sweat
on my twitching lips.)

Not a youngster is taken for larceny but I go up too, and am tried
and sentenced.
Not a cholera patient lies at the last gasp but I also lie at the last gasp,
My face is ash-color'd, my sinews gnarl, away from me people retreat.

Askers embody themselves in me and I am embodied in them,
I project my hat, sit shame-faced, and beg.

Folsom Commentary

We began our journey through Whitman's Civil War writings at the end, with Whitman's extended and literal "death sentence," a summing and a summoning of the hundreds of thousands who died in America's Civil War. Now we go back before the war, to Whitman's 1855 poem eventually titled "Song of Myself," a poem that celebrates an expansive, absorptive, unified self—a person and a nation that can contain contradictions and still remain united. The Civil War would explode this dream of unity-in-diversity, and Whitman would spend the rest of his life dealing with the shattering aftereffects of what he often thought of as the "War to Preserve the Union."

It is instructive, then, to return to "Song of Myself," where we discover that years before the Civil War, he was already cataloging the dead from America's earlier wars. In sections 33 through 36 of the poem, Whitman confronts and absorbs the Revolutionary War and the Mexican War, the two wars that at the time loomed largest in Whitman's imagination and in his own experience (he lived for three months in New Orleans just as the Mexican War ended, and he talked to many returning soldiers). Toward the end of his long catalog in section 33, death and suffering and pain begin to take over, as the soul of the speaker of "Song of Myself" enters into the torture felt by those suffering and near death: "Agonies are one of my changes of garments," the poet says: "I do not ask the wounded person how he feels, I myself become the wounded person." This section of "Song," which began with such a buoyant embrace of the ever-changing world, ends with the stuttered beginnings of dark narratives of death, pain, and loss. And Whitman's "I" absorbs the hatred and factionalism of war.

War is by definition about division. What one side in a war calls aggression and hatred and evil, of course, the other side sees as justice and valor and heroism: one side's "massacre" is the other side's just response to what it sees as its enemy's brutality. The inescapable reality of war is that "young men" (and, increasingly, women) on both sides are maimed and murdered, and that their sacred bodies—the sensory apparatus of living souls—are reduced to ash.

Section 34 is a historical recollection of a mass death in one of the battles over Texas independence that led to the Mexican War. The emphasis here is not on the winners and losers, but on physical loss, the loss of physicality itself, as war takes its inevitable toll on the bodies of those who have been convinced or coerced to fight. In sections 35 and 36, the narratives of war continue, now telling of the Revolutionary War sea battle off the British coast between John Paul Jones's *Bon Homme Richard* and the British ship *Serapis*: both the British and the Americans lost over half their crews in the battle. The story Whitman tells of the "old-time sea-fight" turns darker and darker. It is night; the ship is sinking; "formless stacks of bodies" are all around, as is the gore of the battle itself—"dabs of flesh upon the masts and spars." Again, the emphasis is not on victory but on the awful bloody aftermath of battle. There's a corpse of a child who served in the ship's cabin and the corpse of a beautiful old sailor. At the end, amid the "delicate sniffs of sea-breeze," there are the ominous sounds of "the hiss of the surgeon's knife" and "the gnawing teeth of his saw" as the grisly work of amputation takes place.

A few years after "Song of Myself" was first published, the Civil War would become the war of amputation, with tens of thousands of soldiers returning home without arms or legs, and Whitman would reflect upon how war was after all primarily an attack upon the living body. Even those who survived often did so without the means of moving freely in the world or without the means to create, write, paint, make things. Amputation had the effect of cutting off the soul's access to the world by taking away the body's means of moving and expressing the soul. This section ends by looking unflinchingly at the "swash of falling blood" and listening to the screams and the groans as the amputations of the Revolutionary War prefigure those of the Civil War.

Whitman's haunting final line, "These so, these irretrievable," captures the blank horror of the loss: when a body is destroyed, it cannot be regained. It is as if the poet begins to describe the importance and vitality of what has been lost—"These so . . ." (so beautiful? so brave? so strong?)—but then stops in the moment of recognizing the futility of trying to reconstitute, even in words, that which has been forever taken away: "these irretrievable." Whitman captures an unforgettable scene of loss, agony, and pain against the backdrop of the ultimate composter, the lapping ocean, awaiting the feast of death it is about to receive when it accepts the bodies and limbs that will be deposited there. The ocean will recycle them into other life but never again into the specific human forms that were lost in battle; those complete bodies are beyond retrieval, beyond experiencing whatever it is they thought they died for. Here, then, over a decade before he wrote "The Million Dead, Too, Summ'd Up," he was already facing the darkest truths of war.

Merrill Commentary

Whitman's vivid re-creation of dramatic scenes from the Revolutionary War and the Mexican War, in sections 33–36 of "Song of Myself," testify to the powers of his imagination, in the same way that Stephen Crane brought to life in his novel *The Red Badge of Courage* the experiences of a terrified soldier in the Civil War, though he was born six years after Confederate general Robert E. Lee surrendered to Union general Ulysses S. Grant at the Appomattox Court House in Virginia. For great writers create believable portraits of people, places, and events from the past, if not out of whole cloth from the imagination. Strange to think that in his otherwise optimistic "Song of Myself" Whitman described some of the same gruesome facts of war that would shape his future, prefiguring, so to say, his own destiny. Thus, during his hospital ministry (he titled one Civil War notebook "Walt Whitman, Soldier's Missionary") he was a bearer of "death messages given in charge to survivors," absorbing in his every fiber the measure and meaning of "The hiss of the surgeon's knife, the gnawing teeth of his saw, / Wheeze, cluck, swash of falling blood, short wild scream, and long, dull, tapering groan." No wonder his health gave out before peace came to the land, forcing him to recuperate for several months in Brooklyn.

Did he have an inkling of what was to come when he resurrected the story of 412 young men massacred in Texas, then fashioned a seaman's monologue about John Paul Jones's command of the *Bon Homme Richard* in "an old-time sea-fight" with the British ship *Serapis*? Impossible to say with any degree of certainty. But the world was shifting underfoot in the decade leading up to the Confederate secession from the Union, and the war scenes in "Song of Myself" suggest that Whitman not only understood the centrality of conflict in the unfolding of history but also that his vow to sing into being the whole of existence would be for naught if he did not account for the human propensity to destroy what we hold most dear. "Agonies are one of my changes of garments," he wrote, as if to try on a pair of clothes, perhaps aware in the hidden depths of his soul that one day he himself would "become the wounded person." Caring for wounded and dying soldiers, he discovered how to turn his love for them into original ways of honoring the irretrievable: poetry and prose for the new world that would rise out of the ashes of war.

3

"Poem of Wonder at The Resurrection of The Wheat" / "This Compost"

SOMETHING startles me where I thought I was safest,
I withdraw from the still woods I loved,
I will not go now on the pastures to walk,
I will not strip my clothes from my body to meet my lover the sea,
I will not touch my flesh to the earth, as to other flesh, to renew me.

How can the ground not sicken of men?
How can you be alive, you growths of spring?
How can you furnish health, you blood of herbs, roots, orchards, grain?
Are they not continually putting distempered corpses in the earth?
Is not every continent worked over and over with sour dead?
Where have you disposed of those carcasses of the drunkards and gluttons
of so many generations?
Where have you drawn off all the foul liquid and meat?
I do not see any of it upon you today—or perhaps I am deceived,
I will run a furrow with my plough—I will press my spade through the sod, and
turn it up underneath,
I am sure I shall expose some of the foul meat.

Behold!
This is the compost of billions of premature corpses,
Perhaps every mite has once formed part of a sick person,
Yet Behold!
The grass covers the prairies,
The bean bursts noiselessly through the mould in the garden,
The delicate spear of the onion pierces upward,
The apple-buds cluster together on the apple-branches,
The resurrection of the wheat appears with pale visage out of its graves,
The tinge awakes over the willow-tree and the mulberry-tree,
The he-birds carol mornings and evenings, while the she-birds sit on their nests,

The young of poultry break through the hatched eggs,
The new-born of animals appear, the calf is dropt from the cow, the colt from the
        mare,
Out of its little hill faithfully rise the potato's dark green leaves,
Out of its hill rises the yellow maize-stalk;
The summer growth is innocent and disdainful above all those strata of sour dead.

What chemistry!
That the winds are really not infectious!
That this is no cheat, this transparent green-wash of the sea, which is so amorous
        after me!
That it is safe to allow it to lick my naked body all over with its tongues!
That it will not endanger me with the fevers that have deposited themselves in it!
That all is clean, forever and forever!
That the cool drink from the well tastes so good!
That blackberries are so flavorous and juicy!
That the fruits of the apple-orchard, and of the orange-orchard—that melons,
        grapes, peaches, plums, will none of them poison me!
That when I recline on the grass I do not catch any disease!
Though probably every spear of grass rises out of what was once a catching disease.

Now I am terrified at the earth! it is that calm and patient,
It grows such sweet things out of such corruptions,
It turns harmless and stainless on its axis, with such endless successions of
        diseased corpses,
It distils such exquisite winds out of such infused fetor,
It renews with such unwitting looks, its prodigal, annual, sumptuous crops,
It gives such divine materials to men, and accepts such leavings from them at last.

Folsom Commentary

In the 1840s and 1850s, Walt Whitman was reading about and absorbing the latest advances in the sciences and learning how to turn them into poetry. "Hurrah for positive science!," he wrote in the 1855 poem that would later be called "Song of Myself," where he then directly addressed scientists: "Your facts are useful, and yet they are not my dwelling, / I but enter by them to an area of my dwelling." One of the sciences that most fascinated him was chemistry, and in an 1847 review of a new book on organic chemistry by Justus Liebig, he celebrated the new revelations that the book opened up to him: "Chemistry! the elevating, beautiful study! which only the vulgar think technical, because they have not delved into its capacious recesses. Chemistry—that involves the essences of creation, and the changes, and the growths, and formations and decays, of so large a constituent part of the earth, and the things thereof!" So, in 1856, five years before the Civil War broke out, in his second edition of *Leaves of Grass*, Whitman published a poem about chemistry, based on the facts he had read. He entered through those facts into the realm of poetic truth—a realization that nonstop change, growth, formation, and decay are the "essence of creation." The poem was called "Poem of Wonder at The Resurrection of The Wheat," later titled "This Compost," and at the heart of it was the same wondrous exclamation he had made when he read Liebig's book: "What chemistry!"

In this poem, Whitman most clearly expresses his central faith: spirituality as a compost heap. The soul as endlessly recycling material. Every atom belonging to me as good belonging to you. These spinning atoms that make up each of us were here at the origin of the cosmos and will be here as long as matter exists. Our bodies are a momentary construction of eternal stardust, a continually altering constellation of atoms that, for a period of time, embody Life, then disperse and become the elements of new life. In "The Million Dead, Too, Summ'd Up," as we have seen, Whitman evokes the same composting faith, the same "Nature's chemistry distill'd," but now, as Nature's chemistry processes the hundreds of thousands of dead soldiers, it is working overtime, having to compost death back into life on a more massive scale than ever before. It's an ecological test of Nature's chemical powers, to create food to nurture the nation's future out of the hundreds of thousands of lost soldiers. Whitman's Civil War poetry and the poetry he wrote after the war literally embody that absence, as we shall see.

After the war, Whitman incessantly revised *Leaves of Grass*, working to absorb the poetry of division and loss into what had before the war been a book emphasizing unity and endless expansion. He would sew unbound sheets of *Drum-Taps* into his 1867 edition and then, in succeeding editions, would reorganize and revise poems, scattering the war poetry throughout *Leaves* and bleeding it into every aspect of the book. Sometimes he made major changes to his early poetry; other times the changes could be quite minor. One change he made in 1867 was to rename "Poem of Wonder at The Resurrection of The Wheat": the new title, "This Compost," pointed not only to the world around us, where nature was forever breaking down dead material to turn it into the elements for new life, but also focused our attention on *this* compost, this poem, the very thing we are reading, which is, after all, a *composition* (from the identical roots as *compost*: to put together). This poem, like all poems, is made up of elements, words, that have been used in an endless number of other poems by other poets, but language—like plants and animals—is continually being broken down again into its elements, out of which new compositions grow (the dictionary, for Whitman, was the ultimate linguistic compost heap, where everything ever written in the language existed, broken down again into its constituent parts).

In 1871, Whitman made another seemingly small alteration to this poem: he added to his catalog of all the burgeoning life springing and bursting and piercing upward out of the soil (which is the compost of death) a single quick image, only half a line long—"the lilacs bloom in the dooryards." Here, by bringing in just a tiny fragment of his Civil War elegy on the death of Abraham Lincoln, Whitman invites into this poem all of the massive death from the war. "When Lilacs Last in the Dooryard Bloom'd," as we will see, mourned not only the death of Lincoln but opened itself up to all the "battle-corpses, myriads of them . . . the debris and debris of all the slain soldiers of the war." His prewar poem, then, begins in the years after the war to take part in the somber celebration of the remarkable ability of "Nature's chemistry" to turn the mass death into nutriment for America's future, a future that would have to be made—as all futures are—out of the dead.

Merrill Commentary

Whitman's interest in chemistry, a branch of the physical sciences rooted in the philosopher's quest to understand the nature of the universe and the alchemist's dream of turning base materials into gold, provided him not only with imagery and ideas but also with a method for distilling into versets his vision of the cosmos—a cosmos, centered on the individual self, which in one form or another has existed from time immemorial, descends into the depths of the sea, and reaches beyond the most distant stars, now and in the future, each recombination of words—"the resurrection of the wheat," "the tinge awakes"—reinvigorating the language, inspiring insights about the nature of our journey from the cradle to the grave. His meditation on the mutability of matter thus depends upon an extravagant mixing of elements drawn from literature, philosophy, and science, which serves to change all things into "divine materials." And the constant regeneration of nature, which seems to ceaselessly transform death into life, furnished evidence for Whitman's hypothesis that the end of one life marks the beginning of another.

The carnage of the Civil War tested his hypothesis almost to the breaking point. And it is fascinating to observe his grasp of this long before the first shots were fired, in the poem that came to be titled "This Compost." What startles him in the opening line? The sound of a snapping twig? A voice? A shadow? Whatever the cause may be, he knows that he has entered a death-haunted landscape—which is no different than any place on earth. For the "sour dead" are everywhere, and so he calls out the "growths of spring," anguished by the sudden realization that if he were to plow a furrow here, he would surely turn up corpses. In sickness lie the seeds of health as surely as decomposing flesh delivers nutrients for the living. This is our common inheritance.

Then white space and an imperative: *Behold!* What the poet beholds is the miracle of life, the cataloging of which leads him to see the world anew, enacting the very kind of transformation that proceeds from a chemical reaction. In this new compound, which is made up of poetry and chemistry alike, "all is clean, forever and forever!" For this change of perspective is nothing more, and nothing less, than a model for the exchange of atoms that marks all of life and death, which Whitman would become intimate with during his wartime vigils.

"The whole earth is our hospital," T. S. Eliot wrote in *Four Quartets*, the publication of which sustained Londoners during the German Blitz in World War II, and that is why he believed that "speech impels us / To purify the dialect of the tribe." But it was Whitman who first purified the dialect of a nation torn asunder by civil war, demonstrating why poetry is the right medium for distilling "exquisite winds out of such infused fetor." What chemistry!

4

"Year of Meteors (1859–60)"

YEAR of meteors! brooding year!
I would bind in words retrospective, some of your deeds and signs;
I would sing your contest for the 19th Presidentiad;
I would sing how an old man, tall, with white hair, mounted the scaffold in Virginia;
(I was at hand—silent I stood, with teeth shut close—I watch'd;
I stood very near you, old man, when cool and indifferent, but trembling
with age and your unheal'd wounds, you mounted the scaffold;)
I would sing in my copious song your census returns of The States,
The tables of population and products—I would sing of your ships and their cargoes,
The proud black ships of Manhattan, arriving, some fill'd with immigrants,
some from the isthmus with cargoes of gold;
Songs thereof would I sing—to all that hitherward comes would I welcome give;
And you would I sing, fair stripling! welcome to you from me, sweet boy of England!
Remember you surging Manhattan's crowds, as you passed with your cortege of
nobles?
There in the crowds stood I, and singled you out with attachment;
I know not why, but I loved you . . . (and so go forth little song,
Far over sea speed like an arrow, carrying my love all folded,
And find in his palace the youth I love, and drop these lines at his feet;)
—Nor forget I to sing of the wonder, the ship as she swam up my bay,
Well-shaped and stately the Great Eastern swam up my bay, she was 600 feet long,
Her moving swiftly, surrounded by myriads of small craft, I forget not to sing;
Nor the comet that came unannounced, out of the north, flaring in heaven,
Nor the strange huge meteor procession, dazzling and clear, shooting over our heads,
(A moment, a moment long, it sail'd its balls of unearthly light over our heads,
Then departed, dropt in the night, and was gone;)
—Of such, and fitful as they, I sing—with gleams from them would I gleam
and patch these chants;
Your chants, O year all mottled with evil and good! year of forebodings! year
of the youth I love!

Year of comets and meteors transient and strange!—lo! even here, one equally
transient and strange!
As I flit through you hastily, soon to fall and be gone, what is this book,
What am I myself but one of your meteors?

Folsom Commentary

Newspapers were filled with reports of intense meteor showers during the fall of 1859 and the summer of 1860: it actually *was* a "year of meteors," as Whitman's portentous poem claims. During that last uneasy year before the Civil War began, 1859–60, unexpected spectacular events that seemed to portend something calamitous were taking place with increasing frequency. No event was more ominous than the capture, trial, and hanging of the radical abolitionist John Brown, who had tried to coordinate a slave insurrection that he hoped would initiate a war to end slavery; his attack on Harpers Ferry Armory in western Virginia took place in October 1859. Henry David Thoreau would write that "John Brown's career for the last six weeks of his life was meteor-like, flashing through the darkness in which we live." Herman Melville would begin his own book of Civil War poems, *Battle-Pieces*, with a short poem called "The Portent," picturing Brown "Hanging from the beam, / Slowly swaying," and calling him "The meteor of the war." The spectacular fall meteor shower occurred in November, halfway between Brown's sentencing and his execution, and many newspapers reported the momentous confluence of the two events. Melville called him "Weird John Brown": he was "weird" in the same way Shakespeare's "weird sisters" in *Macbeth* were, agents of prophecy and fate (the word derives from the Old English *wyrd*, meaning "destiny").

In "Year of Meteors," Whitman joins Thoreau and Melville in recognizing the ways that John Brown and meteors signaled the inevitability of the war that so many felt was on the near horizon. In Whitman's poem, he characterizes the year preceding the war as a "brooding year," during which Lincoln was elected president (assuming the nineteenth "Presidentiad," a word Whitman was proud to have invented, meaning a four-year term—a president could serve two presidentiads if reelected, or two presidents could share a presidentiad if one resigned or died while in office). The speaker of Whitman's poem imagines himself present at Brown's hanging, silently witnessing with clenched teeth as the prophetic death becomes a "sign" of many deaths to come.

But then the poem veers off in a completely unexpected direction, recalling the visit of Edward, Prince of Wales, to New York City in October of 1860, just a year after Brown's Harpers Ferry raid. The eighteen-year-old Edward, son of Queen Victoria and the notorious playboy prince, was a hit in North America, greeted by tens of thousands of people at his stops at various American cities. His trip marks the beginnings of America's renewed infatuation with the British royal family. He was the first heir to the British throne to come to the United States, and his attendance at a service in Trinity Church in New York City to hear prayers for the royal family spoken for the first time since the American Revolution was seen as a sign of a new era of friendship between the former antagonists. America's earlier wars with Britain now seemed to be fading into the past just as a new internecine war was shaping up, one that would lead both North and South to seek the vital support and recognition of Great Britain, a country that struggled over which of America's broken halves it should side with and ended up remaining neutral, though many influential Brits favored the Confederacy. In a controversial move, Edward made a quick visit to Richmond, the soon-to-be Confederate capital, but he spent most of his time traveling through the North. He visited President Buchanan in the White House and, in a healing act, visited George Washington's home at Mount Vernon and paid his respects at the tomb of the general who was instrumental in defeating the British and securing American independence.

As Whitman evokes the prince's visit to New York, he echoes the "Calamus" language of male-male affection that he had included in his cluster of poems by that name in his 1860 *Leaves of Grass*, the edition in which he offers up a vision of "a new friendship—It shall be called after my name, / It shall circulate through The States, indifferent of place, / It shall twist and intertwist them through and around each other—Compact shall they be, showing new signs, / Affection shall solve every one of the problems of freedom." This was the "Calamus" affection that he hoped might prevent a civil war, a call for males not to define their relationships with each other by competition and battle but rather through democratic care and concern that would cross and heal regional differences: "The special meaning of the 'Calamus' cluster of 'Leaves of Grass,'" he wrote, "mainly resides in its political significance." It would be "the beautiful and sane affection of man for man, latent in all the young fellows, north and south, east and west" by which "the United States of the future . . . are to be most effectually welded together, intercalated, anneal'd into a living union." So, in "Year of Meteors," he expresses a "Calamus" love for Edward: "I know not why, but I loved you." The love he expresses here for a young man who now represented America's former enemy is a kind of reconciliation that prefigures the reconciliation Whitman would enact toward his Confederate enemies at the end of the Civil War.

Then the speaker recalls another memorable event of the summer of 1860 as the *Great Eastern*, a British iron sailing steamship, at the time the largest ship ever built (Whitman says "she was 600 feet long," but in fact she was 692 feet in length), sails into New York Harbor on her first transatlantic voyage. And from this arrival, the speaker suddenly moves to "the strange huge meteor procession, dazzling and clear, shooting over our heads." Perhaps Whitman now is thinking of the 1860 meteor burst that so captured the nation's attention. But instead of attaching the meteor image to John Brown and the portents of war (as Melville and Thoreau had done), Whitman turns it back on all these events of the year—"evil and good"—and perceives an overarching pattern of comings and goings, of "transient and strange" brightness and darkness, of the ultimate insignificance of all events, even seemingly momentous ones, in the vastness of cosmic time. In the most memorable move, Whitman ends his poem by underscoring the transience of his own work and of himself: "what is this book, / What am I myself but one of your meteors?" The meteor flares up and sails across the sky, then disappears into the dark vastness; Lincoln's presidency comes and suddenly goes; John Brown's plans materialize and collapse; the Prince of Wales visits and leaves; the *Great Eastern* arrives and departs and eventually is dismantled and forgotten (in 1890, two years before Whitman's death, the giant ship would be broken up). Whitman is returning to his faith that only the vastness of time provides the ultimate meaning of all passing events, and he gains some comfort in realizing that the portents of 1859–60 are things that will, in deep time, "flit through . . . hastily." He will continue to try to understand the horrors of the war that is about to come by trusting in the vast restorative power of nature to heal history, to turn mass death back into fertility, to extract a future out of the darkness of the present.

We will see how, throughout the war, Whitman looks to the heavens, not so much for guidance or for signs of what is to come, but rather for the solace that vast time and deep space bring as an eternal backdrop to the comings and goings of the quickly passing human history that seems to our eyes, moment by moment, so vital and important. The horrors Whitman was about to face in the four years of the Civil War would often send his eyes skyward.

Merrill Commentary

In February 2013, a meteor the size of a bus streaked across the sky in the southern Ural region of Russia, a flash of light brighter than the sun, and exploded above the city of Chelyabinsk, sending shock waves over the land, shattering some million square feet of window glass, shards from which injured more than a thousand people, and releasing approximately five hundred kilotons of energy, twenty times the power of the atomic bomb dropped on Hiroshima. An asteroid had passed close to the earth earlier in the day, and while there was no link between the two objects, nevertheless some read portents in this cosmic coincidence, with war raging in the Middle East, terrorist attacks on the rise, and the global economy teetering again on the edge of collapse; within the year Russia would annex Crimea, precipitating an international crisis, which a friend from Moscow blamed, facetiously, on the meteor. Here was proof that something was up in the stars.

Whitman's urge to "bind in words retrospective" is integral to the art of poetry, which seeks to fix for all time the truth of individual experience, fleeting as it may be. What Wordsworth called "emotion recollected in tranquility" acquires another level of meaning in Whitman's determination to catalog decisive events from the year before the start of the Civil War, whether he witnessed them or not: the presidential campaign; the execution of John Brown; the visit of Edward, Prince of Wales; the arrival in New York Harbor of what at the time was the largest ship ever built; the appearance of a comet; the dazzling meteor procession that triggered the poem . . . All is "transient and strange" in the poet's imagination, more so in this "year of forebodings," and what is stranger than his yoking together of such disparate, transitory elements?

Note that Whitman pitches this poem in the conditional: "I would sing"—a pledge at odds with his declaration at the outset of "Song of Myself": "I celebrate myself, and sing myself." What to celebrate on the verge of civil war? Only the recognition that in the scheme of things we are but "poor passing facts," in Robert Lowell's memorable phrase. And this: however long and intensely the flame of our existence flares, it carries meaning—and the possibility of something more. Recall that it was a meteor that brought the building blocks of life to earth. Terrible as the coming war would be, Whitman knew that from its ashes would rise, phoenix-like, a new body politic destined to wing its way into the future, for good or ill, requiring new songs, gleaned and patched together out of a "year all mottled with good and evil." Hear him!

5

"Drum-Taps"

FIRST, O songs, for a prelude,
Lightly strike on the stretch'd tympanum, pride and joy in my city,
How she led the rest to arms—how she gave the cue,
How at once with lithe limbs, unwaiting a moment, she sprang;
(O superb! O Manhattan, my own, my peerless!
O strongest you in the hour of danger, in crisis! O truer than steel!)
How you sprang! how you threw off the costumes of peace with indifferent hand;
How your soft opera-music changed, and the drum and fife were heard in their
stead;
How you led to the war, (that shall serve for our prelude songs of soldiers,)
How Manhattan drum-taps led.

Forty years had I in my city seen soldiers parading;
Forty years as a pageant—till unawares, the Lady of this teeming and turbulent city,
Sleepless, amid her ships, her houses, her incalculable wealth,
With her million children around her—suddenly,
At dead of night, at news from the south,
Incens'd, struck with clench'd hand the pavement.

A shock electric—the night sustain'd it;
Till with ominous hum, our hive at day-break, pour'd out its myriads.
From the houses then, and the workshops, and through all the doorways,
Leapt they tumultuous—and lo! Manhattan arming.

To the drum-taps prompt,
The young men falling in and arming;
The mechanics arming, (the trowel, the jack-plane, the blacksmith's hammer,
tost aside with precipitation;)
The lawyer leaving his office, and arming—the judge leaving the court;
The driver deserting his wagon in the street, jumping down, throwing the reins
abruptly down on the horses' backs;

The salesman leaving the store—the boss, book-keeper, porter, all leaving;
Squads gathering everywhere by common consent, and arming;
The new recruits, even boys—the old men show them how to wear their
accoutrements—they buckle the straps carefully;
Outdoors arming—indoors arming—the flash of the musket-barrels;
The white tents cluster in camps—the arm'd sentries around—the sunrise cannon,
and again at sunset;
Arm'd regiments arrive every day, pass through the city, and embark from the
wharves;
(How good they look, as they tramp down to the river, sweaty, with their guns
on their shoulders!
How I love them! how I could hug them, with their brown faces, and their
clothes and knapsacks cover'd with dust!)
The blood of the city up—arm'd! arm'd! the cry everywhere;
The flags flung out from the steeples of churches, and from all the public
buildings and stores;
The tearful parting—the mother kisses her son—the son kisses his mother;
(Loth is the mother to part—yet not a word does she speak to detain him;)
The tumultuous escort—the ranks of policemen preceeding, clearing the way;
The unpent enthusiasm—the wild cheers of the crowd for their favorites;
The artillery—the silent cannons, bright as gold, drawn along, rumble lightly
over the stones;
(Silent cannons—soon to cease your silence!
Soon, unlimber'd, to begin the red business;)
All the mutter of preparation—all the determin'd arming;
The hospital service—the lint, bandages, and medicines;
The women volunteering for nurses—the work begun for, in earnest—no mere
parade now;
War! an arm'd race is advancing!—the welcome for battle—no turning away;
War! be it weeks, months, or years—an arm'd race is advancing to welcome it.

Mannahatta a-march!—and it's O to sing it well!
It's O for a manly life in the camp!

And the sturdy artillery!
The guns, bright as gold—the work for giants—to serve well the guns:
Unlimber them! no more, as the past forty years, for salutes for courtesies merely;

Put in something else now besides powder and wadding.

And you, Lady of Ships! you Mannahatta!
Old matron of the city! this proud, friendly, turbulent city!
Often in peace and wealth you were pensive, or covertly frown'd amid all your
children;
But now you smile with joy, exulting old Mannahatta!

Folsom Commentary

When Whitman incorporated his Civil War book *Drum-Taps* into *Leaves of Grass,* he kept this poem as the first in what became the cluster of poems called "Drum-Taps." In both his 1870 and 1881 editions of *Leaves*, the "Drum-Taps" cluster is preceded by an 1860 poem called "To the States, To Identify the 16th, 17th, or 18th Presidentiads," and it is one of the angriest poems Whitman ever wrote. Like many Americans, he was fed up with Presidents Millard Fillmore, Franklin Pierce, and James Buchanan, all of whom failed to take the kind of firm and principled action that could have helped prevent the nation from dividing into irreconcilable halves. Whitman expressed his anger in an unpublished political pamphlet called "The Eighteenth Presidency!," where he wrote: "The sixteenth and seventeenth and 18th terms of the American Presidency have shown that the villainy and shallowness of great rulers are just as eligible to These States as to any foreign despotism, kingdom, or empire.... Never were publicly displayed more deformed, mediocre, sniveling, unreliable, false-hearted men! Never were These States so insulted. ... The President eats dirt and excrement for his daily meals, likes it, and tries to force it on The States." In his poem introducing "Drum-Taps," Whitman exclaims, "What a filthy Presidentiad!," and he leaves us with an image of uneasy sleeping: "Then I will sleep awhile yet, for I see that these States sleep, for reasons; / (With gathering murk, with muttering thunder and lambent shoots we all duly awake, / South, North, East, West, inland and seaboard, we will surely awake.)"

This sorry state of affairs, the political corruptions and endless stalemates, lead in the poem "Drum-Taps" to a kind of jubilation when *something* finally begins to happen, when the "scum floating atop of the waters" finally is cleared away by the actions of the awakening citizens, who have decided that they would rise up "at news from the south"—Confederate troops opening fire on the federal garrison at Fort Sumter, South Carolina, on April 12, 1861, the opening shots of the war. At this point, Whitman revels in the energy and the cleansing excitement of his city, "Manhattan," and he feels "pride and joy in my city" as it goes about the activities of "arming" and volunteering and marching to the drum-taps on the "the stretch'd tympanum" (an image of the military drums, but also an image of the ears of the citizens, as the sound of those drums plays on the tympanums of the ears of the citizens, a million tympanic membranes that are vibrating, registering, and responding to those beating drums of war).

There's an odd insistence in this poem on "arms" and "arming": "falling in and arming," "outdoors arming, indoors arming," "arm'd sentries around," "arm'd regiments arrive," "arm'd! arm'd! the cry everywhere"—"War! An arm'd race is advancing!" But this "race" of young men, excited to enter into battle, will soon find that their "lithe limbs" are about to be sacrificed, as the Civil War stretches from "weeks" to "months" to "years" and becomes the great war of amputation. Perhaps only by the end of the poem do we begin to notice how the word "arm'd" is always contracted, missing a letter, carrying an absence, just as so many of these lithe-limbed young men would return to Manhattan missing limbs: once the "silent cannons . . . cease [their] silence," then "soon unlimber'd" begins "the red business." The armed lose arms; the limbed are unlimbed. Built into the excitement of the exhilaration of a fresh start, then, is the dark foreboding of the "hospital service, the lint, bandages and medicines" that Whitman will become so familiar with less than two years later, when he begins moving among the thousands of amputees in the Civil War hospitals of the nation's capital.

Merrill Commentary

Whitman's fervor for the arming of Manhattan, inspired by the electric shock of Confederate forces launching an attack on Fort Sumter, the "news from the south" that jolted the Union awake, may seem perverse considering the impending carnage. Unable to imagine the scale of bloodshed destined to become a defining feature of America, he celebrates a newfound sense of purpose in his fellow citizens, in sharp contrast to the political uncertainty of recent years. Opera music gives way to fife and drum, complex emotions to simple faith in "young men falling in and arming," and in the new dispensation the poet's song is a clarion call to battle, in the tradition of epic bards summoning their brethren down through the ages: "War! an arm'd race is advancing!"

Whitman welcomes this, like a summer thunderstorm that brings relief on a hot and humid afternoon. It will not be long before the drums are muffled for the dead. But for now he catalogs the different ways in which the city rises to the occasion, a hive of activity humming in workshops and houses and streets, all geared to the needs of the regiments and new recruits, "All the mutter of preparation, all the determined arming." This tumult he will turn into song, making common cause not only with the troops but the crowd cheering them on, the mother kissing her son goodbye, the women volunteering for service in the hospitals: "Mannahatta a-march."

War has been a constant in Western literature since Homer commemorated the wrath of Achilles in the *Iliad*, and Whitman's embrace of the military, at least at the outset of hostilities, is hardly unusual. The French poet Guillaume Apollinaire, for example, happily traded his Parisian café life for the barracks during World War I. "I love art so much," he wrote to a friend, "I have joined the artillery." Soldiering, he decided, was his true profession, and he took pleasure in training. "We said farewell to a whole era," he wrote in August 1914, realizing that the first shell fired ushered in a new era, the contours of which he outlined three years later in his essay "The New Spirit and the Poets." Here he coined the term *Surrealism*, the seminal artistic movement of the last century, and what could be more surreal than his realization one day in a trench at the front that the blood dripping onto the newspaper he was reading was his own? The shrapnel removed from his skull scuttled his military career—he never really recovered—and perhaps revealed to him how dream and reality can merge. If war is the great clarifier, concentrating the attention of statesmen, soldiers, and citizens alike, poets praise its glory and mourn its horror. Apollinaire died of Spanish flu two days before the armistice ended the war in November 1918. His poetry endures, marching to the same beat as Whitman's "Drum-Taps."

6

"Beat! Beat! Drums!"

1

Beat! beat! drums!—Blow! bugles! blow!
Through the windows—through doors—burst like a force of ruthless men,
Into the solemn church, and scatter the congregation;
Into the school where the scholar is studying:
Leave not the bridegroom quiet—no happiness must he have now with his bride;
Nor the peaceful farmer any peace, plowing his field or gathering his grain;
So fierce you whirr and pound, you drums—so shrill you bugles blow.

2

Beat! beat! drums!—Blow! bugles! blow!
Over the traffic of cities—over the rumble of wheels in the streets:
Are beds prepared for sleepers at night in the houses?
No sleepers must sleep in those beds;
No bargainers' bargains by day—no brokers or speculators—Would they continue?
Would the talkers be talking? would the singer attempt to sing?
Would the lawyer rise in the court to state his case before the judge?
Then rattle quicker, heavier drums—you bugles wilder blow.

3

Beat! beat! drums!—Blow! bugles! blow!
Make no parley—stop for no expostulation;
Mind not the timid—mind not the weeper or prayer;
Mind not the old man beseeching the young man;
Let not the child's voice be heard, nor the mother's entreaties;
Make even the trestles to shake the dead, where they lie awaiting the hearses,
So strong you thump, O terrible drums—so loud you bugles blow.

Folsom Commentary

At the beginning and the end of the Civil War, Whitman sought a certain comfort in traditional meters and formal verse. His very earliest, pre–*Leaves of Grass* poems were all written in traditional verse patterns and rhyme, so he was well equipped to set aside his free-verse form at any time and pick up patterned writing again. In "Beat! Beat! Drums!" he plays with an insistent spondaic and anapestic meter in order to set up a pounding martial rhythm that plays through three stanzas of seven lines each. Many readers have been drawn to this poem over the years—Ivan Turgenev even translated it into Russian in the 1870s, struggling to maintain that insistent rhythmic beat, and it was one of the most reprinted of Whitman's poems as the war was just getting under way, appearing in newspapers from New York to San Francisco and in the popular *Harper's Weekly* in September 1861.

Like "Drum-Taps," this poem can be heard as a kind of recruitment poem, a poem calling the populace to arms. Whitman's own brother George, an early volunteer in the Union Army, had just reenlisted when Whitman began writing "Beat! Beat! Drums!" Whitman took a draft of the poem with him to Pfaff's beer cellar in Manhattan, where he used to hang out with his bohemian friends, and read it aloud. One Southern friend took exception and began a physical fight with the poet until other friends broke up the scuffle. Tempers were running high after the humiliation of the Union at the First Battle of Bull Run, and Whitman was determined to stoke up support for the Union cause.

Like the first poem (and the *Drum-Taps* collection as a whole), this one plays upon the military drum as it beats the march to war, but we are also always aware of the *other* "Taps" these drums play, the three strong beats to signal the extinguishing of lights at the end of the day in soldiers' camps. It was during the Civil War that "Taps" came to be played at funerals for both Union and Confederate troops—the ultimate extinguishing of the light—often with the familiar bugle accompaniment. So the opening line of each of the three stanzas in this poem—"Beat! beat! drums!—blow! bugles! blow!"—offer three strong beats along with one weak syllable (the second syllable of "bugles")—a single note of hesitation, perhaps, in the otherwise relentless push to war. Just as drums and bugles lead the way to battle, so, too, in playing "Taps," do they lead the soldiers killed there to the grave.

The poem offers a terrifying image of the war-inducing drums and bugles tearing "through the windows—through doors" of the city with a "ruthless force," emptying out civilian society by scattering congregations and classes, clearing workers from the farm fields, pulling the bridegroom away from his bride, and sounding louder and more fiercely at any signs of resistance. Whitman seems to undo the catalogs of city and country life with which he famously filled "Song of Myself": here the infinite variety of activity of the city—"America singing," as he called it in another poem—is drowned out by the singular sound of the drums and bugles that seek to funnel the variety of life into one unabating unitary purpose—to make the lawyers, students, brokers, farmers, and singers all wear the same uniform and conform to this pressing new need. If the war is understood at some level as the way to preserve this glorious and variegated civilian life, then the very thing the war is being fought to preserve must first be entirely undone.

The third and final stanza gives us the voices of the resisters of this intoxicating martial music—the mother, the children, the "timid," the old men, even the dead (who, were they able, might warn the young men not to rush so swiftly toward those beckoning battlefields). "Make no parley," the voice of the poem cries: "to parley" (from the French "to talk") usually means to meet with the enemy to negotiate or settle a dispute, but here the poet tells all his listeners to *avoid* talking with anyone who would stand in the way of the bloodlust, for *they* are the enemy if they try to stop this terrifying, irrepressible march to war.

Merrill Commentary

"Here is something we can all count on," Charles Simic wrote in an essay on the wars of succession in the former Yugoslavia. "Sooner or later our tribe always comes to ask us to agree to murder." Alarmed by the readiness of intellectuals in its constituent republics to espouse separate nationalist causes, he likened the destruction of his homeland to "watching a man mutilate himself in public." No doubt many Americans had similar misgivings about the sundering of their country. (It is worth noting that Yugoslavia had about the same population as the United States during the Civil War—and a quarter of the casualties.) Great poets may be fierce nationalists, as Whitman proves, but for Simic the true poet does not belong to any tribe. "The sole function of the epic poet," he argues, "is to find excuses for the butcheries of the innocent." Against the epic he offers the solitary human voice, the lyric mode, which elevates the dictates of individual conscience above the desires of the tribe—a useful distinction to bear in mind when reading Whitman's clarion call of 1861.

The martial pace of the first line in each of the three sections—"Beat! beat! drums!—Blow! bugles! blow!"—may startle readers accustomed to Whitman's versets, which often wander across the page in a leisurely, even prosaic, fashion, gathering emotions, images, and impressions into a larger vision of the whole. But six stressed syllables out of seven make a different music, shrillness and ferocity invading the solemn church, the scholar's study, the wedding chamber, the harvest, scattering ordinariness to the wind. No time for happiness when there is a war on.

In the second section, Whitman calls into question the routines of daily life, demanding that drums and bugles sound throughout the city, making it impossible for anyone to sleep. For vigilance is the watchword of this new order. And those who would presume to carry on as before, bargaining and speculating, talking and singing and appealing to the judge, will be drowned out, uncertainty giving way to the inexorable logic of war. The voices raised in the final section—the timid and the old, the mother and the child—are as nothing compared to the wild bugles and terrible drums, which will not only call the troops to arms, to march and fight, to rise at daybreak and put out their lights at dusk, but also provide the music for their funerals, such sad music.

7

"Opening of the Secession War"

Attack on Fort Sumter, April, 1861.—What ran through the Land, as if by electric nerves, and show'd itself in stupendous and practical action, immediately after the firing on the Flag at Fort Sumter—the Nation ('till then incredulous) flush'd in the face, and all its veins fiercely pulsing and pounding—the arm'd volunteers instantaneously springing up everywhere—the tumultuous processions of the regiments—Was it not grand to have lived in such scenes and days, and be absorb'd by them, and unloosen'd to them?

The news of the attack on Sumter was receiv'd in New York city late at night, (13th April, 1861,) and was immediately sent out in extras of the newspapers. I had been to the opera in Fourteenth street that night, and after the performance, was walking down Broadway toward twelve o'clock, on my way to Brooklyn, when I heard in the distance the loud cries of the newsboys, who came presently tearing and yelling up the street, rushing from side to side even more furiously than usual. I bought an extra and cross'd to the Metropolitan Hotel (Niblo's,) where the great lamps were still brightly blazing, and, with a small crowd of others, who gather'd impromptu, read the news, which was evidently authentic. For the benefit of some who had no papers, one of us read the telegram aloud, while all listen'd silently and attentively. No remark was made by any of the crowd, which had increas'd to thirty or forty, but all stood a minute or two, I remember, before they dispers'd. I can almost see them there now, under the lamps at midnight again.

"The National Uprising and Volunteering"

The ensuing three Months—The National Uprising and Volunteering. —I have said in another place that the three Presidentiads preceding 1861 show'd how the weakness and wickedness of rulers are just as eligible here in America under republican, as in Europe under dynastic influences. But what can I say of that prompt and splendid wrestling with Secession-Slavery, the arch enemy personified, the instant he unmistakably show'd his face?......The volcanic upheaval of the Nation, after that firing on the flag at Charleston, proved for certain something which had been previously in great doubt, and at once substantially settled the question of Disunion. In my judgment it will remain as the grandest and most encouraging spectacle yet vouchsafed in any age, old or new, to political progress and Democracy.

It was not for what came to the surface merely—though that was important; but what it indicated below, which was of eternal importance.......Down in the abysms of New World humanity there had form'd and harden'd a primal hardpan of National Union Will, determin'd and in the majority, refusing to be tamper'd with or argued against, confronting all emergencies, and capable at any time of bursting all surface-bonds, and breaking out like an earthquake. It is indeed the best lesson of the century, or of America, and it is a mighty privilege to have been part of it....... (Two great spectacles, immortal proofs of Democracy, unequall'd in all the history of the past, are furnish'd by this War—one at the beginning, the other at its close. Those are—the general Voluntary Armed Upheaval—and the peaceful and harmonious Disbanding of the Armies, in the summer of 1865.)

"Contemptuous feeling"

Contemptuous National feeling.—Even after the bombardment of Sumter, however, the gravity of the revolt, and the power and will of the Slave States for a strong and continued military resistance to National authority, was not at all realized through the North, except by a few. Nine-tenths of the people of the Free States look'd upon the rebellion, as started in South Carolina, from a feeling one-half of contempt and the other half composed of anger and incredulity. It was not thought it would be join'd in by Virginia, North Carolina or Georgia. A great and cautious National official predicted that it would blow over "in sixty days," and folks generally believ'd the prediction. I remember talking about it on a Fulton ferry-boat with the Brooklyn Mayor, who said he only "hoped the Southern fire-eaters would commit some overt act of resistance, as they would then be at once so effectually squelch'd, we would never hear of Secession again—but he was afraid they never would have the pluck to really do anything.".......I remember too that a couple of companies of the Thirteenth Brooklyn, who rendezvou'd at the City Armory, and started thence as Thirty Days' Men, were all provided with pieces of rope conspicuously tied to their musket barrels, with which to bring back each man a prisoner from the audacious South, to be led in a noose, on our men's early and triumphal return! [This was indeed the general feeling, and came to the surface. Still, there was a very strong Secession party at the North, as I shall mention in a Note further on.]

Folsom Commentary

The three opening entries of the *Specimen Days* (1882) section on the Civil War were taken from what were originally appended "notes" in *Memoranda During the War* (1876). Whitman reorganizes and reshapes the notes to create in *Specimen Days* a dramatic threshold to the story of the war as Whitman is about to tell it—a narrative that will center the war not on the battlefields but in the hospitals, not on heroic deeds and exciting battles but on horrifying aftereffects.

As Whitman re-creates his initial reactions to the first reports of the outbreak of war, we are struck by the very different way that the media in his time carried and distributed such urgent news. Whitman has just exited an opera, where he had witnessed a grand, sweeping, mythic drama set to intense and soaring music, and he walks out into the late spring night onto Broadway where a very real drama is just now beginning to unfold: the newsboys' furious shouts are the perfect prelude to what will develop into a four-year saga of mass death and heartbreak. One anonymous voice reads aloud, by the lamps of a nearby hotel, the report of the Confederate attack on Fort Sumter, as a small crowd gathers and listens in silence. As the news sinks in, Whitman can already feel "the volcanic upheaval of the nation," "breaking out like an earthquake." The newsboys' shouts seem to have released vast, destructive natural forces that will eventually lead to "the grandest and most encouraging spectacle yet vouchsafed in any age, old or new, to political progress and democracy," as the nation begins a "prompt and splendid wrestling with secession slavery, the arch enemy personified." The grand spectacle of the opera that Whitman has just witnessed fades into the opening act of what will become a far greater democratic spectacle of fighting the archvillain of "secession slavery"—a conflated evil that threatens to tear asunder the still-young democratic republic and set up a competing slave empire. Whitman has wandered out of the opera onto the expanding stage of a national drama that will occupy four years of tumult and claim hundreds of thousands of young lives. No opera could begin to match this vast historical drama whose overture he was witnessing that night.

But Whitman has constructed this memory of the opening of the war only in retrospect. At the time of the firing on Fort Sumter, as he admits in "Contemptuous Feeling," he in fact believed along with most other people that he was not really witnessing the beginning of a massive and long-lasting war but rather only a short, small, contained rebellion that would be put down in weeks, not years. The first companies of soldiers only signed up for thirty days because no one thought they would be needed for longer than that. Few thought the rebellion would expand beyond South Carolina, and government officials were confident everything would be cleared up "in sixty days." Only in retrospect, after the war and its duration and vast death tally were known, could Whitman look back on the "opening of the Secession War."

Indeed, it was only after the war was over that the war could be named, and even then, as Whitman's use of "Secession War" indicates, the very name of the war was still very much in contention. While many writers at the time (including Abraham Lincoln) referred to "a civil war" in the lower case (in his 1863 Gettysburg Address, Lincoln said, "Now we are engaged in a great civil war"), very few were naming it the "Civil War." That name would only emerge during the last decades of the nineteenth century and the first decades of the twentieth. Until then, the name of the war was itself a battleground, and at least fifty different names were used at various times by the two sides. The South preferred "War Between the States" or "War for Southern Independence," while the North most frequently called it the "War of the Rebellion" (or simply "Great Rebellion") or the "War for the Union" (or even the "War to Preserve the Union"). The South was invested in naming the war as a battle between two sovereign states (or a confederacy of states vs. a federation of states), while the North insisted that it was dealing with a rebellion and thus could operate by the Constitution's dictates for how to "suppress Insurrections," turning the rebels into traitors and treating those in the South who remained loyal to the Union as citizens, not enemies. Frederick Douglass, speaking for many freed slaves, named it the "Slaveholders' Rebellion," and other freed slaves referred to it as the "Freedom War."

Whitman, however, chooses here and throughout his Civil War reminiscences to call it the "Secession War." This term gained favor in the 1880s and 1890s, and the name helped temper the idea that Confederate leaders were rebels or insurrectionists (and thus traitors), but rather were statesmen attempting a formal withdrawal from a federation of states they no longer wished to be part of. Whitman, in other words, chooses the term that softens the judgment of Southerners who fought the Union. This is very much in line with Whitman's call at the end of the war for "reconciliation" with (rather than punishment for) the Confederates. For Whitman, the war was very much a "War to Preserve the Union," for his antebellum ideal had been a unified democratic self that could contain contradictions ("Do I contradict myself? / Very well then . . . . I contradict myself; / I am large . . . . I contain multitudes"). The Civil War shattered that ideal, for it suggested that the contradictions at the heart of the American national experiment could not be contained, and he watched those contradictions between slave states and free states explode into open warfare as the Union split in two. His decision, after the trauma, to name it the "Secession War" is part of his desperate attempt to pull the shattered Union back together again, to suture the deep wounds of disunion.

Merrill Commentary

"Naturally, the great seedbed of any poetic renewal is in the field of prose," wrote the Italian poet Eugenio Montale. And the first entries in Whitman's *Memoranda During the War*, reconstructed from notes taken at the start of the "Secession War" (his favored term for the conflict), reveal the seeds of what would shape his poetry for the rest of his life—the shock of the attack on the flag at Fort Sumter; the silent reception of the news spreading at night like wildfire across the land; his elation at the spectacle of volunteers instantly forming armed militias in response to the prospect of disunion—the first sign of national feeling; his dawning realization that Southern opposition to the Union was fiercer and more entrenched than he had expected. Left unspoken was the suspicion that the war would be longer, costlier, and bloodier than anyone had imagined, as so often happens at the outbreak of hostilities. In Whitman's obsessive note-taking, the field of prose he shaped and compiled after the Confederate Army's surrender, we may trace the outlines of what would inform the final, darker version of *Leaves of Grass*, his lifework.

War is the arena in which anything goes, sometimes for good, though mainly for ill—which is why over the last century the international community has established conventions on the lawful conduct of war: to check excesses on the battlefield and in the treatment of prisoners is judged to be necessary for the general welfare of humankind, for when the blood rises, it becomes easier for some to countenance cruel and malicious behavior. This is especially true in civil conflicts, which may be governed by what Freud defined as "the narcissism of minor differences," proximity and similarity in outlook having the potential to exacerbate tensions between people in adjoining lands. Thus it is important to note Whitman's memory of "the volcanic upheaval" of the first shots fired—and his joy at the realization that an era of political stalemate was over. "Was it not grand to have lived in such scenes and days, and be absorb'd by them, and unloosen'd by them?" he writes. Well, yes and no. For while secession resolved the question of whether the North would fight to preserve the Union, inspiring "the general Voluntary Armed Upheaval," it also paved the way to carnage on a massive scale—truths that Whitman would address, in prose and poetry, until the end of his life, determined to reconcile his celebration of the self and its connection to all things in the universe—"for every atom belonging to me as good belongs to you"—with the terrible facts of war. In two spectacles bookending the war, the formation of volunteer militias in the North after Fort Sumter and then the peaceful disbanding of both armies after Appomattox, Whitman found "immortal proofs of Democracy," his great theme. But at what cost, both to himself and his nation, he would not be able to gauge for a very long time to come.

8

"Down at the Front"

FALMOUTH, VA., *opposite Fredericksburgh, December* 21, 1862.—Began my visits among the Camp Hospitals in the Army of the Potomac. Spent a good part of the day in a large brick mansion, on the banks of the Rappahannock, used as a Hospital since the battle—Seems to have receiv'd only the worst cases. Out doors, at the foot of a tree, within ten yards of the front of the house, I notice a heap of amputated feet, legs, arms, hands, &c., a full load for a one-horse cart. Several dead bodies lie near, each cover'd with its brown woollen blanket. In the door-yard, towards the river, are fresh graves, mostly of officers, their names on pieces of barrel-staves or broken board, stuck in the dirt. (Most of these bodies were subsequently taken up and transported North to their friends.)..........The large mansion is quite crowded, upstairs and down, everything impromptu, no system, all bad enough, but I have no doubt the best that can be done; all the wounds pretty bad, some frightful, the men in their old clothes, unclean and bloody. Some of the wounded are rebel soldiers and officers, prisoners. One, a Mississippian—a captain—hit badly in leg, I talk'd with some time; he ask'd me for papers, which I gave him. (I saw him three months afterward in Washington, with his leg amputated, doing well.)..........I went through the rooms, downstairs and up. Some of the men were dying. I had nothing to give at that visit, but wrote a few letters to folks home, mothers, &c. Also talk'd to three or four, who seem'd most susceptible to it, and needing it.

(Everything is quiet now, here about Falmouth and the Rappahannock, but there was noise enough a week or so ago. Probably the earth never shook by artificial means, nor the air reverberated, more than on that winter daybreak of eight or nine days since, when Gen. Burnside order'd all the batteries of the army to combine for the bombardment of Fredericksburgh. It was in its way the most magnificent and terrible spectacle, with all the adjunct of sound, throughout the War. The perfect hush of the just-ending night was suddenly broken by the first gun, and in an instant all the thunderers, big and little, were in full chorus, which they kept up without intermission for several hours.)

"After First Fredericksburg"

December 23 *to* 31.—The results of the late battles are exhibited everywhere about here in thousands of cases, (hundreds die every day,) in the Camp, Brigade, and

Division Hospitals. These are merely tents, and sometimes very poor ones, the wounded lying on the ground, lucky if their blankets are spread on layers of pine or hemlock twigs or small leaves. No cots; seldom even a mattress. It is pretty cold. The ground is frozen hard, and there is occasional snow. I go around from one case to another. I do not see that I do much good, but I cannot leave them. Once in a while some youngster holds on to me convulsively, and I do what I can for him; at any rate, stop with him and sit near him for hours, if he wishes it.

Besides the hospitals, I also go occasionally on long tours through the camps, talking with the men, &c. Sometimes at night among the groups around the fires, in their shebang enclosures of bushes. These are curious shows, full of characters and groups. I soon get acquainted anywhere in camp, with officers or men, and am always well used. Sometimes I go down on picket with the regiments I know best.......As to rations, the army here at present seems to be tolerably well supplied, and the men have enough, such as it is, mainly salt pork and hard tack. Most of the regiments lodge in the flimsy little shelter-tents. A few have built themselves huts of logs and mud, with fireplaces.

"Back to Washington"

WASHINGTON, *January,* '63.—Left camp at Falmouth, with some wounded, a few days since, and came here by Aquia Creek railroad, and so on Government steamer up the Potomac. Many wounded were with us on the cars and boat. The cars were just common platform ones. The railroad journey of ten or twelve miles was made mostly before sunrise. The soldiers guarding the road came out from their tents or shebangs of bushes with rumpled hair and half-awake look. Those on duty were walking their posts, some on banks over us, others down far below the level of the track. I saw large cavalry camps off the road. At Aquia Creek landing were numbers of wounded going North. While I waited some three hours, I went around among them. Several wanted word sent home to parents, brothers, wives, &c., which I did for them, (by mail the next day from Washington.) On the boat I had my hands full. One poor fellow died going up.

I am now remaining in and around Washington, daily visiting the hospitals. Am much in Patent Office, Eighth street, H street, Armory Square and others. Am now able to do a little good, having money, (as almoner of others home,) and getting experience........To-day, Sunday afternoon and till nine in the evening, visited Campbell Hospital; attended specially to one case in Ward 1; very sick with pleurisy and typhoid fever; young man, farmer's son, D. F. Russell, Company E, Sixtieth New York; downhearted and feeble; a long time before he would take any interest; wrote a letter home to his mother, in Malone, Franklin County, N. Y., at his request;

gave him some fruit and one or two other gifts; envelop'd and directed his letter, &c. Then went thoroughly through Ward 6; observ'd every case in the Ward, without, I think, missing one; gave perhaps from twenty to thirty persons, each one some little gift, such as oranges, apples, sweet crackers, figs, &c.

Thursday, Jan. 21.—Devoted the main part of the day to Armory Square Hospital; went pretty thoroughly through Wards F, G, H, and I; some fifty cases in each Ward. In Ward F supplied the men throughout with writing paper and stamp'd envelope each; distributed in small portions, to proper subjects, a large jar of first-rate preserv'd berries, which had been donated to me by a lady—her own cooking. Found several cases I thought good subjects for small sums of money, which I furnish'd. (The wounded men often come up broke, and it helps their spirits to have even the small sum I give them.) My paper and envelopes all gone, but distributed a good lot of amusing reading matter; also, as I thought judicious, tobacco, oranges, apples, &c. Interesting cases in Ward I; Charles Miller, bed No. 19, Company D, Fifty-third Pennsylvania, is only sixteen years of age, very bright, courageous boy, left leg amputated below the knee; next bed to him, another young lad very sick; gave each appropriate gifts. In the bed above, also, amputation of the left leg; gave him a little jar of raspberries; bed No. 1, this Ward, gave a small sum; also to a soldier on crutches, sitting on his bed near.......(I am more and more surprised at the very great proportion of youngsters from fifteen to twenty-one in the army. I afterwards found a still greater proportion among the Southerners.)

Evening, same day, went to see D. F. R., before alluded to; found him remarkably changed for the better; up and dress'd—quite a triumph; he afterwards got well, and went back to his regiment.........Distributed in the Wards a quantity of note-paper, and forty or fifty stamp'd envelopes, of which I had recruited my stock, and the men were much in need.

Folsom Commentary

When any war begins, most people think it will be over quickly. Many people can still remember the 2003 comments of U.S. Secretary of Defense Donald Rumsfeld, on the eve of the Iraq War, a war that lasted eight years: "It is unknowable how long that conflict will last. It could last . . . six days, six weeks. I doubt six months." Vice President Richard Cheney agreed that "it'll go relatively quickly, . . . weeks rather than months." It was no different for Walt Whitman on the front edge of the Civil War, as we saw in the previous texts we examined. Like the United States initiating a war in Iraq that one of the president's advisors blithely predicted would be a "cakewalk," most Northern and Southern observers predicted the Civil War would be a brief and clean little war, over in a matter of weeks if not days. "A great and cautious national official," Whitman recalled, "predicted that it would blow over 'in sixty days,' and folks generally believ'd the prediction." Civil War histories are full of the stories of people who packed picnic lunches to go sit on the hills to watch the Battle of Bull Run, only to be shocked into horror as the Northern troops beat a retreat into Washington. "Where are the vaunts, and the proud boasts with which you went forth?" Whitman asked after Bull Run. "Where are your banners, and your bands of music, and your ropes to bring back your prisoners? Well, there isn't a band playing—and there isn't a flag but clings ashamed and lank to its staff."

A year and a half later, Whitman was down at the war front, in Fredericksburg, Virginia, looking after his injured soldier-brother, George, and was now wondering how long this suddenly very bloody quagmire would last. Like most Americans who were not on the battlefields, Whitman spent time each day looking at the growing list of casualties that newspapers printed—the lists of the dead and wounded that, as those lists got longer and longer, became increasingly *amputated names,* names of the dead that were now forever cut off from the young lives they so recently signified. Mass death came to be, as inevitably it has to, *anonymous* death. We can't keep track of the cascading faces and names: think of the vast black slabs of the Vietnam memorial in Washington, D.C., with its endless rows of names. That memorial captures what Americans during the Civil War would have experienced as the newspaper arrived each day, invading their homes with these lists of names now severed from their living identities.

It was from just such a list of casualties in the *New York Herald* that Whitman picked out his brother George's name, the name itself mangled ("Whitmore" instead of "Whitman") just like the soldier it indicated, which that led Walt to the Fredericksburg battlefield and changed the course of his life and his poetry. As he arrived and approached the mansion used as a hospital, he passed by "a heap of amputated feet, legs, arms, hands, &c., a full load for a one-horse cart." It was the first indication he had that this would be a war of amputation, eventually severing an entire generation of American males from the country's future. That pile of body parts Whitman encountered, like some grotesque parody of his life-affirming poetic catalogs, became the stubborn reality he would have to learn to incorporate in his radically altered post-1860 poetry: now—as we saw in "The Million Dead, Too, Summ'd Up"—instead of celebrating an expanding self and nation and cosmos in his affirmative song, he would begin cataloging mass death and horrifying wounds. For the poet of the body, who believed the soul only existed when it took on flesh and bone, when it gained a body so it could act in the world—for this poet, the war was an attack on the American soul, leaving a generation of American men dead or disfigured. How could the soul of a generation function without legs, the very means of locomotion, of moving in the world, or without hands and arms, the means of doing work in the world?

To his relief, Whitman found his brother George with only a minor facial wound. George would heal and go on to take part in many of the key battles of the war, rising to the rank of major and spending time as a prisoner of war in Danville, one of the most notorious Confederate prisoner camps. But many of George's comrades in the Battle of Fredericksburg were badly wounded, and Whitman began caring for them while he was at his brother's camp: "I go around from one case to another. I do not see that I do much good to these wounded and dying; but I cannot leave them." Just sitting with them, touching them, holding them, he discovered, provided comfort, and when Whitman took a train back to Washington, he rode with the wounded on their way to the hospitals in the nation's capital. Whitman found that many of these soldiers wanted him to write letters to "parents, brothers, wives, &c." At this point, Whitman already had found his calling for the rest of the war. He abruptly gave up plans to return to New York and took up residence in Washington to tend to the endless stream of wounded and dying soldiers who came there. "America," he wrote to Ralph Waldo Emerson, was "already brought to Hospital in her fair youth"; the nation's capital and its monumental buildings (many of them, like the Capitol itself, still under construction) were turned into a vast network of hospitals. And, for the next two and a half years, Whitman would occupy those hospitals, caring for soldiers from the North and South and East and West, black soldiers as well as white—the vast variety of the nation's youth brought to hospital, which for Whitman became the very center, the locus, of the war.

Merrill Commentary

"Too old to carry arms and fight like the others," Zbigniew Herbert writes in "Report from a Besieged City," a critical poem from the period of martial law in Poland (ca. 1982), "they graciously gave me the inferior role of chronicler / I record—I don't know for whom—the history of the siege." This was the position that Whitman found himself in at the start of the Civil War, and in these excerpts from *Memoranda During the War* we see him discovering his wartime vocation—ministering to wounded and dying soldiers from the North and South alike, dispensing gifts, making a record of his encounters. "Am now able to do a little good," he wrote of his daily visits to Washington-area hospitals, where "the men were much in need," and in his new role as almoner to them, distributing money and food, note paper, and stamped envelopes, he also documented the consequences of war, gaining the experience necessary to write about it in an original fashion.

"The real war will never get in the books," Whitman wrote, though in fact he chronicled a sizable portion of it with an exacting eye. It is in the nature of literature to suggest the contours of an event, to engage the reader's imagination in an approximation of reality—which is, of course, no substitute for what happened on the battlefield, in the hospital wards, or anywhere else; absolute fidelity to the emotional, physical, political, social, or spiritual dimensions of any moment in time is impossible, particularly when it concerns events of civilizational importance, like the Civil War; hence the number of books on the subject still being published 150 years later. It remains a rich lode to mine for poets and writers, historians and scholars, as Whitman himself may have foreseen. "Each line, each scrawl, each memorandum, has its history," he wrote of the notes he compiled, some of them stained with blood. "Some pang of anguish—some tragedy, profounder than ever poet wrote. Out of them arise active and breathing forms"—the long dead who continue to nourish American literature, scholarship, and mythology.

Sound and sight inspired in different ways the pair of crises—personal and political—that defined Whitman's body of work. The musical imperative of his poetic breakthrough, the versets in "Song of Myself," which in the run-up to the Civil War were designed to suggest the whole of the cosmos, gave way to images of carnage, which governed his voyage into the dark heart of America. The visual component of his writings during and after the war, rooted in the new art form of photography, proved to be as critical to the future of American literature as the cadences thrumming in the original edition of what became *Leaves of Grass.* He taught us how to hear and see afresh, for what he heard and saw among groups of soldiers huddled around campfires, on trains and boats, and in the hospitals summon "myriad varied scenes of day or night—the graphic incidents of field or camp," which forever changed the world.

9

"Cavalry Crossing a Ford"

A LINE in long array, where they wind betwixt green islands;
They take a serpentine course—their arms flash in the sun—Hark to the musical clank;
Behold the silvery river—in it the splashing horses, loitering, stop to drink;
Behold the brown-faced men—each group, each person, a picture—the negligent rest on the saddles;
Some emerge on the opposite bank—others are just entering the ford;
The guidon flags flutter gaily in the wind.

Folsom Commentary

This little six-line poem was the third poem in the 1865 *Drum-Taps* and the first to present an image of troops in the midst of the war. But the imagery here is remarkably calm, and, unlike the prose descriptions of battle that appear in *Memoranda During the War*, where the battles are often very specific and very bloody, the scene in this poem is oddly generalized and serene. The poem gives us no information about where we are geographically or why the troops are crossing a ford, nor does it even indicate whether we are watching Union or Confederate troops. Whitman has numerous very short poems like this in *Drum-Taps*, precursors to what in the early twentieth century would come to be called "imagist" poems—short, condensed, intense, terse observations that engrave themselves on the reader's imagination. The sources of Whitman's Civil War poems are numerous, and during the war he began drawing more and more on descriptions that soldiers in the hospitals provided him of their various experiences, often taking on their point of view and creating soldier personae to narrate the poems so that we experience the speaker not as the Whitmanian "I" that we came to expect from his prewar poetry, but rather as specific soldiers recalling war experiences. In "Cavalry Crossing a Ford," however, there is no "I" but rather a kind of omniscient narrator who seems to see this cavalry from a heightened perspective, looking down on the maneuver as if from above.

In the late 1990s, a critic named Betty Barrett made a remarkable discovery about the source of this poem. While reading through the 1868 *Rebellion Record*, a collection of documents detailing Southern Civil War experiences, she came across the records for an 1864 twelve-day Union strike deep into Alabama, one of the southernmost maneuvers the Union army made during the war, as General Lovell Rousseau guided 2,500 cavalry from Decatur, Alabama, as far south as Tuskegee, destroying bridges and railways before eventually meeting up with General Sherman's forces in Georgia. The idea was to cut off supplies to Confederate troops defending Atlanta. Among the documents that Barrett found was an anonymous news report about the expedition, filed by a Union correspondent and published in the *New York Herald* on July 27, 1864. The report covered the entire campaign, but one description—of the Union cavalry crossing the Coosa River at Ten Islands Ford—stood out to Barrett because it so closely echoed Whitman's little poem, or, more precisely, Whitman's 1865 poem echoed it:

"The ford being clear, the column commenced crossing. The passage of the river was a beautiful sight. The long array of horsemen winding between the green islands and taking a serpentine course across the ford—their arms flashing back the rays of the burning sun, and guidons gaily fluttering along the column, formed a bright picture, recalling the days of romance, and contrasting strongly with the stern hardships and vivid realities of the every-day life on the duty march."

It is clear that Whitman borrowed key phrases—"long array," "between green islands," "taking a serpentine course," "their arms flashing back the rays of the burning sun," "guidons gaily fluttering"—in order to construct his poem, giving us a "bright" imagistic "picture," and also offering us an early example of what would in the twentieth century come to be called "found poetry," poems that are created by using text found somewhere else—in a newspaper or advertisement or law report or instruction manual—and refashioning those texts into poems by rearranging lines, phrases, and images. (Indeed, as the databases of newspapers and periodicals from the nineteenth century continue to grow, scholars are discovering more and more of Whitman's poems that borrow lines and key phrases from articles he read.) In the case of "Cavalry Crossing a Ford," we might say that it was not until the late 1990s that we knew the specific place and reason for the event that Whitman's poem recalls, but it would be more accurate to say that Whitman took a newspaper account of a specific event that occurred with Union troops in a specific place in Alabama in 1864, and then stripped that event of most of its identifying markers, leaving us with a striking and timeless image of soldiers moving in a kind of organic and synchronous movement with the landscape, their movements directed by the contours of the land as they follow "a serpentine course," with each individual soldier melding into the "brown-faced men": every single soldier merging with the group ("each group, each person a picture"), the group merging with the landscape. What is unspoken here but implied by the poems that follow, is that the landscape the soldiers move through now will eventually absorb many of those same soldiers, as the battles leave the dead to merge into the green islands and sink into the silvery river.

In *Memoranda During the War*, Whitman offers us a similar vision of watching, "for more than an hour," "long strings of cavalry, several regiments, very fine men and horses, four or five abreast," an "inspiriting" sight, with "our men . . . generally well mounted, feel[ing] good, . . . young, gay on the saddle, their blankets in a roll behind them, their sabres clanking at their side." But what Whitman includes in his prose yet leaves out of the poem is an equally powerful "line in long array" heading in the opposite direction: "Then just as they had all pass'd, a string of ambulances commenc'd from the other way, . . . slowly wending along, bearing a large lot of wounded to the hospitals." For every inspiriting line of cavalry heading one way, there is an equally dispiriting line heading back the other way, bearing the wounded and dying to the hospitals, where Whitman would position himself, and which he would come to see as the war's very cynosure.

Merrill Commentary

On New Year's Eve 1995, just after the Dayton Peace Accords were signed, I traveled to Županje, Croatia, to watch American peacekeeping forces cross the Sava River into Bosnia and Herzegovina—thirty thousand soldiers and hundreds of tanks, Bradley armored vehicles, and Humvees. The bridge across the river had been destroyed at the start of the war, and now speedboats held in place the longest floating bridge built by the U.S. military since the spanning of the Rhine in World War II. On the riverbank, above the roar of idling vehicles and helicopters hovering overhead, I heard the commanding officer say he was having fun. This seemed to hold for the townspeople watching the soldiers follow a serpentine course across the bridge, which recalled Whitman's "Cavalry Crossing a Ford." Moving troops have been integral to warfare and to war literature since Greek forces sailed to Troy, and when the Iraqi Army used a floating bridge to cross the Euphrates River in its recent campaign to retake the strategic city of Ramadi, I realized that Whitman's genius lay in his ability to find timeless images for basic facts of life—in this case, a military operation.

That Whitman adopted the outline of his poem and some of its language from a newspaper account reminds us that he possessed a magpie sort of imagination, gathering phrases and stray bits of language from what he read or heard, then arranging and rearranging them into poetry—a precursor of a certain strain of contemporary poetic practice. An exercise in erasure, for example, in which words are removed from an existing text, which may be quite banal, until a poem emerges, follows Whitman's lead in recognizing that other meanings may lie buried in otherwise ordinary language. The artist is the one who can reveal beauty hiding in plain sight.

"Immature poets imitate; mature poets steal," said T. S. Eliot; "bad poets deface what they take, and good poets make it into something better, or at least different." One must thus admire Whitman's theft in "Cavalry Crossing a Ford," which went undetected for over a century—long enough to ensure its place in the literary canon. But the rise of the internet and the development of software to check for plagiarized content make it difficult to disguise material lifted from another source—a challenge, one imagines, that Whitman might have welcomed. For poetry demands of its practitioners the ability to overcome resistance. No doubt he would have devised creative ways to make use of found materials on the World Wide Web.

There is a larger point to make. Think of his stripped-down version of the original text as a form of abstraction. Just as Georgia O'Keeffe painted the same landscape over and over, removing identifying details from each successive canvas in order to distill the spirit of the place, so Whitman abstracts the essence of a specific event to suggest its timeless qualities. Wallace Stevens achieved a similar effect in his poem "Metaphors of a Magnifico," which begins:

Twenty men crossing a bridge,
Into a village,
Are twenty men crossing twenty bridges,
Into twenty villages,
Or one man
Crossing a single bridge into a village.

Stevens concludes that "This is old song / That will not declare itself." It may be that in this instance "meaning escapes," but in fact he has captured an essential truth about what soldiers experience in war: they belong to a collective entity, designed to erase any hint of individuality, and yet it is as individuals that they will meet their fate. Each one dies alone.

10

"When I Heard the Learn'd Astronomer"

WHEN I heard the learn'd astronomer;
When the proofs, the figures, were ranged in columns before me;
When I was shown the charts and the diagrams, to add, divide, and measure them;
When I, sitting, heard the astronomer, where he lectured with much applause in
    the lecture-room,
How soon, unaccountable, I became tired and sick;
Till rising and gliding out, I wander'd off by myself,
In the mystical moist night-air, and from time to time,
Look'd up in perfect silence at the stars.

Folsom Commentary

This little poem initially does not seem like it belongs in *Drum-Taps*. The poem's subject is obviously not the Civil War, but the tenor of the war times is nonetheless reflected in the speaker's desire to escape a place of fragmentation (where the unified cosmos is broken down and divided into "columns") and to regain a sense of wholeness. Union and oneness, pulling back together that which has been separated—these are the subjects of many of the *Drum-Taps* poems, and they are also the focus of this poem. In addition, newspapers during the war printed daily a macabre set of "proofs" and "figures" in "columns"—the list of the names of the dead and injured, casualty lists like the ones Whitman examined to ascertain that his brother George had been injured at Fredericksburg. It was a time of "columns" of soldiers fighting, with many of them then appearing in the casualty "columns" of newspapers, all part of a horrifying war mathematics accumulating numbers as vast as the astronomer's calculation of the universe—"the million dead."

The first half of "Astronomer" consists of four anaphoric lines of steadily increasing length; the insistent repetition of the opening "When" joins with the accumulating verbiage to build to a peak point of exacerbation, after which the speaker expresses in a final group of four brief lines his relief at getting out of the "lecture-room" and into "the mystical moist night-air." The two halves of the poem, then, imitate the contrasting sounds of the scene: the first four lines (evoking the astronomer's lecture) contain sixty-four noisy syllables, while the last four (moving toward the speaker's "perfect silence") contain only fifty syllables and diminish into the relative quiet of the final ten-syllable line with its hushed concluding fourfold sibilance ("silence at the stars").

As the speaker moves from the lecture-room—with its demonstration of book learning—out into the night, he repeats a familiar pattern in Whitman's poetry, as when the speaker of "Song of Myself" puts "Creeds and schools in abeyance" and leaves the "Houses and rooms" to "go to the bank by the wood." The erudite astronomer presents the cosmos as an intellectual abstraction—a series of proofs and figures and diagrams—and receives applause for, in effect, having broken the cosmos down into charts and moved it into a lecture-room, where the only brilliance the audience can see belongs to the astronomer, not to the stars. One has to go outside to see the actual stars, which speak their proofs in "perfect silence." The speaker of the poem becomes "unaccountable . . . tired and sick" of the lecture, and the term "unaccountable" resonates with the speaker's desire to experience the cosmos again as "uncountable," as beyond the clever adding, dividing, and theorizing of the scientist.

And yet, as the speaker looks up at the sky, he does not forget the lessons he learned in the lecture-room. He describes how he looked "from time to time" into the heavens, and what at first seems to be a kind of throwaway phrase suddenly signals one of the newly formulated concepts that the astronomer would have explained in his lecture: that light takes time to travel, and when we look at the stars, we are not only looking across vast distances of space but vast distances of time as well. When we look at the night sky, we are looking from our time to the light from distant pasts, "from time to time." Whitman followed the work of astronomers carefully and would have been aware of the formulation of light-years through the work of Cincinnati astronomer Ormsby MacKnight Mitchel (1810–62), who gave a series of lectures in New York in the late 1840s (many of Whitman's poetic images of the cosmos derive from Mitchel's work) and who later became a major general in the Union Army, where he was known, fittingly, as "Old Stars."

As so often happens in Whitman, the scientist's lessons are not rejected but are absorbed by the poet, who employs them in surprising ways to create poetic truth. "Hurrah for positive science!," Whitman writes in "Song of Myself"; "Your facts are useful, and yet they are not my dwelling, / I but enter by them to an area of my dwelling." In the "Astronomer" poem, the science enhances the poet's experience of looking at the night sky. Astronomers' discovery of the speed of light and the vast distances of the cosmos even gives Whitman the idea that his own poems can be like starlight, traveling through time, able to reach readers in the twenty-first century who did not even exist when the poems were written by a poet who himself now no longer exists, just as we may be looking at stars in the sky that actually no longer exist but appear to be there because their distant light is still traveling to our eyes. The stars and planets often form a kind of vast and oddly comforting sense of permanence in Whitman's Civil War poetry—an eternal backdrop (deep time and deep space) against which the horrors of war in one country on a tiny planet become temporary disturbances that will resolve themselves and even eventually disappear in the healing cosmic cycles of time.

Merrill Commentary

What a terrible beauty—this was my first thought at the sight of tracer rounds during the siege of Sarajevo. Then I shook with terror, for the lights streaking across the night sky brought only death and destruction to the city encircled by Serbian forces. A bookish man who finds himself in a war zone is quickly disabused of his inclination to read his surroundings in symbolic terms—after all, one function of the tracer rounds used by gunners on both sides was to improve targeting—though I was still prone to stargazing there on clear nights. The bullets flew by at a fraction of the speed of the shooting star I saw above Mount Igman (the only escape route from the city), whose velocity was as nothing compared to that of the seemingly motionless stars revolving in the constellations overhead. This was what came to mind in Sarajevo when I realized that I knew by heart Whitman's exquisite little poem "When I Heard the Learn'd Astronomer." It had become for me a touchstone, recalibrating in just eight lines my perspective on our place in the scheme of things, and when I considered the stars in the sky lit up by tracers my terror subsided.

Twenty years after the signing of the Dayton Peace Accords, the poem resonates for me in other ways. Whitman's ability to suggest in a single sentence the scale of the universe, absorb and recast scientific proofs and diagrams, and reveal the gulf between theory and reality remind us that in the interest of compression a poet can accelerate thought to the speed of light. Recite these lines, and the world may begin to hum and shimmer with meaning.

Here a question arises: Why does the speaker glide into the "mystical moist night-air," if in fact he is "tired and sick"? Indeed, it sounds as if he is preparing to traverse the heavens, one star in a multitude of stars. The tidal rhythm that governed "Song of Myself," the surging and ebbing lines that match the movement of his journey outward to the edge of the universe and inward into the depths of his soul, is echoed in the countermotions of "When I Heard the Learn'd Astronomer," the lines expanding in the first half of the poem until applause erupts in the lecture-room and then contracting in the second half into the speaker's gaze "in perfect silence at the stars." How far he will wander from the earthbound crowd to orbit not in the firmament but among wounded soldiers, who will instruct him in the true costs of division and fragmentation, the prelude to his reconstruction of a poetic vision large enough to contain both war and peace.

An unpaved forest road on Mount Igman, the site of the ski jump competition in the 1984 Winter Olympic Games, was the only overland supply route into Sarajevo during the siege. And it was on an icy stretch of that road, in the winter of 1995, that an armored personnel carrier (APC) pulled over to make room for a truck carrying French peacekeepers to the airport—the front line between Bosnian and Serb forces. I was in that APC, en route to the port city of Split, Croatia, and when one young soldier fixed his eyes on mine I shuddered involuntarily with dread. Soon after, so I learned upon reaching the coast, the truck skidded off the road and plunged down the heavily mined hillside, killing nine peacekeepers—the worst incident of its kind in the war. That night I gazed at the stars above the Adriatic Sea in utter incomprehension.

11

Walt Whitman to Margaret S. Curtis, October 4, 1863

Washington, | Armory Sq Hospital,
Sunday evening Oct 4
Dear Madam,
Your letter reached me this forenoon with the $30 for my dear boys, for very dear they have become to me, wounded & sick here in the government hospitals—As it happens I find myself rapidly making acknowledgment of your welcome letter & contribution from the midst of those it was sent to aid—& best by a sample of actual hospital life on the spot, & of my own goings around the last two or three hours—As I write I sit in a large pretty well-fill'd ward by the cot of a lad of 18 belonging to Company M, 2d N Y cavalry, wounded three weeks ago to-day at Culpepper—hit by fragment of a shell in the leg below the knee—a large part of the calf of the leg is torn away, (it killed his horse)—still no bones broken, but a pretty large ugly wound—I have been writing to his mother at Comac, Suffolk co. N Y—She must have a letter just as if from him, about every three days—it pleases the boy very much—has four sisters—them also I have to write to occasionally—Although so young he has been in many fights & tells me shrewdly about them, but only when I ask him—He is a cheerful good-natured child—has to lie in bed constantly, his leg in a box—I bring him things—he says little or nothing in the way of thanks—is a country boy—always smiles & brightens much when I appear—looks straight in my face & never at what I may have in my hand for him—I mention him for a specimen as he is within reach of my hand & I can see that his eyes have been steadily fixed on me from his cot ever since I began to write this letter.

There are some 25 or 30 wards, barracks, tents, &c in this hospital—This is ward C, has beds for 60 patients, they are mostly full—most of the other principal wards about the same—so you see a U S general hospital here is quite an establishment—this has a regular police, armed sentries at the gates & in the passages &c.—& a great staff of surgeons, cadets, women & men nurses &c &c. I come here pretty regularly because this hospital receives I think the worst cases & is one of the least visited—there is not much hospital visiting here now—it has become an old story—the principal here, Dr Bliss, is a very fine operating surgeon—sometimes he performs several amputations or other operations of importance in a day—

amputations, blood, death are nothing here—you will see a group absorbed [in] playing cards up at the other end of the room.

I visit the sick every day or evening—sometimes I stay far in the night, on special occasions. I believe I have not missed more than two days in past six months. It is quite an art to visit the hospitals to advantage. The amount of sickness, and the number of poor, wounded, dying young men are appalling. One often feels lost, despondent, his labors not even a drop in the bucket—the wretched little he can do in proportion. I believe I mentioned in my letter to Dr Russell that I try to distribute something, even if but the merest trifle, all round, without missing any, when I visit a ward, going round rather rapidly—& then devoting myself, more at leisure, to the cases that need special attention. One who is experienced may find in almost any ward at any time one or two patients or more, who are at that time trembling in the balance, the crisis of the wound, recovery uncertain, yet death also uncertain. I will confess to you, madam, that I think I have an instinct & faculty for these cases. Poor young men, how many have I seen, & known—how pitiful it is to see them—one must be calm & cheerful, & not let on how their case really is, must stop much with them, find out their idiosyncrasies—do any thing for them—nourish them, judiciously give the right things to drink—bring in the affections, soothe them, brace them up, kiss them, discard all ceremony, & fight for them, as it were, with all weapons. I need not tell your womanly soul that such work blesses him that works as much as the object of it. I have never been happier than in some of these hospital ministering hours.

It is now between 8 & 9, evening—the atmosphere is rather solemn here tonight—there are some very sick men here—the scene is a curious one—the ward is perhaps 120 or 30 feet long—the cots each have their white musquito curtains—all is quite still—an occasional sigh or groan—up in the middle of the ward the lady nurse sits at a little table with a shaded lamp, reading—the walls, roof, &c are all whitewashed—the light up & down the ward from a few gas-burners about half turned down—It is Sunday evening—to-day I have been in the hospital, one part or another, since 3 o'clock—to a few of the men, pretty sick, or just convalescing & with delicate stomachs or perhaps badly wounded arms, I have fed their suppers—partly peaches pealed, & cut up, with powdered sugar, very cool & refreshing—they like to have me sit by them & peal them, cut them in a glass, & sprinkle on the sugar—(all these little items may-be may interest you).

I have given three of the men, this afternoon, small sums of money—I provide myself with a lot of bright new 10ct & 5ct bills, & when I give little sums of change I give the bright new bills. Every little thing even must be taken advantage of—to give bright fresh 10ct bills, instead of any other, helps break the dullness of hospital life—

Folsom Commentary

Whitman wrote about the Civil War in many forms, contexts, and situations. He kept notes in multiple small notebooks he carried with him while he visited wounded and sick soldiers in the teeming hospitals of the nation's capital. Often, while sitting by the bed of a suffering soldier, he would jot down what the soldier told him. Out of these notebooks—which record his visits to thousands of soldiers, listing their names, their home states, their wounds or illnesses, and often noting the stories of their lives on the march or in battle—he crafted many of his Civil War poems. He also mined these notebooks for the dispatches he wrote for multiple newspapers (including the *New York Times*) about the war and about his work in the hospital. Then he used those journalistic pieces to create his *Memoranda During the War* and *Specimen Days*. He also returned to those notebooks when he wrote his letters, which contain some of his most powerful Civil War writing. For Whitman, the borders between informal notebook writing, journalism, poetry, and correspondence were porous, and we can often find the same images appearing in prose and poetry, in scrawled notes and in published poems. Whitman's tendency to meld and merge poetry and prose is evident from the 1850s on, but it increases during the years he experienced the war in Washington, D.C. Passages from his poetry frequently sound as if they could be from his letters or his newspaper writing, and passages in his letters can often be lined to form poetry.

Whitman's remarkable letter to Margaret Curtis is in response to a letter she wrote to him on October 1. She sent the poet $30 and explained how she and her husband, a Boston counselor, had listened to someone reading aloud a letter that Whitman had written to Dr. LeBaron Russell, a Boston physician who also had sent Whitman money to support his hospital work: "It was with exceeding interest that Mr Curtis & I listened to the letter you lately wrote to Dr. Russell, which came to us through my sister Miss Stevenson. Its effect was to make us desire to aid you in the good work you are engaged in,—caring for the sick & wounded soldiers. We inclose thirty dollars, & feel very glad to have the opportunity to minister to their comfort." What we see here, as the critic Martin Buinicki has recently demonstrated, is an early fundraising network. Whitman's letters to donors present the often heartbreaking details of soldiers' suffering and underscore the efficacy of the small gifts that Whitman was able to distribute in the hospitals as a result of the money he received. Whitman presents the horrific details of the hospitals so that people like Dr. Russell and Margaret Curtis will read these letters to their friends, pass them around so that others may read them, and thus encourage an ever-broadening group to support the poet's work. Whitman's youngest brother,

Jeff, who never served in the war, often coordinated his brother's fundraising work, reminding Walt to write letters—the more detailed the better—to every donor. As Buinicki shows, Whitman and his brother developed an informal fundraising network that anticipated the more sophisticated, mechanized networks that charities use to raise money today. The raw emotion of Whitman's letters, expressed with aching sincerity, brought in just enough money to allow Whitman to carry on a quite miraculous series of hundreds of exhausting hospital visits, ultimately taking him to the bedsides of as many as 100,000 soldiers, distributing modest treats and providing something far more important—deep affection for stranger after stranger.

Whitman was given an appointment by the U.S. Christian Commission, an organization run by Protestant ministers and established to aid soldiers in hospitals (unlike the more formally constituted U.S. Sanitary Commission, which devoted itself more to mending soldiers in order to return them to the battlefields). Whitman's notoriety as an "immoral" poet and his lack of church membership made his affiliation with the Christian Commission a tenuous one, however, and he ended up operating very much on his own, distributing an unsanctioned array of gifts, from brandy to small amounts of money to candy, ice cream, and fruit: religious comfort was not what Whitman offered, opting instead for the physical, bodily comforts of touch. He sat and held severely wounded soldiers—what he called "the cases that need special attention"—and kissed them, and he developed a complex and multifaceted relationship with many of them—partly paternal, partly fraternal; partly erotic; and, importantly, partly maternal, as he nurtured the wounded, prepared their food, and fed them: "One must be calm & cheerful, & not let on how their case really is, must stop much with them, find out their idiosyncrasies—do any thing for them—nourish them, judiciously give the right things to drink—bring in the affections, soothe them, brace them up, kiss them, discard all ceremony, & fight for them, as it were, with all weapons." In Whitman's mind, he was fighting a war every night in the army hospitals, but his weapons were the healing arts of affection and love, the delight of small gifts and casual kisses. And the object in Whitman's war was life, not death, though death often came. Whitman could sense that his work—taking him to the hospitals where the fewest people visited—was ultimately the work of a "womanly soul" that gave him perhaps the most surprising gift of all, the gift of *happiness* in a place of "amputations, blood, death": "I need not tell your womanly soul," he writes to Margaret Curtis, "that such work blesses him that works as much as the object of it. I have never been happier than in some of these hospital ministering hours."

Merrill Commentary

To read a poet's correspondence is to be reminded of the gulf that lies between life and art. For if poetry is language in its most condensed form, a distillation of words and phrases and sentences into a musical arrangement capable of quickening the heart and mind, then letters composed or dashed off (as the case may be) by a poet whose eyes are not fixed on eternity may reveal the secret sources of his or her enduring literary works. This is certainly true of Whitman's correspondence, which like that of most poets is a mixture of business, gossip, ideas, information, and reflections. He submitted poems to editors, often with an imperious air; solicited help in securing employment (his letter of recommendation from Ralph Waldo Emerson to Secretary of State William H. Seward is a model of tact); and detailed what he saw and heard. His letter thanking Margaret S. Curtis for her gift of $30 to be distributed among the wounded soldiers is no ordinary thank-you note; for he describes at some length what life is like on the wards, offering his benefactress an accounting of the uses to which he puts her largesse and a vision of the tragic reality wrought by war. His courtesy serves as both a lubricant for his supplication and an excuse to pay closer attention to men whose lives hang in the balance, leavened by the gifts he bestows on them.

"It is quite an art to visit the hospitals to advantage," Whitman writes, by which he means finding ways to make himself useful amid so much suffering. His ability to identify those who would appreciate what he had to offer was inseparable from his poetic instinct—the skill set born of talent, sympathy, and experience that he brought to the page; another advantage of his caring for the wounded thus accrued to the literature of war. "Every little thing even must be taken advantage of—to give bright fresh 10ct bills, instead of any others, helps break the dullness of hospital life." Poetry can do that, too, burnishing small details until they shine.

"I have been thinking of Whitman's huge sweep," Robert Lowell wrote to Elizabeth Bishop in the summer of 1966, "mostly in his thirties and forties, lines pouring out, a hundred poems a year, yet with long, idle afternoons of sauntering, chatting, at ease nearly with what the eye fell on." With his fiftieth birthday approaching, Lowell dreamed of taking a long break, his life having grown altogether too complicated. But Whitman must have felt the same during the war, his days of ease giving way to the frenetic routine that ultimately ruined his health. Both men, broken by the years, nevertheless managed to turn their pain into art.

Whitman's attention to the soldiers was not uniformly welcomed by hospital staff. "There comes that odious Walt Whitman to talk evil and unbelief to my boys," one nurse wrote to her husband. That feeling persists in some quarters, prompting the poet Norman Dubie to write: "I worked on the wards for years, and have no patience with individuals who despise, as erotic, Whitman's nursing practices in the field hospitals of Washington. The very best nursing I witnessed was done by women with a major obsession and grace that were both founded by Eros." To Margaret Curtis, Whitman confided that "such work blesses him that works as much as the object of it. I have never been happier than in some of these hospital ministering hours." There are worse ways to spend an evening than comforting someone in pain.

12

"The Dresser"

An old man bending, I come, among new faces,
Years looking backward, resuming, in answer to children,
Come tell us old man, as from young men and maidens that love me;
Years hence of these scenes, of these furious passions, these chances,
Of unsurpass'd heroes, (was one side so brave? the other was equally brave;)
Now be witness again—paint the mightiest armies of earth;
Of those armies so rapid, so wondrous, what saw you to tell us?
What stays with you latest and deepest? of curious panics,
Of hard-fought engagements, or sieges tremendous, what deepest remains?

O maidens and young men I love, and that love me,
What you ask of my days, those the strangest and sudden your talking recals;
Soldier alert I arrive, after a long march, cover'd with sweat and dust;
In the nick of time I come, plunge in the fight, loudly shout in the rush of
successful charge;
Enter the captur'd works . . . . yet lo! like a swift-running river, they fade;
Pass and are gone, they fade—I dwell not on soldiers' perils or soldiers' joys;
(Both I remember well—many the hardships, few the joys, yet I was content.)

But in silence, in dream's projections,
While the world of gain and appearance and mirth goes on,
So soon what is over forgotten, and waves wash the imprints off the sand,
In nature's reverie sad, with hinged knees returning, I enter the doors—(while for
you up there,
Whoever you are, follow me without noise, and be of strong heart.)

Bearing the bandages, water and sponge,
Straight and swift to my wounded I go,
Where they lie on the ground, after the battle brought in;
Where their priceless blood reddens the grass, the ground;
Or to the rows of the hospital tent, or under the roof'd hospital;

To the long rows of cots, up and down, each side, I return;
To each and all, one after another, I draw near—not one do I miss;
An attendant follows, holding a tray—he carries a refuse pail,
Soon to be fill'd with clotted rags and blood, emptied, and fill'd again.

I onward go, I stop,
With hinged knees and steady hand, to dress wounds;
I am firm with each—the pangs are sharp, yet unavoidable;
One turns to me his appealing eyes—(poor boy! I never knew you,
Yet I think I could not refuse this moment to die for you, if that would save you.)

On, on I go—(open, doors of time! open, hospital doors!)
The crush'd head I dress, (poor crazed hand, tear not the bandage away;)
The neck of the cavalry-man, with the bullet through and through, I examine;
Hard the breathing rattles, quite glazed already the eye, yet life struggles hard;
(Come, sweet death! be persuaded, O beautiful death!
In mercy come quickly.)

From the stump of the arm, the amputated hand,
I undo the clotted lint, remove the slough, wash off the matter and blood;
Back on his pillow the soldier bends, with curv'd neck, and side-falling head;
His eyes are closed, his face is pale, he dares not look on the bloody stump,
And has not yet looked on it.

I dress a wound in the side, deep, deep;
But a day or two more—for see, the frame all wasted and sinking,
And the yellow-blue countenance see.

I dress the perforated shoulder, the foot with the bullet wound,
Cleanse the one with a gnawing and putrid gangrene, so sickening, so offensive,
While the attendant stands behind aside me, holding the tray and pail.

I am faithful, I do not give out;
The fractur'd thigh, the knee, the wound in the abdomen,
These and more I dress with impassive hand—(yet deep in my breast a fire, a
burning flame.)

Thus in silence, in dream's projections,
Returning, resuming, I thread my way through the hospitals;
The hurt and the wounded I pacify with soothing hand,

I sit by the restless all the dark night—some are so young;
Some suffer so much—I recall the experience sweet and sad;
(Many a soldier's loving arms about this neck have cross'd and rested,
Many a soldier's kiss dwells on these bearded lips.)

Folsom Commentary

On the granite walls of the Dupont Circle Metro station in Washington, D.C., lines from Whitman's "The Wound-Dresser" (originally, in the first edition of *Drum-Taps*, titled simply "The Dresser") are engraved in a semicircle around the escalators, engulfing those who enter or exit the station: "Thus in silence in dreams' projections, / Returning, resuming, I tread my way through the hospitals, / The hurt and wounded I pacify with soothing hand, / I sit by the restless all the dark night, some are so young, / Some suffer so much, I recall the experience sweet and sad . . ." The quoted lines—from the final section of the poem—stop there. What is missing are the final two parenthetical lines of the poem: "(Many a soldier's loving arms about this neck have cross'd and rested, / Many a soldier's kiss dwells on these bearded lips.)" Whitman's lines were chosen to honor the many doctors, nurses, and volunteer health-care workers who had, at great risk to themselves, cared for AIDS victims during the years of the scourge of that disease. The Dupont Circle area has long been a center of the gay population in the capital, and Whitman's poem about nursing the suffering and dying young men in Civil War hospitals resonated with the AIDS crisis of the 1980s through the mid-1990s, when over forty thousand people a year died from the disease before medical advances cut the mortality rate dramatically. While there was general acclaim for the public display of Whitman's poem, many in the gay community were troubled by the decision to excise the final lines, since they underscored the homoerotic nature of the act of caring in "The Wound-Dresser," emphasizing the importance of physical contact between the caregiver and the patient, affirming the crucial hug and kiss that turned dispassionate medical care into compassionate caring.

Whitman's entire poem is an urgent flow of words continually interrupted by parenthetical asides, the syntactical equivalent of the action of the wound-dresser that the poem traces: "I onward go, I stop." That onward thrust, brought on by the necessity of dealing with so many patients, is impeded by the need of each individual soldier to be tended, to have the wound-dresser stop with him, talk with him, touch him. To be an effective caregiver, the wound-dresser has to be "firm with each" and keep moving on to the next case, but he feels the "sharp yet unavoidable" "pangs" as each patient "turns to me his appealing eyes" and makes the wound-dresser want "to die for you, if that would save you." It is this Christ-like expression of a willingness to sacrifice himself, combined with a clear sense that such a sacrifice would be useless, that makes the wound-dresser's job so vexing. To maintain his effectiveness, the wound-dresser has to contain and repress his emotional response to what he experiences, for his skill requires a steady and "impassive hand," no trembling, "hinged knees" that can remain steady and flexible to do the work of kneeling and rising without buckling, an ability to be "straight and swift" in his duties, though everything about his work makes him tremble inside and threatens to melt his "impassive" hand into the gentle touch of compassion. "I am faithful," he says; "I do not give out." That statement is rife with the wavering ambiguity that marks the entire poem: to be "faithful" to his work, he must not allow himself to physically or emotionally waver, to "give out." But to be "faithful" to each suffering patient, he *wants* to "give out" in the sense of giving generously, radiating his love outward from his body that must in fact hold back in order to move on. And so, while he moves inexorably from one horror to the next—from "the amputated hand" and the "bloody stump" to the "wound in the side" to the "perforated shoulder" and the "putrid gangrene," on to the "fractur'd thigh, the knee, the wound in the abdomen"—he has to quell within himself (just as he literally *contains* in the poem with his parentheses) the "fire, a burning flame" that rages in his "breast." He works to heal, to soothe, even when he knows such care is ultimately useless ("But a day or two more, for see the frame all wasted and sinking"). He dresses the "crush'd head" and examines the "neck" with "the bullet through and through" (in one side and out the other), and while his "impassive hand" nurses the wounds, deep in his breast (and deep in parentheses) he is calling for an end to this unbearable suffering ("Come sweet death!").

While this poem is often taken to be a clear autobiographical statement—especially with Whitman's framing of the poem as the recollection of an "old man" answering "children" who are curious about what the war was like—it is important to remember that Whitman was never a wound-dresser in the hospitals, though he certainly watched and came to know such people. As with his Civil War poems that offer the perspective of soldiers, this poem is built on a persona, as Whitman imagines—based on his observations of wound-dressers' work and his talks with them—what these tireless health workers must have felt, what they would carry with them for the rest of their lives (what would "deepest remain"). Of course, Whitman himself *did* witness horrendous wounds inflicted on the thousands of soldiers he visited, and he recorded in his notebooks how he—like the wound-dresser—learned to suppress his revulsion: "It is curious: when I am present at the most appalling scenes, deaths, operations, sickening wounds (perhaps full of maggots,) I keep cool and do not give out or bulge, although my sympathies are very much excited; but often, hours afterward, perhaps when I am home, or out walking alone, I feel sick."

What Whitman finds most powerfully embedded in the memory, though, since he experienced the magical effects of personal touch with the wounded and dying soldiers, is what the inscription of the poem at the Dupont Circle Metro station—not far from where Whitman visited wounded and sick soldiers 150 years earlier—left off: the final parenthetical two lines, the things the wound-dresser now (long after the war is over) knows meant even more to the soldiers than his careful medical care—the embrace and the kiss, body to body, mouth to mouth, the physical touch of love, held in a parenthetical moment, amidst otherwise overwhelming pain, loss, and death.

Merrill Commentary

It is sometimes difficult to remember that for all the advances in medical science, the healing arts still depend to some degree on touch—which governs the movement of "The Dresser," Whitman's fictional re-creation of a soldier and wound-dresser, told in the form of an old man's recollections of his service during the war. "The hurt and the wounded I pacify with soothing hand," he remarks in the last stanza, after cataloging a variety of gruesome wounds he dressed—a crushed head; bullet holes in the shoulder and neck, abdomen and foot; fractures and gangrene and worse. "From the stump of the arm, the amputated hand, / I undo the clotted lint, remove the slough, wash off the matter and blood," he says. The unimaginable suffering he witnesses even leads him at one point to plead with death—sweet, beautiful, merciful death—to deliver from agony a cavalryman with a glazed eye and rattling breath. His compassion knows no bounds.

Juxtaposed with grisly descriptions—blood-soaked rags dumped in a refuse pail, the putrid odor of gangrene—is an image of the wound-dresser methodically working his way down the long rows of cots, bearing "bandages, water and sponge" to salve the men's pain with "impassive hand" and burning heart. Just as hospice volunteers know that touch can alleviate the anxiety experienced by patients nearing the end of their lives, so the wound-dresser attends to the dying, pacifying them with his presence, the touch of his hand, a kiss, his personal feelings supplanting his professional obligations. For compassion means to suffer with, and so he does, again and yet again.

There is a religious aspect to his ministrations, his laying-on of hands. He describes himself as being faithful to the suffering and to his calling; the wound he dresses in the side of one soldier brings to mind the spear that a praetorian guard thrust into Christ's side to hasten His death on the Cross; and when he exclaims, "On, on I go—(open, doors of time! open, hospital doors!)," one hears an echo of Jesus preaching to His disciples: "Ask, and it shall be given you; seek, and ye shall find; knock, and it shall be opened unto you." His practice of loving-kindness, Myles Coverdale's inspired translation of the Hebrew term for a quintessential religious virtue frequently invoked in the Psalms, mingles with the erotic, reminding us of the ancient connection between sexuality and the divine. That his most urgent pleas and revelations occur in parenthetical asides points to the division between his professional duties and his personal feelings—a division that at every turn threatens to dissolve into love. Which is what he remembers now.

13

"Patent-Office Hospital"

Feb. 23.—I must not let the great Hospital at the Patent Office pass away without some mention. A few weeks ago the vast area of the second story of that noblest of Washington buildings, was crowded close with rows of sick, badly wounded and dying soldiers. They were placed in three very large apartments. I went there many times. It was a strange, solemn and, with all its features of suffering and death, a sort of fascinating sight. I go sometimes at night to soothe and relieve particular cases. Two of the immense apartments are fill'd with high and ponderous glass cases, crowded with models in miniature of every kind of utensil, machine or invention, it ever enter'd into the mind of man to conceive; and with curiosities and foreign presents. Between these cases are lateral openings, perhaps eight feet wide, and quite deep, and in these were placed the sick; besides a great long double row of them up and down through the middle of the hall. Many of them were very bad cases, wounds and amputations. Then there was a gallery running above the hall, in which there were beds also. It was, indeed, a curious scene at night, when lit up. The glass cases, the beds, the forms lying there, the gallery above, and the marble pavement under foot—the suffering, and the fortitude to bear it in various degrees—occasionally, from some, the groan that could not be repress'd—sometimes a poor fellow dying, with emaciated face and glassy eye, the nurse by his side, the doctor also there, but no friend, no relative—such were the sights but lately in the Patent Office. The wounded have since been removed from there, and it is now vacant again.

"Inauguration Ball"

March 6—*Inauguration Ball.*—I have this moment been up to look at the gorgeous array'd dance and supper-rooms, for the Inauguration Ball, at the Patent Office, (which begins in few hours;) and I could not help thinking of those rooms, where the music will sound and the dancers' feet presently tread—what a different scene they presented to my view a while since, fill'd with a crowded mass of the worst wounded of the war, brought in from Second Bull Run, Antietam and Fredericksburgh. To-night, beautiful women, perfumes, the violins' sweetness, the polka and the waltz; but then, the amputation, the blue face, the groan, the glassy eye of the dying, the clotted rag, the odor of wounds and blood, and many a mother's son amid strangers, passing away untended there, (for the crowd of the badly hurt was great, and much for nurse to do, and much for surgeon.)

Folsom Commentary

The United States Patent Office Building was one of the first large governmental buildings to be constructed in Washington (after the Capitol and the White House); it was begun in the mid-1830s and completed at the end of the Civil War. In 1865, Whitman would work in this building as a clerk in the Bureau of Indian Affairs (which was housed in the basement of the Patent Office), but two years earlier—within days of arriving in the capital after he finished caring for his soldier-brother George at Fredericksburg, Virginia—he had visited sick and wounded soldiers who were housed here. It is where he made his commitment to devote himself to these soldiers in the hospitals that were proliferating throughout Washington, so many that it seemed to him as if the entire nation (as he wrote to Ralph Waldo Emerson) had been "brought to Hospital in her fair youth—brought and deposited here in this great, whited sepulchre of Washington itself." America's great white capital city that was still being built seemed to Whitman to have already become so many tombs—literal tombs of dying soldiers and figurative tombs of a dying nation, a nation broken and wounded and yet still so young, just like the endless streams of injured boyish soldiers who flooded into Washington. Whitman traveled from Virginia to Washington on a train full of wounded soldiers from the bloody Battle of Fredericksburg, and he wrote to Emerson about this "freight of helpless worn and wounded youth, genuine of the soil," many of them from the promising new western part of the nation, a "convincing western crop, prophetic of the future, proofs undeniable to all men's ken of perfect beauty, tenderness and pluck." The capital's grand, new, still unfinished white marble government buildings were appropriated as barracks for soldiers and as hospitals for the wounded. The Patent Office served both purposes, first as temporary housing for troops preparing to leave for battle, and then, all too quickly, as a hospital for the battered remnants that returned. And so Whitman began his daily visits, he told Emerson, and found "Death there up and down the aisle, tapping lightly by night or day here and there some poor young man, with relieving touch."

The two brief sections that Whitman devotes to the U.S. Patent Office Building —one near the beginning of *Memoranda During the War* and one near the end— illustrate his keen sense of irony about the quickly shifting nature of the city and the phantasmagoric way that one building could contain such a conflicting, altering, and compressed panorama of the nation's abrupt transformations. The Patent Office was set up to show off human inventiveness, to celebrate the progress of civilization through the development of new tools, implements, and machines. The second story of the building had display cases throughout the hall, some lit by gaslight, displaying "models in miniature of every kind of utensil, machine or invention, it ever enter'd into the mind of man to conceive" (inventors at the time were required to submit such miniature models in order to apply for a patent). Some of those models were of the latest and ever more efficient weapons that were now being deployed on the Civil War battlefields. So Whitman subtly develops in the "Patent Office Hospital" section the cruel irony surrounding the word *cases*: he describes the "high and ponderous glass cases" that contained the models of man's invention, and then he tells us that "between these cases" in the "lateral openings" "were placed the sick, besides a great long double row of them up and down through the middle of the hall." "Many of them," Whitman tells us, "were very bad cases, wounds and amputations." "It was, indeed, a curious scene," Whitman says, made all the more curious because of the juxtaposition of one set of "cases" celebrating the latest weaponry and another set of "cases" revealing the horrific results of the use of those inventions. The building that was created to show off the fruits of civilization now displayed instead the bloody results—cases surrounding cases—as a nation just beginning to take its place as a model of New World civilization descended into barbarism.

When Whitman goes back to the Patent Office in 1865 to begin his clerkship, he once again views the exhibition hall, which in March of that year was set up to house the gala dinner and ball for President Lincoln's second inauguration. The subtle irony of the "Patent Hall Hospital" section now hardens into the sarcasm and cynicism of the "Inauguration Ball" paragraph: "I could not help thinking, what a different scene [the rooms] presented to my view a while since, fill'd with a crowded mass of the worst wounded of the war." The stark contrast between "beautiful women, perfumes, the violins' sweetness" and "the glassy eye of the dying, the clotted rag, the odor of wounds and blood" is more than Whitman can take. "Civilization" now appears to have reclaimed the building, and the cases of inventions are surrounded by music, dancing, and fine food, but Whitman knows it is a façade: he can no longer enter this building without seeing, hearing, and smelling the now invisible but still palpable *other* cases, the worst cases, "the crowd of the badly hurt" that will haunt him for the rest of his life.

Merrill Commentary

These two entries about the Patent Office, from *Memoranda During the War*, serve as palimpsests for Whitman, who discerns in each instance another layer of history, a darker truth: that a space dedicated to human ingenuity was requisitioned early in the war to house sick, wounded, and dying soldiers; their suffering not only colored his view of American society and institutions, calling into question the very idea of progress, but called him to care for them and their wounded brethren. For when "that noblest of Washington buildings," home to the agency charged with measuring and protecting the inventiveness of the American people, was transformed into a site "of suffering and death," a new political and social reality was patented, in which death took dominion. And when that space was used for Lincoln's second inaugural ball, the rooms filling with beautiful perfumed women, music, and dance, the poet could not forget "the amputation, the blue face, the groan, the glassy eye of the dying, the clotted rag, the odor of wounds and blood, and many a mother's son amid strangers, passing away untended there"—a catalog of horrors that brought into sharp relief the inherent complications of Lincoln's electoral promise to prevail in the war and then stitch the Union back together. This, too, would be patented in Whitman's writings.

He was haunted by what he witnessed in the makeshift hospital, and in his invocation of the men's ghostly presence he recapitulates one of his working methods, adding layers of grief and complexity to his observations, like scars. Ed Folsom notes that "Whitman often literally cut and pasted poems and essays together," turning his manuscripts into palimpsests, which are sometimes difficult to categorize and transcribe, crossed-out words and phrases jostling with new lines and ideas. The same holds for successive versions of some of his writings, which he filtered through a gauze of memory and desire. No wonder he could not stop revising *Leaves of Grass*: each detail suggested the tragic scale of the war, the most enduring invention of his time.

"The past is never dead," William Faulkner wrote in his novel *Requiem for a Nun*. "It's not even past." The persistent influence of the past in shaping belief and behavior in the present, which governed Faulkner's chronicles of postwar life among the descendants of the defeated in Mississippi, took center stage in the recent controversy over the flying of the Confederate flag in public spaces in the South. Stories passed down through the generations, of valor and betrayal and loss, ensure the continuity of certain ways of thinking about one's place in the world—which is why aftershocks from the Civil War continue to rock the American body politic. The wounded and dying would be removed from the Patent Office, but not from the troubled conscience of the poet, who would document in granular detail the consequences of secession—which are still with us.

14

"Mother and Babe"

I SEE the sleeping babe, nestling the breast of its mother;
The sleeping mother and babe—hush'd, I study them long and long.

Folsom Commentary

Scattered through *Drum-Taps* are some very short proto-imagist poems that initially seem to have nothing to do with the Civil War. The critic Ted Genoways has shown how Whitman's attempt to maximize the use of space in his self-published book (and to minimize the number of pages, since the price of paper during the war had increased exponentially) led him to disperse the shorter poems somewhat randomly at the last moment before printing, wherever there was a small open space left on a page. Initially, some of these brief imagist pieces seem out of place in a book of poems about the war. Still, many of the resulting juxtapositions of shorter and longer poems are quite suggestive: the very brief "Mother and Babe" coming just before "Vigil Strange I Kept on the Field One Night" is a case in point.

We begin with a tender and intimate two-line observation of a sleeping mother nursing her sleeping baby, with the "hush'd" poet "study[ing] them long and long." This is the primal scene of maternal intimacy, the baby's first experience of the secure bond of nurture and love, a bond so close and sensual that the act of nursing allows both participants to peacefully sleep: only the poet is awake, in fact wide awake—"I see," "I study." The poet is so attentive because, during the war, as he watches so many very young men die alone, far removed from their families, he takes on himself that role of nurturing parent, to tenderly hold and kiss these dying boys, to be the loving and caring presence that they so desperately need at that moment. That babe nursing at its mother's breast is not that many years removed from the suffering soldiers at whose bedside Whitman sat: it is as if Whitman absorbed the original scene of nurture and worked to re-create it time and again in the hospitals he visited. He wrote about one young New York soldier he visited: "I often come and sit by him in perfect silence; he will breathe for ten minutes as softly and evenly as a young babe asleep."

But what of the soldiers who died on the battlefield? Did they depart without care or love? Most, of course, did, but, as Whitman listened to the stories that wounded soldiers told him of their experiences in battle, he jotted down in the notebooks he carried with him on his hospital visits soldiers' recollections of the intense love they felt for their comrades, and he was particularly taken with one story he heard. That is the story of the poem that follows this one in *Drum-Taps,* which we will consider next, a poem in which the soldier/narrator, standing in for the missing mother, puts his loving "son" to bed one final time.

Merrill Commentary

The image of a poet assembling a book by spreading his or her poems around the floor to see which ones go where endures in the literary imagination, even in the Age of the Internet, when poets are inclined to save their work in electronic files. Robert Frost said that in a book of twenty-four poems, the twenty-fifth one should be its arrangement, a challenge that rewards artfulness and imagination. For while a slim volume of poetry may amount to little more (or less) than a collection of individual poems, it can also be structured in the form of an aesthetic argument, defined in lyrical, meditative, or narrative terms (or some combination thereof), suitable for exploring personal, philosophical, political, or social themes. A book may follow an arc, musical or otherwise, with poems grouped together by images, ideas, or motifs. Or the poet may seek to create sparks between poems, linking them by means of subject and sound, texture and color, or putting some distance between poems that treat similar subjects, inviting readers to forge their own connections. Then again, serendipity may guide the selection and order of the poems, the laying out of which can reveal gaps for the poet to fill with new work. There are myriad ways to organize a book.

Whitman was forever adding, removing, and reordering poems in *Leaves of Grass,* which was published in six different editions in his lifetime, presenting an evolving understanding of his work, its measure and meaning. The arrangement of *Drum-Taps,* which can be described as an argument against the needless carnage of sectarian strife incorporated eventually into *Leaves of Grass,* gains power from the inspired pairing of "Mother and Babe" and "Vigil Strange I Kept on the Field One Night." To juxtapose a two-line imagistic poem on maternal love with a fictional rendering of a nocturnal vigil for a dead soldier may create in the reader's mind the right conditions for a meditation on the ways in which a loving gaze extends into eternity. For the one who studies "long and long" the sleeping mother and child at her breast performs a similar function when he bends over the cold body of his dead comrade, "son of responding kisses (never again on earth responding)," keeping watch through the night. Birth and death, yin and yang—the central duality of the human condition acquires greater significance in the pairing of these poems.

When my father-in-law passed away on the morning of my older daughter's fifth birthday, the hospice chaplain suggested that for the bedside service it might be wise to honor the life of the departed and then celebrate the future of the girl holding my hand.

"This is everything, isn't it?" said the chaplain. "She's learning that at an early age."

Among Whitman's virtues as a poet was his grasp of the intimate connection between the beginning and the end—of, well, everything.

15

"Vigil Strange I Kept on the Field One Night"

VIGIL strange I kept on the field one night,
When you, my son and my comrade, dropt at my side that day,
One look I but gave, which your dear eyes return'd, with a look I shall never forget;
One touch of your hand to mine, O boy, reach'd up as you lay on the ground;
Then onward I sped in the battle, the even-contested battle;
Till late in the night reliev'd, to the place at last again I made my way;
Found you in death so cold, dear comrade—found your body, son of responding kisses, (never again on earth responding;)
Bared your face in the starlight—curious the scene—cool blew the moderate night-wind;
Long there and then in vigil I stood, dimly around me the battle-field spreading;
Vigil wondrous and vigil sweet, there in the fragrant silent night;
But not a tear fell, not even a long-drawn sigh—Long, long I gazed;
Then on the earth partially reclining, sat by your side, leaning my chin in my hands;
Passing sweet hours, immortal and mystic hours with you, dearest comrade—Not a tear, not a word;
Vigil of silence, love and death—vigil for you, my son and my soldier,
As onward silently stars aloft, eastward new ones upward stole;
Vigil final for you, brave boy, (I could not save you, swift was your death,
I faithfully loved you and cared for you living—I think we shall surely meet again;)
Till at latest lingering of the night, indeed just as the dawn appear'd,
My comrade I wrapt in his blanket, envelop'd well his form,
Folded the blanket well, tucking it carefully over head, and carefully under feet;
And there and then, and bathed by the rising sun, my son in his grave, in his rude-dug grave I deposited;
Ending my vigil strange with that—vigil of night and battle-field dim;
Vigil for boy of responding kisses, (never again on earth responding;)
Vigil for comrade swiftly slain—vigil I never forget, how as day brighten'd,
I rose from the chill ground, and folded my soldier well in his blanket,
And buried him where he fell.

Folsom Commentary

In one of his Civil War notebooks, Whitman wrote down the particulars of what he heard from one soldier about how soldiers cared for each other on the battlefield: "William Giggee, Sept 18th '62. I heard of poor Bill's death—he was shot on [Union General John] Pope's retreat—Arthur took him in his arms, and he died in about an hour and a half—Arthur buried him himself—he dug his grave." Recent research by the critic Martin G. Murray has revealed that William Giggee (or Giggie) and Arthur Giggie were privates in the same New York regiment, and, though they share an uncommon last name, they were not related; Murray suggests that Arthur Giggie may in fact have taken William's last name in order to allow the two young men to claim a brotherly relationship and thus not to draw attention to what may have been a homoerotic relationship. In any case, Arthur's tender gesture of care for William stayed with Whitman, who, a year later, began drafting lines for what would become "Vigil Strange," as he imagined himself as the soldier burying his "loving comrade": "Carefully wrapt in my blanket there I buried my soldier / Buried my loving comrade boy of responding kisses, there on the field, never again responding." Another draft began: "I wrapt him in his blanket / A Soldier's death when death arrives / When my darling & comrade fell, / Not a tear I shed."

Eventually Whitman developed the idea of an all-night vigil and worked his way toward the striking syntactical reversal of the first line: "Vigil strange I kept on the field one night." The usual syntax, of course, would be "I kept a strange vigil on the field one night." Whitman puts object before subject, adjective after noun. Like some other *Drum-Taps* poems, this one is a single long meandering sentence, moving from beginning to end with no stop until the final line, where everything comes to a literal dead end: "And buried him where he fell." As Whitman revised the poem, he replaced the original semicolons at the ends of lines with commas, emphasizing all the more the relentless and unbroken attentiveness of the speaker's all-night vigil. The more we look as we wander through this sentence, the more inversions we come across: "One look I but gave"; "Then onward I sped"; "to the place at last again I made my way"; "Long there and then in vigil I stood, dimly around me the battle-field spreading." Reversed phrasings proliferate, and the inverted syntax permeates the poem. One of Whitman's Civil War notebooks contains six pages of trial lines for this poem, many of them crossed out. We can see in that notebook how Whitman edges his way toward the inverted syntax: the manuscript's "I wrapt my comrade in his blanket," for example, becomes in the final version "My comrade I wrapt in his blanket." It is as if the whole narrative is oddly off kilter, out of the usual sequence of time, off balance, "strange" indeed: the dead object seems to be in control of the living subject. The sentence pushes on, but phrase after phrase circles back, creating a kind of syntactic resistance to the forward thrust, extending the vigil, lengthening the night and delaying the inevitable dawn, when the burial will become necessary. The inversion in the title and first line ("Vigil strange I") allows the adjective, surprisingly, to adhere to the noun that follows it in the syntactic order ("strange I"), creating this estranged "I," this soldier-narrator who has left behind his fallen comrade, has gone on to fight a battle, then has returned to his dead "brave boy" (in the manuscript, "my darling") to narrate a strange vigil in eddying syntax that keeps reversing the very flow of time that the overall sentence tracks.

The three parenthetical statements join in this slowing of time by creating pauses (but not stops): they are in some sense the linguistic equivalent of the blanket, the place where the narrator folds or envelops things into enclosures apart from the rest of the inexorable syntactical flow. One parenthetical is his attempt to offer himself consolation by addressing the dead comrade and expressing the hope that "we shall surely meet again," but the two shorter parentheticals that frame the consolatory one underscore the finality of the comrade's death—"(never again on earth responding)." Taken together, the parenthetical interruptions destabilize the serenity that the soldier otherwise feels in the presence of his comrade's body, a "body . . . of responding kisses" that "never again" will respond to kiss or touch. The boy's "living" body has stopped "responding" to the "kisses" of his comrade. The dead soldier is, at the end of the poem, being enclosed and set off from the ongoing flow of the war and of life, and the sentence has nothing to do but to end.

In the original *Drum-Taps*, this poem came three poems after "Come Up from the Fields Father," but in Whitman's final arrangement of the "Drum-Taps" cluster in *Leaves of Grass*, he placed the poem immediately after "Come Up from the Fields," emphasizing the close tonal and imagistic relationships between the two works. In "Come Up," we get an enveloped letter sent to a family in Ohio, and that letter contains (and communicates) an absent identity, a son whose inevitable death is confirmed by the "strange hand" that wrote the letter and sent it to the family. In "Vigil Strange," the speaker (a "strange I") sits by a corpse all night before "enveloping" the dead soldier's "form" in a blanket, as if he too is putting a letter in an envelope. The "I" of this poem "folds" the soldier into the blanket, as if putting his "son" to sleep, but this time a final sleep: the soldier's dead body is itself now the radical sign of absence. As the burial takes place, we get one last long line of inverted syntax—"And there and then, and bathed by the rising sun, my son in his grave, in his rude-dug grave I deposited"—where the "rising sun" illuminates the descending "son" lowered to his grave as mourning gives way to morning. Then the poem concludes with abruptly straightforward syntax, subjects and objects suddenly back in their proper places, as the march of time (and the march of the living soldiers) goes on: "I rose from the chill ground, and folded my soldier well in his blanket, / And buried him where he fell." The dead letter "deposited," the living soldier can now resume his march; in the final arrangement of "Drum-Taps," the poem that follows this one is, fittingly, "A March in the Ranks Hard-Prest, and the Road Unknown," where another soldier-narrator is stopped momentarily by the death of a young soldier before "falling in" and pressing on.

Merrill Commentary

It is a solemn religious duty that Whitman performs in his night-long vigil for a fallen soldier, proceeding by means of a single sentence governed by a twelvefold repetition in the body of the poem of the word *vigil,* which is not only the first word of the title but the form of the ceremony the grieving poet enacts for his comrade, keeping watch in the starlight, with a cool wind blowing over the battlefield, spreading the fragrance of death in the silence that follows the din of another horrific battle; and as he gazes upon the face of the one he loved, faithfully, then sits beside him, preparing for a sacred feast at dawn, which will celebrate death, not life, inverting the promise of the Easter vigil kept in anticipation of the revelation that Christ is risen, Christ will come again, a dramatic theological turn that is reinforced by the plethora of syntactical inversions propelling the forward motion of the poem, he confesses to passing "sweet hours, immortal and mystic hours" with his beloved son and soldier, in a "Vigil of silence, love and death," believing they will meet again, if not in Heaven then underground, where sometime in the future, after the poet himself has passed on, they will be linked again at the atomic level, "earth to earth, ashes to ashes, dust to dust"; hence the essential strangeness of this vigil, which is at odds with the night office or a death watch in the family parlor, betokening instead a new dispensation, wherein there is no difference between the living and the dead, only new stars rising in the East at the break of day and a grave large enough to hold all those who fought on both sides of the Civil War, those who cared for the wounded and mourned the dead, those who argued for or against the issues dividing the country, those who remained indifferent or oblivious, and those who tried to stay above the fray, imagining they might be spared the judgment of history, if not of God, determined to overlook the fact that in the end no one can escape their fate, slave and slave-master, priest and penitent, judge and criminal—all are subject to the immutable laws of the universe, which bind us one to another, just as the aging poet knew, folding a blanket over the boy who died too young and must be buried.

16

"A March in the Ranks Hard-Prest, and the Road Unknown"

A MARCH in the ranks hard-prest, and the road unknown;
A route through a heavy wood, with muffled steps in the darkness;
Our army foil'd with loss severe, and the sullen remnant retreating;
Till after midnight glimmer upon us, the lights of a dim-lighted building;
We come to an open space in the woods, and halt by the dim-lighted building;
'Tis a large old church, at the crossing roads—'tis now an impromptu hospital;
—Entering but for a minute, I see a sight beyond all the pictures and poems ever made:
Shadows of deepest, deepest black, just lit by moving candles and lamps,
And by one great pitchy torch, stationary, with wild red flame, and clouds of smoke;
By these, crowds, groups of forms, vaguely I see, on the floor, some in the pews laid down;
At my feet more distinctly, a soldier, a mere lad, in danger of bleeding to death, (he is shot in the abdomen;)
I staunch the blood temporarily, (the youngster's face is white as a lily;)
Then before I depart I sweep my eyes o'er the scene, fain to absorb it all;
Faces, varieties, postures beyond description, most in obscurity, some of them dead;
Surgeons operating, attendants holding lights, the smell of ether, the odor of blood;
The crowd, O the crowd of the bloody forms of soldiers—the yard outside also fill'd;
Some on the bare ground, some on planks or stretchers, some in the death-spasm sweating;
An occasional scream or cry, the doctor's shouted orders or calls;
The glisten of the little steel instruments catching the glint of the torches;
These I resume as I chant—I see again the forms, I smell the odor;
Then hear outside the orders given, *Fall in, my men, Fall in*;
But first I bend to the dying lad—his eyes open—a half-smile gives he me;
Then the eyes close, calmly close, and I speed forth to the darkness,
Resuming, marching, as ever in darkness marching, on in the ranks,
The unknown road still marching.

Folsom Commentary

This is another poem that grew out of Whitman's Civil War notebooks, where he recorded talks he had with soldiers about their experiences in the war. This time it was a Maine soldier named Milton Roberts, who, from his hospital bed after having his left leg amputated, told Whitman of a "scene in the woods on the peninsula": "after the battle of White Oaks church, on the retreat, the march at night—the scene between 12 & 2 o'clock that night at the church in the woods, the hospital show at night, the wounded brought in—previous the silent stealthy march through the woods, at times stumbling over the bodies of dead men in the road." Whitman writes down all the grisly details of Roberts's narrative about what the soldier saw as his unit finally came to the opening in the woods: "In this opening was a pretty good sized old church used impromptu for a hospital for the wounded of the battles of the day thereabout—with these it was filled, all varieties, horrible beyond description—the darkness dimly lit with candles, lamps, torches, moving about, ~~but dark~~ but plenty of darkness & half darkness.—the crowds of wounded, bloody & pale, the surgeons operating—the yards outside also filled—they lay on the ground some on blankets, some on stray planks." Roberts described to the poet how in the "murky darkness" he could discern "the doctors operating, the scent of chloroform, the glisten of the steel instruments as the flash of lamps fell upon them." Whitman transfers many of these details directly into "A March in the Ranks Hard-Prest," as he takes on the voice of Roberts, imagining him arriving at "an open space in the woods" to find "a large old church . . . now an impromptu hospital," "dim-lighted," where, inside, among "Shadows of deepest, deepest black, just lit by moving candles and lamps," is "a sight beyond all the pictures and poems ever made," with "surgeons operating, . . . the smell of ether, the odor of blood."

It is a horrifying spectacle that Whitman imagines here and re-creates, one that seems beyond the power of art to capture: no "pictures or poems ever made" have absorbed *this*, and yet Whitman's poem will try, although he can only make out "the group of forms vaguely" because of the dim and wavering light amidst the dark shadows that protect him from confronting the full horror. Whitman carried his copy of Dante's *Inferno* with him in the hospitals and jotted notes on Dante right next to his descriptions of the wounded soldiers he was visiting; it was as if he knew, as he traversed the rows of beds in Washington's makeshift hospitals, that he was experiencing his own descent into hell, faced with horrors that a year or so earlier would have been unimaginable. Like "A Vigil Strange," this poem is one long unbroken sentence, originally with semicolons at the end of most lines (later replaced with commas), underscoring the inexorable march of words that match the "hard-prest" march that these words record. But the "hard-prest" march pauses for a moment at this hellish church-turned-hospital, and two small parenthetical pauses in the long march of the poem's sentence make us pause, too, as we read.

By the time we reach those two brief parenthetical pauses, we realize that Whitman has added one significant detail to Milton Roberts's narrative of his experience: he has imagined a very young, mortally wounded soldier ("a mere lad") who captures the narrator's attention and makes him pause amidst the murky horror. This boy soldier takes shape out of the vague forms—"more distinctly a soldier"—and is there only for three short lines before the narrator returns to the surrounding "obscurity" and then goes outside to join the ranks for the ongoing march. The two parentheticals in those three lines enact a syntactic pause in the sentence's march. The first is a clinical and unpoetic frank appraisal of the soldier's grievous wound: "(He is shot in the abdomen)." Gut wounds in the Civil War were among the most fatal, producing massive bleeding and quickly spreading infection: the narrator knows immediately the boy is "in danger of bleeding to death." But then comes a remarkable line: "I staunch the blood temporarily, (the youngster's face is white as a lily)." We move from the clinical description of the first parenthetical to the poem's one "poetic" moment, buried in the second parenthetical—the only metaphorical statement amidst all the horror. But we realize with a start that this poetic moment in fact emerges directly from the clinical observation: the boy's face can be described as a white lily only *because* he has been shot in the abdomen and is bleeding out of his gut, draining the blood from his face as he dies. The most the narrator can do is stop the flow "temporarily"—an awkward word that is difficult to say and that takes time, five syllables that slow down the poem incrementally, that buy a precious extra moment of the boy's life. And, our ears tell us, that awkward word "temporarily" rhymes, surprisingly, with "lily," forming a moment of consonance, of fleeting stasis in the march and flow. There are several marches and flows going on in this poem: the march of the soldiers (put on pause for a brief time by the stop at the church/hospital), the march or flow of the nonstop long sentence that extends across all the lines of the poem (paused momentarily by the parentheticals), and the flow of the young soldier's blood out of his body (staunched by the narrator but only "temporarily").

Like a cut flower, this boy is already dead, and he achieves his ultimate lily-beauty as (and because) his life is draining from him. As the narrator goes back outside the church and hears "the orders given, *Fall in, my men, fall in*," we can hear the dark pun: "*Fallen, my men, fallen*." For this is the nature of a military march: it is "hard-prest," and the men who remain capable fall into formation to push ahead "in darkness marching . . . the unknown road," while the men who have fallen stay behind in the church/hospital or are abandoned along the road.

Soldiers either "fall in" or they are "fallen." So as the narrator hears the order to prepare to march, he thinks again of the boy whose fatal flow of blood he had momentarily staunched, and he recalls the final moment before death: "his eyes open, a half-smile gives he me." This tender moment produces a syntactical inversion, as we get the odd grammatical situation of subject and object nestling directly next to each other—"he me": a perfect rhyme, subject and object sitting intimately on the same side of the verb, "gives he me." The narrator, marching again into the darkness, now carries with him a gift from the dead soldier, whose tentative smile breaking in his lily-white face gives something to the narrator—a moment of shared subjectivity, of deep union captured in the juxtaposed "he me." This boy has, in some very real sense, given the marching soldier back to himself; his death has delivered a moment of deep sharing and love, and, in a place overwhelmed by death, his death has given the narrator *life*. Easter lilies in church, we recall, are the flower of resurrection and new life, and that new life comes only through death.

Merrill Commentary

The researcher from Human Rights Watch, who was taking testimony from an Albanian victim of abuse at the hands of Serbian paramilitaries, impressed me with his methodical questioning and equanimity. Pristina, Kosovo, 1992. The war raging in Bosnia and Croatia had displaced millions of men, women, and children, many of them living precariously in refugee camps in the republics of the former Yugoslavia, and the consensus among foreign policy experts and journalists was that it was only a matter of time before the fighting spread to Kosovo. Reporting from the camps, I also encountered journalists, investigators from the United Nations High Commissioner for Refugees (UNHCR) and the War Crimes Tribunal at The Hague, and humanitarians from a variety of NGOs, all of whom faced the challenge of recording stories of unimaginable suffering. In their own ways they were carrying on the tradition of Whitman's hospital note-taking, which formed the basis of his *Memoranda During the War* and *Drum-Taps*. But only Whitman could have written "A March in the Ranks Hard-Prest," the dramatic monologue of a sojourner in Hell.

Whitman adopts the fictional persona of a soldier marching through dark woods, a Dantean mask that grants him the freedom to invent a scene, drawn from his notes, in which he joins the ranks of a retreating army approaching a dimly lit building in an open space—a church that offers no salvation because it has been converted into a field hospital. Here is "a sight beyond all the pictures and poems ever made"; for war creates a new reality, which demands new forms of writing to account for the bloodletting. He surveys a congregation of dead and dying souls, some lying in the pews instead of kneeling, sacrificed for the Union, and then temporarily staunches the bleeding of a gut-shot soldier, whose "face is white as a lily." In his brief time inside a place defined by shadows he can neither save the wounded man nor absorb the full weight of the scene—"postures beyond description," surgeons barking orders, their "little steel instruments catching the glint of the torches." His attention to the dying is a light in the darkness, which calls to mind Robert Frost's dictum: "Every poem is a momentary stay against the confusion in the world."

The religious element in the poem is unmistakable. The metaphor of the lily invokes critical passages from the Old and New Testaments: "My beloved is mine, and I am his," we hear in the Song of Solomon; "he feedeth among the lilies." And in the Gospel of Matthew Jesus preaches to His disciples: "Consider the lilies of the field, how they grow: they toil not, they spin not; and yet I say unto you, that Solomon in all his glory was not arrayed like one of these." What the speaker chants to the young man in his final moments is a kind of benediction born of the love that priests bestow in God's name on their parishioners—the love that most of us experience at some point in our lives, given and received: a form of grace reserved for the living and the dead. It is what marks the ministrations of the humanitarians who care for refugees from Iraq and Syria, Yemen and Somalia, Burundi and the Congo; the chronicles of the journalists who bear witness to the tragedies of our time; the prayers of all who find themselves on "The unknown road still marching."

17

"A Sight in Camp in the Day-Break Grey and Dim"

A SIGHT in camp in the day-break grey and dim,
As from my tent I emerge so early, sleepless,
As slow I walk in the cool fresh air, the path near by the hospital-tent,
Three forms I see on stretchers lying, brought out there, untended lying,
Over each the blanket spread, ample brownish woolen blanket,
Grey and heavy blanket, folding, covering all.

Curious, I halt, and silent stand;
Then with light fingers I from the face of the nearest, the first, just lift the blanket:
Who are you, elderly man so gaunt and grim, with well-grey'd hair, and flesh
all sunken about the eyes?
Who are you, my dear comrade?

Then to the second I step—And who are you, my child and darling?
Who are you, sweet boy, with cheeks yet blooming?

Then to the third—a face nor child, nor old, very calm, as of beautiful yellow-
white ivory:
Young man, I think I know you—I think this face of yours is the face of the Christ
himself;
Dead and divine, and brother of all, and here again he lies.

Folsom Commentary

In the original 1865 *Drum-Taps*, "A Sight in Camp in the Day-Break Grey and Dim" shared a page with another of Whitman's brief imagistic poems, called "A Farm Picture," consisting of two impressionistic lines: "Through the ample open door of the peaceful country barn, / A sun-lit pasture field, with cattle and horses feeding." This serene glimpse through an open barn door of a fertile farm reveals a sunny field with livestock feeding on the pasture, another scene of "leaves of grass," where the animals are eating the grass that grows up from the soil, which is always simply composted death. As Whitman so often reminds us, the farm fields of America often became battle-fields during the war, and they were often the place where soldiers' bodies were quickly buried after the fighting was over. As we saw in "A Million Dead, Too, Summ'd Up," those fields often reminded people how every grain of wheat we ate after the war contained the blood of soldiers, and so this peaceful pastoral scene captures the transformation of the dead back into life, as these animals feed on the vegetation emerging from death, and the living survivors in America feed on the cattle and harness the horses, completing the cycle of turning the massive Civil War death into the nation's future life. After the war, Whitman added a third line to this tiny poem—"And haze and vista, and the far horizon fading away"—emphasizing how the nation's future (what Whitman would come to call its "democratic vistas") depended on and stretched out from this innocent scene of the cycle of life out of death.

So the poem just preceding "A Farm Picture" offers us another glimpse—"A sight in camp"—perhaps of the same field a few days earlier or months later: the field occupied by soldiers' tents and a "hospital-tent," outside of which are "three forms on stretchers lying," corpses, each covered with a blanket. Those blankets are "grey" like the poem's light, in contrast to the "sun-lit pasture field" of "A Farm Picture." The light is "dim," and we can feel the narrator's burden as he lifts each "heavy" blanket "with light fingers": the lightness of the narrator's touch contrasts with the heaviness of the grey blankets, and his touch in fact brings some "light" along with an expression of affection and recognition for each dead soldier. The first lifted blanket reveals an "elderly man," "gaunt and grim, with well-grey'd hair," almost fading into the "grey and dim" atmosphere: the narrator blesses him with the name "dear comrade." The second soldier is very young, "with cheeks still blooming," cut off in the first flowering of his life, and he becomes for the narrator "my child and darling." Then he lifts the blanket from the third corpse and finds a "beautiful yellow-white ivory" face, one that resembles paintings and pictures of Jesus, and he is stunned to think "this face is the face of the Christ himself," and the narrator names him the "brother of all."

These three soldiers will soon join many others buried in the field, but first they receive a gesture of affection and recognition from the poet, whose identification of the third soldier as Christ does not so much single out this particular soldier as special, but rather renders him representative of *all* the dead soldiers, because they are all (so the narrator suddenly realizes) part of a vast ritual of sacrifice, all dying so that we, the survivors, can live. It is what we tell ourselves about soldiers in any war: they sacrificed their lives for us; they died for our freedom; they died so we could live. They are, then, all Christ figures, but the mass Crucifixion of the war does not yield a new atonement with God but rather reveals the divinity in each and every slain soldier. Whitman makes us feel here the senselessness of the loss, even as we experience its inevitability. *This* young man's death—like the boy-soldier's death, like the elderly soldier's death, like every soldier's death—is as significant as any in human history, even Christ's. There is divinity deep within all of us, and in war we see that divinity snuffed out with a frightening carelessness—war's endless thousands of bloody crucifixions.

Merrill Commentary

During the Nazi occupation of Warsaw, the future Nobel laureate Czesław Miłosz wrote a poem in twenty parts, in the style of a school primer, "The World: A Naïve Poem," proposing an idyllic vision of nature in counterpoint to what he would later call the poetry of witness, also collected in his postwar book *Rescue*. The question posed in "Dedication," the last poem in that book—"What is poetry which does not save / Nations or people?"—Miłosz answered in different ways during his long career, directly in this poem—"A connivance with official lies, / A song of drunkards whose throats will be cut in a moment, / Readings for sophomore girls"—and indirectly in "The World," which recalls his childhood in the countryside, as in the opening quatrain of "The Porch:"

The porch whose doors face the west
Has large windows. The sun warms it well.
From here you can see north, south, east, and west,
Forests and rivers, fields and tree-lined lanes.

Suffice to say the poet could see none of this during the occupation of Warsaw, which by the end of the war would lie in ruins, and in his poignant invocation of nature, juxtaposing pastoral visions with testimony about the tragic consequences of armed conflict, he achieves a similar effect as Whitman does in his pairing of "A Sight in Camp in the Day-Break Grey and Dim" and "A Farm Picture," placing side by side disparate images of truth, eternal and temporal, inviting readers to reflect on the relationship between the two orders of being.

What the poet records in "A Sight in Camp in the Day-Break Grey and Dim" is steeped in religion: the last of the three corpses laid out on stretchers near the hospital-tent has "the face of the Christ himself; / Dead and divine, and brother of all, and here again he lies." But there is no sense that the dead will be resurrected, even within the precincts of this poem. And the question that Whitman puts to the first two corpses—"Who are you?"—suggests not only the anonymity of the fallen in the Civil War, many of whom carried no identification, but also his fear of what he might find. He was looking for his brother, George, in the aftermath of the Union defeat at the Battle of Fredericksburg, and this sight made a deep impression on him.

The waste of blood would not be redeemed, unless a more perfect Union was established; hence every resource—military, economic, political, poetic—would have to be brought to bear to defeat the Confederate forces and create a more sustainable polity. Christ's sacrifice and promise of a new covenant between God and humankind offered a template for the new order that Whitman believed must come to pass if the sacrifice of so many young men was not to be in vain. Which helps to explain the power of "A Farm Picture"; for it presents a vision of the future as if glimpsed in a dream—a field restored to pasturage, thick with the blood of the slain: "Through the ample open door of the peaceful country barn, / A sunlit pasture field with cattle and horses feeding, / And haze and vista, and the far horizon fading away."

18

"The Wounded from Chancellorsville, May '63"

The Wounded from Chancellorsville, May, '63.—As I write this, the wounded have begun to arrive from Hooker's command from bloody Chancellorsville. I was down among the first arrivals. The men in charge of them told me the bad cases were yet to come. If that is so I pity them, for these are bad enough. You ought to see the scene of the wounded arriving at the landing here foot of Sixth street, at night. Two boat loads came about half-past seven last night. A little after eight it rain'd a long and violent shower. The poor, pale, helpless soldiers had been debark'd, and lay around on the wharf and neighborhood anywhere. The rain was, probably, grateful to them; at any rate they were exposed to it. The few torches light up the spectacle. All around—on the wharf, on the ground, out on side places—the men are lying on blankets, old quilts, &c., with bloody rags bound round heads, arms, and legs. The attendants are few, and at night few outsiders also—only a few hard-work'd transportation men and drivers. (The wounded are getting to be common, and people grow callous.) The men, whatever their condition, lie there, and patiently wait till their turn comes to be taken up. Near by, the ambulances are now arriving in clusters, and one after another is call'd to back up and take its load. Extreme cases are sent off on stretchers. The men generally make little or no ado, whatever their sufferings. A few groans that cannot be suppress'd, and occasionally a scream of pain as they lift a man into the ambulance........To day, as I write, hundreds more are expected, and to-morrow and the next day more, and so on for many days. Quite often they arrive at the rate of 1000 a day.

Folsom Commentary

The Battle of Chancellorsville (April 30–May 6, 1863) was, at its conclusion, the bloodiest battle in American history, with over 30,000 casualties (just two months later, the Battle of Gettysburg would exceed it with over 46,000 dead and wounded). Chancellorsville was one of the most crucial battles in the war, with 130,000 Union troops led by Major General Joseph "Fighting Joe" Hooker confronting a Confederate army of less than half that size led by General Robert E. Lee. Lee's surprising decision to have his vastly outnumbered troops attack the Union army caught Hooker by surprise, as did General Thomas J. "Stonewall" Jackson's initial flank move that caused the first of multiple Union retreats (it also resulted in Jackson's death after he was shot by his own troops in a costly incident of friendly fire). Lee's victory, at a cost of over 13,000 casualties for the South (the North lost over 17,000), shook the Union. Hooker soon resigned, just as Lee and his Army of Northern Virginia headed north toward Gettysburg. It now looked to many Northerners as if the Confederacy was going to win the war, and everyone realized that, at the very least, the fighting was going to drag on longer, and get far bloodier, than anyone had previously imagined.

Whitman positions himself at the receiving end of this battle's bloody production line, the place where those staggering casualty figures become haunting actual broken human presences on the streets of the nation's capital. "Hooker's command"—suspect as it had quickly become—had produced a seemingly endless stream of "wounded arriving at the landing here," at night, spreading out on the "foot of Sixth street." Whitman's straightforward narration of the scene disguises his artistry as he carefully creates an atmosphere of silent horror, with a heavy and "violent" rain drenching the wounded as they scatter themselves "around on the wharf and neighborhood anywhere," re-creating a littered battlefield throughout the capital, becoming, like the sudden rainstorm, an onslaught of violence drenching the streets. The spring rains of 1863 were not bringing fresh hope and new birth, but rather burgeoning carnage, as the bloodied soldiers lie "exposed" to the elements, momentarily "grateful" for the cleansing shower. This onslaught of wounded bodies now covering Washington's streets has already become such a familiar sight that few residents of the city even pay much attention, as they harden themselves (literally "grow callous") to the bleeding multitudes strewn in their path, "with bloody rags bound round heads, arms, and legs," as common as a spring rainstorm in the night. By morning, they will have disappeared as quickly as the rain, picked up by the "clusters" of ambulances, each carting a "load" of wrecked bodies to the growing number of crowded hospitals that the capital seemed to be turning itself into. Just a few months earlier, Whitman had written to Ralph Waldo Emerson, explaining this transformation: "I go a great deal into the Hospitals. Washington is full of them—both in town and out around the outskirts. Some of the larger ones are towns in themselves." He tells Emerson he intends to write a book—what would ultimately become *Memoranda During the War*—about "this phase of America."

Only at the very end of Whitman's section on Chancellorsville is the eerie silence of that dim-lit night broken—"a few groans . . . occasionally a scream of pain." And then, suddenly, it is the next morning, but what Whitman now realizes, as he picks up his pen on a new day, is that the previous night was only the first of an ever more violent series of deluges to come. We circle back to the beginning—to Whitman's initial description as the wounded materialize: "the wounded have begun to arrive"; these are "the first arrivals." *Begun. First.* Now, in the dawning of the new spring day, "hundreds more are expected, and to-morrow and the next day more, and so on for many days," a thousand a day, coming harder, relentlessly, accumulating until they will become "the million dead, too, summ'd up."

Merrill Commentary

A Bosnian librarian once described for me his code of conduct during the siege of Sarajevo: "This is all that counts in a dangerous time," he said. "Good humor while you wait in the road to fetch water, a joke, wearing a nice tie, a clean shirt, perfume, or makeup. We were in such a small area, so I told my wife we cannot get angry at someone because in the years to come we will meet them again." Rare as such clarity may be in the darkest days of civil war, it is precisely what can shape better prospects for postwar reconstruction and reconciliation. Whitman's decision to record in the sparest terms the arrival of the wounded from the Battle of Chancellorsville reminds us that a writer's equanimity in the face of unspeakable tragedy may combat despair. Whitman understood that "the wounded are getting to be common, and people grow callous," which must have fueled his determination to document the consequences of the war without resorting to the kinds of ornate prose that would needlessly heighten the horror. His sober reckoning of a scene fit for Dante's *Inferno* possessed the power not only to startle readers out of their indifference but also to help lay the groundwork for the rebuilding of America, imperfect and unfinished as it is.

Note, too, the calm demeanor and patience of the wounded lying in the rain, who "generally make little or no ado, whatever their sufferings." It is as if Whitman took his bearings from these men in great pain, sometimes extraordinary pain, the memory of which would shape his future work; his writings from the war served a similar function as "the few torches light[ing] up the spectacle" on the wharf, revealing the dimensions and significance of the wound at the heart of the American experience. Think of this short entry in *Memoranda During the War* as an imperative, literary and moral: "You ought to see the scene of the wounded arriving at the landing here foot of Sixth Street, at night," Whitman declares. And we do. Indeed we do.

19

Walt Whitman to Mr. and Mrs. S. B. Haskell, August 10, 1863

Washington
August 10 1863
Mr and Mrs Haskell,
Dear friends, I thought it would be soothing to you to have a few lines about the last days of your son Erastus Haskell of Company K, 141st New York Volunteers. I write in haste, & nothing of importance—only I thought any thing about Erastus would be welcome. From the time he came to Armory Square Hospital till he died, there was hardly a day but I was with him a portion of the time—if not during the day, then at night. I had no opportunity to do much, or any thing for him, as nothing was needed, only to wait the progress of his malady. I am only a friend, visiting the wounded & sick soldiers, (not connected with any society—or State.) From the first I felt that Erastus was in danger, or at least was much worse than they in the hospital supposed. As he made no complaint, they perhaps [thought him] not very bad—I told the [doctor of the ward] to look him over again—he was a much [sicker boy?] than he supposed, but he took it lightly, said, I know more about these fever cases than you do—the young man looks very sick, but I shall certainly bring him out of it all right. I have no doubt the doctor meant well & did his best—at any rate, about a week or so before Erastus died he got really alarmed & after that he & all the doctors tried to help him, but without avail—Maybe it would not have made any difference any how—I think Erastus was broken down, poor boy, before he came to the hospital here—I believe he came here about July 11th—Somehow I took to him, he was a quiet young man, behaved always correct & decent, said little—I used to sit on the side of his bed—I said once, You don't talk any, Erastus, you leave me to do all the talking—he only answered quietly, I was never much of a talker. The doctor wished every one to cheer him up very lively—I was always pleasant & cheerful with him, but did not feel to be very lively—Only once I tried to tell him some amusing narratives, but after a few moments I stopt, I saw that the effect was not good, & after that I never tried it again—I used to sit by the side of his bed, pretty silent, as that seemed most agreeable to him, & I felt it so too—he was generally opprest for breath, & with the heat, & I would fan him—occasionally he would want a drink—some days he dozed a good deal—sometimes when I would come in, he woke up, & I would lean down & kiss him, he would reach out

his hand & pat my hair & beard a little, very friendly, as I sat on the bed & leaned over him.

Much of the time his breathing was hard, his throat worked—they tried to keep him up by giving him stimulants, milk-punch, wine &c—these perhaps affected him, for often his mind wandered somewhat—I would say, Erastus, don't you remember me, dear son?—can't you call me by name?—once he looked at me quite a while when I asked him, & he mentioned over in[audibly?] a name or two (one sounded like [Mr. Setchell]) & then, as his eyes closed, he said quite slow, as if to himself, I don't remember, I dont remember, I dont remember—it was quite pitiful—one thing was he could not talk very comfortably at any time, his throat & chest seemed stopped—I have no doubt at all he had some complaint besides the typhoid—In my limited talks with him, he told me about his brothers & sisters by name, & his parents, wished me to write to his parents & send them & all his love—I think he told me about his brothers living in different places, one in New York City, if I recollect right—From what he told me, he must have been poorly enough for several months before he came to Armory Sq[uare] Hosp[ital]—the first week in July I think he told me he was at the regimental hospital at a place called Baltimore Corners not many miles from White House, on the peninsula—previous to that, for quite a long time, although he kept around, he was not at all well—couldn't do much—was in the band as a fifer I believe—While he lay sick here he had his fife laying on the little stand by his side—he once told me that if he got well he would play me a tune on it—but, he says, I am not much of a player yet.

I was very anxious he should be saved, & so were they all—he was well used by the attendants—poor boy, I can see him as I write—he was tanned & had a fine head of hair, & looked good in the face when he first came, & was in pretty good flesh too—(had his hair cut close about ten or twelve days before he died)—He never complained—but it looked pitiful to see him lying there, with such a look out of his eyes. He had large clear eyes, they seemed to talk better than words—I assure you I was attracted to him much—Many nights I sat in the hospital by his bedside till far in the night—The lights would be put out—yet I would sit there silently, hours, late, perhaps fanning him—he always liked to have me sit there, but never cared to talk—I shall never forget those nights, it was a curious & solemn scene, the sick & wounded lying around in their cots, just visible in the darkness, & this dear young man close at hand lying on what proved to be his death bed—I do not know his past life, but what I do know, & what I saw of him, he was a noble boy—I felt he was one I should get very much attached to. I think you have reason to be proud of such a son, & all his relatives have cause to treasure his memory.

I write to you this letter, because I would do something at least in his memory—his fate was a hard one, to die so—He is one of the thousands of our unknown

American young men in the ranks about whom there is no record or fame, no fuss made about their dying so unknown, but I find in them the real precious & royal ones of this land, giving themselves up, aye even their young & precious lives, in their country's cause—Poor dear son, though you were not my son, I felt to love you as a son, what short time I saw you sick & dying here—it is as well as it is, perhaps better—for who knows whether he is not better off, that patient & sweet young soul, to go, than we are to stay? So farewell, dear boy—it was my opportunity to be with you in your last rapid days of death—no chance as I have said to do any thing particular, for nothing [could be done—only you did not lay] here & die among strangers without having one at hand who loved you dearly, & to whom you gave your dying kiss—

Mr and Mrs Haskell, I have thus written rapidly whatever came up about Erastus, & must now close. Though we are strangers & shall probably never see each other, I send you & all Erastus' brothers & sisters my love—

Walt Whitman

I live when home, in Brooklyn, N Y. (in Portland avenue, 4th door north of Myrtle, my mother's residence.) My address here is care of Major Hapgood, paymaster U S A, cor 15th & F st, Washington D C.

Folsom Commentary

Whitman wrote many letters for sick and injured Civil War soldiers that he met in the various hospitals he visited in Washington, D.C.: some he wrote as if he were the soldier, speaking in the soldier's voice and signing the soldier's name, and others he wrote in his own name, reporting on the soldier's condition to members of his family. This letter to the parents of a young soldier named Erastus Haskell—a carpenter from Elmira, New York, and a fife player for his infantry band—is remarkable both for its length and for the variety of relationships that the poet claims to have had with Erastus. "I am only a friend," Whitman tells Mr. and Mrs. Haskell toward the beginning of his letter, but, as he recounts the intensity of his care for Erastus, we can feel his sense of the relationship deepen: "Somehow I took to him," Whitman says, and, by the time he describes his continuing visits to the sick young man's bedside (Erastus was suffering from typhoid fever), we sense something beyond friendship—"sometimes when I would come in, he woke up, & I would lean down & kiss him, he would reach out his hand & pat my hair & beard a little, very friendly, as I sat on the bed & leaned over him." As the soldier's mind begins to go, Whitman's voice would take on a paternal tone: "Erastus, don't you remember me, dear son?" And the more the young man sinks toward death, the more Whitman's feelings intensify: "I felt he was one I should get very much attached to." As Whitman describes Erastus's death to his parents, he cannot help falling at one point into an apostrophe (as we saw him do in "The Million Dead, Too, Summ'd Up"), turning away from addressing Mr. and Mrs. Haskell to directly addressing, now, the dead soldier who has somehow been transformed into his own departed son—"Poor dear son, though you were not my son, I felt to love you as a son, what short time I saw you sick & dying here." It is as if Erastus in fact had three parents, the two absent ones back in New York and the surrogate one who was fully present at his bedside, who was there to hold him as he died; it was Whitman, after all, "to whom you gave your dying kiss."

The critic Peter Coviello has written movingly of how Whitman, through "his acts of surrogacy" in the hospital, queered and blurred the usual relational roles of "mother, father, nurse, lover, confidant, scribe," and began to imagine a new kind of family emerging out of his "project of queer generation," one that was realized when a couple of the soldiers he had nursed, held, kissed, mothered, fathered, loved, and even dreamed of buying a small house with and living together when the war ended, ended up naming their sons after Walt, as if to recognize and honor a double paternity—the queer offspring of a love born in the rank squalor of the Civil War hospitals.

When, late in his life, Whitman came across a draft of this letter, he offered it to his young friend Horace Traubel to read, telling him that Erastus "was a pitiful, though after all only a specimen, case: they died all about us there just about in the same way—noble, sturdy, loyal boys." Whitman recalls to Traubel that, while in the hospitals, he "always kept an outward calm in going among them—I had to, it was necessary, I would have been useless if I hadn't—but no one could tell what I felt underneath it all—how hard it was for me to keep down the fierce flood that always seemed threatening to break loose." We sense here the same necessary repression of emotion that we experienced in "The Wound-Dresser," where the narrator contained and controlled—literally held in—his emotions in a series of parentheticals. When Traubel read the letter, Whitman was touched by his young friend's strong emotional reaction and gently said, "I see that you understand it. Well, I understand it too. I know what you feel in reading it because I know what I felt in writing it. When such emotions are honest they are easily passed along." Traubel asked: "Do you go back to those days?" And Whitman answered: "I do not need to. I have never left them. They are here, now, while we are talking together—real, terrible, beautiful days!"

Whitman's "terrible, beautiful" oxymoron says it all: those intense days of the war, roaming the hospitals that were filled with the wounded and dying, that were filled with young men like Erastus Haskell in need of a mother, father, comrade, and lover, were as "terrible" as they were "beautiful"—a time when the intensity of passion was everything, when, among the dying, the poet most completely experienced love. Whitman wrote one more time to Mr. Haskell, a month after Erastus's death, affirming that "death has not blotted out my love for him, the remembrance will be not sad only but sweet." This heartbreaking tension defined the war for Whitman—a thing of sadness and sweetness, terror and beauty, in which the horror could never be extricated from the love. This was the very fabric—the warp and woof—of Whitman's war.

Merrill Commentary

Imagine what the parents of Erastus Haskell must have felt upon receiving this letter detailing his final days. Grief, certainly. Then surprise, and bewilderment, and perhaps anger as questions rose inevitably in their minds. Who is this Walt Whitman? What was his relationship to Erastus? Who or what granted him the license to speak at such length, in such a familiar tone? Why did the doctor refuse to heed his warnings about their son's deteriorating health? What more could have been done to save his life? How will we live without him?

It was not uncommon during the Civil War for a soldier to write to a fallen comrade's loved ones, assuring them that at the time of his death he remained faithful to God and thus was destined to be rewarded in the afterlife. While Whitman affirms in his letter to the Haskells that they have every reason to be proud of their son, his description of Erastus's state of mind contains no hint of religiosity, for he had another aim in mind: "I write to you this letter, because I would do something at least in his memory—his fate was a hard one, to die so—He is one of the thousands of our unknown American young men in the ranks about whom there is no record or fame, no fuss made about their dying so unknown, but I find in them the real precious & royal ones of this land, giving themselves up, aye even their young & precious lives, in their country's cause." Royalty for this advocate of democracy resides in the blood of the soldiers who gave their lives to the radical cause of freedom, the cornerstone of the American experiment—and of Whitman's poetics.

His condolences take a strange turn with his declaration of love, first in a familial sort of way, as he assumes the role of doting father, and then as the recipient of Erastus's dying kiss. If for this poet freedom flourished in a union of comrades and kindred spirits, which was at the same time a microcosm of the Union shattered by the Confederate secession, then it is easy to understand why he pinned all his hopes on young men like Erastus, whose suffering and death permanently marked him. No wonder the momentum of his writing carried him beyond the occasion, and beyond decorum, impelling him to directly address the dead: "So farewell, dear boy." The Haskells must have read these lines in shock—and then inconsolable grief. How could they know when they set the letter down that their lives would be inextricably intertwined with someone they would never meet—a gray-bearded poet who took the time to tell them something true?

20

"Year That Trembled and Reel'd Beneath Me"

YEAR that trembled and reel'd beneath me!
Your summer wind was warm enough—yet the air I breathed froze me;
A thick gloom fell through the sunshine and darken'd me;
Must I change my triumphant songs? said I to myself;
Must I indeed learn to chant the cold dirges of the baffled?
And sullen hymns of defeat?

Folsom Commentary

This brief six-line poem captures concisely and starkly the momentous change that Whitman was experiencing in his life, his poetic career, and his nation's history in the tumultuous year of 1863, which began for him with his decision to take up residence in the nation's capital and to devote himself to visiting and caring for the endless thousands of wounded soldiers in the war hospitals that were now everywhere in Washington. With Stones River in Tennessee producing nearly 25,000 casualties at the start of the year, to Chancellorsville in Virginia with over 30,000 in May, then Gettysburg in Pennsylvania with over 45,000 in July, and Chickamauga in Georgia with another 35,000 in September, the year did in fact seem to tremble and reel, as blasting artillery and raging battles produced maimed bodies throughout the country. Just as the May showers in Washington in the days after the Battle of Chancellorsville brought no spring growth but rather a violent storm of bloodied bodies, so in this poem do the 1863 warm summer winds uncannily bring air frozen with fear and death, and the summer sunshine eerily darkens rather than illuminates, like the thick smoke of those ghastly battlefields obliterating the light. New words enter Whitman's poetic vocabulary now, as he discovers the confident "triumphant songs" of his prewar editions of *Leaves of Grass* shifting tonality to "the cold dirges of the baffled"—his optimistic celebrations of unity sinking to "sullen hymns of defeat."

Before, Whitman sang *songs*—the song of himself, the song of the open road, the song of the rolling earth—but those acts of celebratory singing now turn (like the sunshine becoming darkness, like warm winds freezing the lungs) to baffled *cold dirges*. In this somber poem, Whitman continues to speak to himself, just as he had done in his earlier "triumphant songs" ("I celebrate myself"), but now the tone is doubtful, querulous, resistant—"Must I change my triumphant songs? said I to myself." In "Song of Myself," Whitman had rejected "what the talkers were talking, the talk of the beginning and the end": "I do not talk of the beginning or the end," he wrote, because life and death seemed to him one ongoing endless process without division or separation. "There was never any more inception than there is now, / Nor any more youth or age than there is now": life is always life, emerging eternally from what we call death, so there is no need for dirges; there is only "Urge and urge and urge, / Always the procreant urge of the world."

The critic Garrett Stewart years ago reminded us of how, when we *listen* to a poem instead of simply *reading* it, we can often hear words that don't appear in print, words that our "reading voices" vocalize by the linguistic phenomenon of "transegmental drift," when the end of one word adheres to the beginning of the next word to create a new word, unseen but heard. In "Song of Myself," for example, Whitman's lines about "the hounded slave" contain the striking image of "my gore dribs thinned with the ooze of my skin." Most readers, if they are listening to the poem aloud, hear the beginning of that phrase as "my gored ribs" (and some editions of Whitman's poem have even mistakenly printed it that way)—the transegmental drift ("gor*e d*ribs") alters the subject/verb to an adjective/noun, and we *hear* something different from what we *see* (we *see* the dribbling gore, and we *hear* where on the body that wound occurred). Whitman often plays with these unseen but heard words in his poetry. Hidden in that 1855 triple-urge sexual chant ("Urge an*d ur*ge and urge")—disguised by the transegmental drift of the *d* of "and" adhering to the *u* of "urge" that allows us to hear in that push of desire the proleptic echo of the inevitable death that accompanies any birth—is "urge *and dirge* and urge." It is as if Whitman, in 1855, is invisibly embodying in the very sounds of his procreant song the word that would emerge as so central to his Civil War experience of mass death. Every procreant urge will ultimately result in a death-dirge as the body is recycled into compost that eventually will urge out new life again. That is why beginnings always have ends, yet the ends never really are endings but always beginnings again: "*urge and dirge and urge.*"

So, in this brief Civil War poem about sensing deep in his own body the shifting tones of his life's work, Whitman once again allows us to hear an unseen echo of his earlier work: in "col*d d*irges" we can hear the "col*d u*rges" that the war has frozen into him, turning sunshine and warmth to ice and darkness. Whitman and the nation have emerged from a period of warm "urges" into a period of cold "dirges," endless thousands of premature death-songs, and Whitman's new songs now register that deep change, even as they and he and the nation realize they will have to seek a way out of the time of dirge back to the procreant urge of trying to reconstruct a renewed nation. This will be the excruciating work of Whitman and the Re-united States in the years following the war—to find ways to re-chant the hundreds of thousands of funeral songs into a reunified song of new birth.

Merrill Commentary

"I like middles," John Updike said. "It is in middles that extremes clash, where ambiguity restlessly rules." Whitman wrote "Year That Trembled and Reel'd Beneath Me" midway through the defining year of the Civil War, in the capital of a divided nation, in the middle of his literary career. Here at the intersection of North and South, one hundred miles north of the Eastern Seaboard's midpoint, the Confederate capital of Richmond, he wonders how the war will affect his writing—which is to say, his soul; the consequences of the clashing extremes that sundered the nation, which he is recording in both poetry and prose, bearing witness to the suffering of the wounded and dying on his regular visits to the city's hospitals, will change him. Ambiguity surely rules his reflections on the fact that his full-throated "triumphant songs" in *Leaves of Grass* may give way to the writing of "cold dirges of the baffled," if not "sullen hymns of defeat." (Those hymns, as it happens, would be sung not in the Union but in former Confederate strongholds during Reconstruction—and they remain in vogue in more precincts of the land than we might imagine.)

It is noteworthy that a poem auguring such a profound change in Whitman's bearing toward his work is just six lines long, neatly divided into three descriptions of his state of mind and three questions about the direction of his writings. What he glimpsed in his prewar "Year of Meteors," which was for him a year of love and forebodings, "transient and strange," has turned into a hellish vision of the poet freezing in a summer wind, his outlook darkening in a "thick gloom" of sunlight. Think of this poem as the hinge connecting his celebrations of the American experiment in liberty in "Song of Myself" and the Dantesque scenes inscribed in *Memoranda During the War*. The scale of carnage left Whitman reeling in the summer of 1863; for the smoke rising from the battlefields in Chancellorsville and Gettysburg and Chickamauga obscured the darkest truth of all—that a nation "dedicated to the proposition that all men are created equal," as Abraham Lincoln would declare in his Gettysburg Address that November, might not endure. No wonder American poets have never stopped chanting "the cold dirges of the baffled."

21

"Give Me the Splendid Silent Sun"

1

GIVE me the splendid silent sun, with all his beams full-dazzling;
Give me juicy autumnal fruit, ripe and red from the orchard;
Give me a field where the unmow'd grass grows;
Give me an arbor, give me the trellis'd grape;
Give me fresh corn and wheat—give me serene-moving animals, teaching content;
Give me nights perfectly quiet, as on high plateaus west of the Mississippi,
and I looking up at the stars;
Give me odorous at sunrise a garden of beautiful flowers, where I can walk
undisturb'd;
Give me for marriage a sweet-breath'd woman, of whom I should never tire;
Give me a perfect child—give me, away, aside from the noise of the world, a
rural domestic life;
Give me to warble spontaneous songs, reliev'd, recluse by myself, for my own ears only;
Give me solitude—give me Nature—give me again,
O Nature, your primal sanities!
—These, demanding to have them, (tired with ceaseless excitement, and rack'd by
the war-strife;)
These to procure, incessantly asking, rising in cries from my heart,
While yet incessantly asking, still I adhere to my city;
Day upon day, and year upon year, O city, walking your streets,
Where you hold me enchain'd a certain time, refusing to give me up;
Yet giving to make me glutted, enrich'd of soul—you give me forever faces;
(O I see what I sought to escape, confronting, reversing my cries;
I see my own soul trampling down what it ask'd for.)

2

Keep your splendid silent sun;
Keep your woods, O Nature, and the quiet places by the woods;

Keep your fields of clover and timothy, and your corn-fields and orchards;
Keep the blossoming buckwheat fields, where the Ninth-month bees hum;
Give me faces and streets! give me these phantoms incessant and endless along
the trottoirs!
Give me interminable eyes! give me women! give me comrades and lovers by the
thousand!
Let me see new ones every day! let me hold new ones by the hand every day!
Give me such shows! give me the streets of Manhattan!
Give me Broadway, with the soldiers marching—give me the sound of the
trumpets and drums!
(The soldiers in companies or regiments—some, starting away, flush'd and reckless;
Some, their time up, returning, with thinn'd ranks—young, yet very old, worn,
marching, noticing nothing;)
—Give me the shores and the wharves heavy-fringed with the black ships!
O such for me! O an intense life! O full to repletion, and varied!
The life of the theatre, bar-room, huge hotel, for me!
The saloon of the steamer! the crowded excursion for me! the torch-light procession!
The dense brigade, bound for the war, with high piled military wagons following;
People, endless, streaming, with strong voices, passions, pageants;
Manhattan streets, with their powerful throbs, with the beating drums, as now;
The endless and noisy chorus, the rustle and clank of muskets, (even the sight of
the wounded;)
Manhattan crowds with their turbulent musical chorus—with varied chorus and
light of the sparkling eyes;
Manhattan faces and eyes forever for me.

Folsom Commentary

In the writings that we have read so far, we have frequently seen the intense pressures and tensions that the Civil War forged in Whitman's work, often leaving him with no recourse but to celebrate his oxymoronic reactions to the mix of "sweetness" and "sadness" he found in his war experiences, or the blend of beauty and horror, love and death, he experienced in the war hospitals. This 1865 poem embodies another of those irresolvable tensions—the way the war made Whitman want to escape to a solitary rural retreat far from the urban space he inhabited, with its continual noise and incessant reminders of the war, and the way the war simultaneously made him want to even more fully embrace the militarized city and its raucous sociability. Oddly, he feels an equally strong pull toward silence and noise, toward "solitude" and "faces and streets," and he is drawn toward composing his own "spontaneous songs" written "for my ears only" at the same time that he wants to record and broadcast the "strong voices, passions, pageants" and the very public "powerful throbs" of "Manhattan streets."

This is another poem in which the real power and poignancy are contained in parentheses—first, at the end of the opening section, when Whitman's two-line parenthetical insertion pauses to articulate the bewildering but inevitable pressures that make him desire such contradictory things: he sees what he "sought to escape" now confronting him and "reversing my cries"—"I see my own soul trampling down what it ask'd for." His desire to retreat is forcefully countered by the even stronger desire to engage. Then, in the second section of the poem, as he passionately rejects what he had just so fervently sought, and as he embraces what he had just so firmly rejected, he pauses parenthetically again to dwell on the spectacle of "the soldiers marching" and "the sound of the trumpets and drums," and he realizes how "flush'd and reckless" the soldiers heading off to battle are, and what a contrast they provide to the "returning . . . thinn'd ranks": those ranks are "thinn'd" by the absent soldiers who will never return, and those ranks put on display the oxymoronic "young, yet very old, worn" soldiers who *do* return but who come back in utter distraction, "noticing nothing." Youth, exposed to war, no longer equates with freshness and vitality. Whitman exits this parenthetical pause to generate yet another catalog of urban excitement—another "brigade bound for the war" as part of "the endless and noisy chorus." But one final quiet and brief parenthetical pause—"(even the sight of the wounded)"—brings him back to his deeply draining and yet inspiriting experience of caring for the soldiers in the hospitals. It is a final short aside, quickly swallowed up in the "turbulent musical chorus" of "Manhattan faces and eyes forever for me" in the final lines.

These three parentheticals make us realize that, as Whitman wanders among the Manhattan crowds—"these phantoms incessant and endless along the trottoirs"—all the eyes and faces of the urban masses around him are in fact phantoms, here today and gone tomorrow; it's just that the "thinn'd ranks" of the "returning" regiments and the memory of the countless "wounded" underscore for the poet just how quickly any "crowd" can dissipate into a phantom memory. Retreat, confrontation; excitement, despair; energetic youth, careworn age; silence, noise; presence, absence: it is the endlessly pulsating, oxymoronic experience of war.

Merrill Commentary

During the war, Whitman must often have wished to flee "the noise of the world," as he proposes to do in the first part of "Give Me the Splendid Silent Sun." Nature's "primal sanities" were a balm for his soul, and the images he conjures of rural contentment—the warbling of birds, the fragrance of flowers in the garden, the sight of the stars—fortify him in the city, to which he still adheres. Exhausted by his ministry to the wounded, he beseeches the sun to give him strength, which in the second half of the poem allows him to once again appreciate "comrades and lovers," soldiers on parade, black ships in the wharves, the endless procession of people streaming past, full of passion: "O such for me! O an intense life! O full to repletion and varied!"

From retreat to engagement—this movement recalls the ebb and flow of certain passages in "Song of Myself," the tidal rhythm that bespeaks the sea and also the beating of the heart, systole and diastole, the mechanism by which blood circulates through the arteries and veins. Whitman understood at an elemental level how the waves breaking on shore mimic the motions of the heart.

"In the years of Buchenwald and Auschwitz," the Greek poet Odysseus Elytis writes in "Chronicle of a Decade," much of which is set in Nazi-occupied Athens, "[Henri] Matisse painted the juiciest, rawest, most enchanting flowers and fruits ever made, as if the miracle of life itself discovered it could compress itself inside them forever. Today, they speak more eloquently than any macabre necrology." Elytis suggests that "an entire contemporary literature made the mistake of competing with events and succumbing to horror instead of balancing it, as it should have done." Indeed, his poems oscillate between the poles of the pastoral tradition (with a surrealist inflection) and the work of witnessing—the same tension that animates "Give Me the Splendid Silent Sun." For poets must decide at critical moments in their lives, in peacetime and at war, whether to retreat or engage: a defining feature of the human condition. One step back then one step forward, and vice versa, over and over again; in that interval lie our hopes and fears.

22

"Over the Carnage Rose Prophetic a Voice"

OVER the carnage rose prophetic a voice,
Be not dishearten'd—Affection shall solve the problems of Freedom yet;
Those who love each other shall become invincible—they shall yet make Columbia victorious.

Sons of the Mother of All! you shall yet be victorious!
You shall yet laugh to scorn the attacks of all the remainder of the earth.

No danger shall balk Columbia's lovers;
If need be, a thousand shall sternly immolate themselves for one.

One from Massachusetts shall be a Missourian's comrade;
From Maine and from hot Carolina, and another an Oregonese, shall be friends triune,
More precious to each other than all the riches of the earth.

To Michigan, Florida perfumes shall tenderly come;
Not the perfumes of flowers, but sweeter, and wafted beyond death.

It shall be customary in the houses and streets to see manly affection;
The most dauntless and rude shall touch face to face lightly;
The dependence of Liberty shall be lovers,
The continuance of Equality shall be comrades.

These shall tie you and band you stronger than hoops of iron;
I, extatic, O partners! O lands! with the love of lovers tie you.

Were you looking to be held together by the lawyers?
Or by an agreement on a paper? or by arms?
—Nay—nor the world, nor any living thing, will so cohere.

Folsom Commentary

In the years following the Civil War, many novels and stories appeared that portrayed the marriage of a Northerner and a Southerner. John William DeForest's *Miss Ravenal's Conversion from Secession to Loyalty* (1867) was perhaps the best known of these works that employed the power of fiction to help Southerners and Northerners imagine a new kind of bond that would heal the divisions and lingering enmity of the war: by figuring a marriage between two people from opposite sides of the Civil War, these writers created an imaginary space that helped readers think their way toward the possibilities of a Re-united States. Whitman had already begun imagining a different kind of cross-sectional affection that he originally believed—when he first published his "Calamus" poems in 1860—might prevent a civil war from happening. His "Calamus" poems had explored the possibilities of a more public and accepted expression of a national affection between males, a freeing of homoerotic feelings from the repressive and repressed dungeons to which they had long been cast. While women were free to express their strong affection for other women—to hold hands, walk arm-in-arm, embrace and kiss, even write passionate letters to each other—most males were disciplined into withholding such expressions of love for other men. Men were taught that their relationships to other men needed to be based on manly competition, starting as schoolboys on athletic fields and carrying over into the capitalistic survival-of-the-fittest economy that rewarded self-reliance, ambition, and, increasingly, a ruthlessness that might result in business victories over competitors. For democracy to flourish, Whitman believed, this dangerous faith in manly competition had to be offset with the encouragement of affection between men. He saw the developing hatred between North and South as the perverse flowering of manly competition gone mad. When he published the "Calamus" poems as a new cluster in his 1860 *Leaves of Grass*, he hoped the book might help avert a war by proposing a simple solution—"affection"—to all the problems the young nation was facing.

When that attempt failed, Whitman revised one of his "Calamus" poems and repurposed it as a Civil War poem. He published it in *Drum-Taps*, adding a new first line—"Over the carnage rose prophetic a voice"—and made it clear that the prophetic voice was his own, the same voice that he had raised five years earlier, when that voice implicitly warned of the carnage that would result from men's failure to love and respect the bodies of other men. That carnage had now, by the time the poem was published, manifested itself in one and a half million casualties, the horrifying fruit of untrammeled competition: America now could *only* speak "over the carnage," because dead and maimed male bodies were scattered throughout the American landscape (many still being buried in the first years after the war) and in town squares all across the nation, where, for decades, amputees from the war gathered. The war, then, intensified the urgency of Whitman's belief that there needed to be a radical reconception of America's ideas of affection and a new emphasis on and acceptance of intimacy between men: "It shall be customary in the houses and streets to see manly affection." America's public spaces, in Whitman's prophecy, would welcome the sight of men touching "face to face lightly," welcoming instead of recoiling from physical touch with each other. All the political problems of union, secession, and reunification would be solved, he believed, not by legal or military means but by a release of repressed physical affection: "Affection shall solve the problems of Freedom yet." Those looking for constitutional remedies for regional hatred and division were missing the root cause: no "agreement on paper" or laws enforced "by arms" would allow the fragile nation, "nor any living thing," to cohere. Instead of military "arms," the newly reconstituted nation needed the "arms" of its young men embracing.

So, what had in the 1860 "Calamus" poems been a desperate attempt to call young men of the North and South to recognize the affectional bonds that united them in order to tamp down the enmity that was flaring up and threatening war, now became in 1865 Whitman's attempt to offer an imaginary healing space similar to, and yet radically different from, the post–Civil War marriage fiction that united a Southern belle with a Union veteran: Whitman, instead, offers the healing figure of men expressing affection for each other across formerly warring regions—"One from Massachusetts shall be a Missourian's comrade; / From Maine and from hot Carolina, and another an Oregonese, shall be friends triune." It is a vision of a reunited nation, sustained and held together not so much by legal remedies as by the remedy of a new homoerotics—men loving men. As we have seen, Whitman experienced in the Civil War hospitals a deepening expression of affection among the wounded and dying young soldiers; he observed the camaraderie of soldiers that had been forged on the battlefield, their growing comfort with physical touch with other men, even the easy camaraderie of Confederate soldiers in those hospitals with their Union counterparts. It was Whitman's crazy and powerful notion that the love he experienced then would survive the war and help remake the nation.

Merrill Commentary

Columbia is the name that Whitman invokes for postbellum America in "Over the Carnage Rose Prophetic a Voice," signaling a spiritual union grounded in affection between males: comradeship. The name derives, of course, from Christopher Columbus, the Italian explorer and colonizer of the New World, and it was bestowed on many towns, things, and institutions in America, including Columbia University, the District of Columbia, a river in the Pacific Northwest, a record company, the command module that landed the first men on the moon, a radio and television network, a film studio, and the ill-fated space shuttle that in 2003 disintegrated upon reentry into the atmosphere. A variation of the word, Columbiad, was the name given to a cannon deployed on both sides of the Civil War, and to the fictional space gun in Jules Verne's 1865 novel, *From the Earth to the Moon,* which could fire an aluminum ball capable of carrying people to the moon. In short, a name rich in associations, which in the poet's hands becomes a figure for uniting men North and South, turning combatants into comrades, enemies into lovers.

The grammatical inversion in the first line (added five years after the poem was published in the 1860 edition of *Leaves of Grass*) contains a visual pun: "carnage rose" can be read as a noun and a verb or as a compound noun—a cultivar, if you will, created especially for the soil of the battlefields thick with human remains. The mind makes the necessary correction with the next word, "prophetic," even as it retains an image of the flower that symbolizes love and death. It is also an emblem of purity and passion, change and perfection: key elements of Whitman's poetics and philosophy. Rooted in this charged earth, his prophecy—"Affection shall solve the problems of Freedom yet"—is thus a rebuke to the despair that customarily takes hold in the aftermath of war. What he proposes is a radically new understanding of the bonds that will hold together the society rising from the ashes of sectarianism—a blossoming of homoerotic love.

Which begins with "friends triune," a secular version of the Holy Trinity, uniting comrades (gods) from three points of the compass: north and south and west. Call them Liberty, Equality, and Fraternity: the slogan of the French Revolution. Law in this conception of America is neither the governing idea of a land composed of disparate peoples nor the final arbiter of right and wrong: a paper agreement can be ripped up; flaws can be written into a constitution; the breakdown of the social contract can lead to war. But love? "America I'm putting my queer shoulder to the wheel," Allen Ginsburg declared, obeying Whitman's imperative. There lies the future.

23

"Come Up from the Fields Father"

Come up from the fields, father, here's a letter from our Pete;
And come to the front door, mother—here's a letter from thy dear son.

Lo, 'tis autumn;
Lo, where the trees, deeper green, yellower and redder,
Cool and sweeten Ohio's villages, with leaves fluttering in the moderate wind;
Where apples ripe in the orchards hang, and grapes on the trellis'd vines;
(Smell you the smell of the grapes on the vines?
Smell you the buckwheat, where the bees were lately buzzing?)

Above all, lo, the sky, so calm, so transparent after the rain, and with wondrous
clouds;
Below, too, all calm, all vital and beautiful—and the farm prospers well.

Down in the fields all prospers well;
But now from the fields come, father—come at the daughter's call;
And come to the entry, mother—to the front door come, right away.

Fast as she can she hurries—something ominous—her steps trembling;
She does not tarry to smooth her white hair, nor adjust her cap.

Open the envelope quickly;
O this is not our son's writing, yet his name is sign'd;
O a strange hand writes for our dear son—O stricken mother's soul!
All swims before her eyes—flashes with black—she catches the main words only;
Sentences broken—*gun-shot wound in the breast, cavalry skirmish, taken to hospital,*
At present low, but will soon be better.

Ah, now the single figure to me,
Amid all teeming and wealthy Ohio, with all its cities and farms,
Sickly white in the face and dull in the head, very faint,
By the jamb of a door leans.

Grieve not so, dear mother, (the just-grown daughter speaks through her sobs;

The little sisters huddle around, speechless and dismay'd;)
See, dearest mother, the letter says Pete will soon be better.

Alas, poor boy, he will never be better, (nor may-be needs to be better,
　　that brave and simple soul;)
While they stand at home at the door, he is dead already;
The only son is dead.

But the mother needs to be better;
She, with thin form, presently drest in black;
By day her meals untouch'd—then at night fitfully sleeping, often waking,
In the midnight waking, weeping, longing with one deep longing,
O that she might withdraw unnoticed—silent from life, escape and withdraw,
To follow, to seek, to be with her dear dead son.

Folsom Commentary

During the last decade of Whitman's life, his famous poem about Abraham Lincoln's assassination—"O Captain! My Captain!"—became his most reprinted and most anthologized piece, as the United States emerged from the era of Reconstruction and as Lincoln came to be revered and idolized as the "Great Emancipator." But during the Reconstruction years, "Come Up from the Fields Father" was the Whitman poem that was most often included in the early literature anthologies and textbooks that were appearing with ever greater frequency in the United States in the decade after the Civil War. Telling the story of a mother receiving a letter informing her of her soldier-son's battle injury, the poem neatly fit the conventions of a literature of sentimentality: it was made to elicit tears with its meditation on death, motherly love, and dashed hopes (one textbook writer said the poem's power was in its "vivid and touching home scene"). Whitman even received letters from young women who recalled hearing their teachers recite it; one young woman named Lizzie Westgate wrote to Whitman about her memory of hearing the poem: "We, boys & girls were young, and merry, but we all felt the fresh country air, and later the deep pathos. . . . I do not think that any of us moved for a moment after the poem was ended, and then such a spontaneous, unpremeditated burst of applause, rose from girlish & boyish hearts, and surprised our teacher." Another young woman, Amelia Bates, recalled how she "had been brave enough" to recite the poem herself and ended up moving her audience to tears. Whitman's poem captured the deep sense of personal loss that hundreds of thousands of families across the nation were feeling in those tense, sad years of Reconstruction, and the poem helped to remake Whitman's image. He was still the radical experimentalist—this poem was, after all, unrhymed and without a recognizable metric pattern—but it nonetheless affirmed for many readers a reassuringly conservative set of values and evoked a socially sanctioned emotional response.

Whitman sets the poem in Ohio, a state which escaped having any major battles fought within its borders, but one that sent well over 300,000 of its young men to the war. Many thousands never returned, and this poem captures the effect of one representative death on one representative Ohio family. The farm fields of many states had turned into battle fields and killing fields, where dead soldiers were buried and composted back into the soil, adding their blood and decomposing bodies to all the future nutriment of the country (as Whitman reminded us in "The Million Dead, Too, Summ'd Up"). In Ohio, however, the fields were not mixed with the dead, and the fall harvest was not haunted by the corpses of soldiers; instead, as the poem opens, all is "calm, all vital and beautiful, and the farm prospers well." But no place in the nation would remain untouched by the war's massive death, and now the son of this farm family, Pete, will never return to take over the maintenance of this fertile place from his father. As one of the daughters of the family calls the father up from the fields because a letter from Pete has arrived, the father simply vanishes from the poem as we enter into the domestic space of the farmhouse, where now the mother and daughters gather around to open Pete's letter.

What had been the safe and sonorous sounds of that Senecan word "Ohio" suddenly fracture into verbal shards of grief, as the "O's" are amputated from the state's name and become the isolated cries of the mother: "O this is not our son's writing, yet his name is sign'd, / O a strange hand writes for our dear son, O stricken mother's soul." We have seen how Whitman's writing of letters for injured and dying soldiers was one of his ongoing services in the Washington hospitals, and this poem could only have been written by someone who had thought deeply about the impact that his own letters, written on behalf of soldiers too sick or debilitated to write for themselves, would have when they reached the soldiers' families, who would immediately see that the letter was written in a "strange hand." We recall how Whitman would sometimes sign the soldier's name to those letters, since many had lost their hands or arms or were simply too weak to write on their own. In this poem, Whitman probes deeply and imagines the horror of opening a letter that, because the writing is physically severed from the body that should have been doing the writing, betrays the fact that the soldier's body is already lifeless by the time the letter arrives—as absent in fact as the absence of the familiar hand in the letter's script. The very name of the soldier appears in a "strange hand,"

and that severance of name and body signals a loss of identity. When the mother in the poem tries to read the letter, it too fragments: "All swims before her eyes, flashes with black, she catches the main words only, / Sentences broken." She can only pick up disembodied pieces of the text, amputated phrases, and so the letter appears to her to be the reflection of what she now knows is her son's broken body, damaged beyond repair. What she *cannot* see in the letter is the word "I," because, though it must be there, it too is written in that "strange hand," and the brokenness of the letter, the absence of Pete's body's attachment to the words that claim to be his, prevents the mother from perceiving a cohesive identity. Though the "letter" *says* that Pete will "soon be better," the mother knows he is already gone. The broken form of the letter speaks louder and more truly than the words themselves.

All the nutriment of that fertile Ohio farm in the lush "autumn," the season of harvest, now can sustain no one. The father has vanished on his way up from the fields (just as Pete has vanished coming up from other fields), and the mother now leaves "her meals untouch'd," rejecting the farm's fertility and heading inexorably toward the same "withdrawal" that Pete has enacted—the dissipation of identity that the letter, like so many that it was Whitman's sad duty to write, revealed simply by being in the hand of Whitman instead of that of the soldier.

Merrill Commentary

Poetic influence is notoriously difficult to trace. Spiritual affinities, temperament, taste, language, geography, ethnicity, sexual identity, politics—all combine in mysterious ways to form a poet's inheritance, which he or she may not claim or even recognize. A notable exception is the Jesuit priest and poet Gerard Manley Hopkins. "I always knew in my heart Walt Whitman's mind to be more like my own than any other man's living," he wrote to a friend in 1882. "As he is a very great scoundrel this is not a pleasant confession." Although "Come Up from the Fields Father" was one of only three Whitman poems that Hopkins admitted reading, the alliteration and abrupt stresses in its title and opening line helped inspire him to develop his own distinctive "sprung rhythm," a prosodic advance as important for poetry in English as Whitman's free verse. Hopkins dismissed Whitman's line as "irregular rhythmic prose," but his expanded understanding of iambic rhythms was no less radical; from both sides of the Atlantic these men opened new acoustic spaces in which to hear poetry, reinvigorating an art form that had gone stale.

A poet may be influenced by another poet's inferior work, delighting in a single phrase or cadence or combination of sounds: the alliteration of "fields, father," for example, may have been rattling around in Hopkins's auditory imagination when he composed "The Windhover," which begins, "I caught this morning morning's minion, king- / dom of daylight's dauphin, dapple-dawn-drawn Falcon," and ends with "Fall, gall themselves, and gash gold-vermillion." The subject matter of these two poems, and indeed the quality, could not be more dissimilar: Hopkins's ecstatic praise song to Christ our Lord is a masterful essay on the ways in which his "heart in hiding / Stirred for a bird—the achieve of, the mastery of a thing," while Whitman's fictional (and rather more conventional) rendering of a family's reaction to the delivery of their son's last letter home elicits more somber emotions. The distraught mother, who like the Virgin Mary has lost her only son, will find no religious solace, no outlet for her grief, no reason not to follow the dead into the earth. The letter in a stranger's hand, thousands of which Whitman himself wrote, arrives during the fall harvest, the fertility of these fields a stark reminder that other fields are filled with the remains of Union and Confederate soldiers: the grimmest harvest imaginable.

Whitman's depiction of the mother's shock—"Sickly white in the face and dull in the head, very faint, / By the jamb of a door leans"—echoes two crucial lines in "Song of Myself": "Unscrew the doors themselves from their jambs!" and "I lean and loafe at my ease observing a spear of summer grass." In his conflation of ideas central to his prewar poetics he steers close to Hopkins, who one morning would "wake and feel the fell of dark, not day." The very premise of Whitman's celebration of the self and the universe was upended by the war that left countless grieving men and women desperate to "withdraw unnoticed—silent from life."

Sing that.

24

"The Veteran's Vision"

WHILE my wife at my side lies slumbering, and the wars are over long,
And my head on the pillow rests at home, and the mystic midnight passes,
And through the stillness, through the dark, I hear, just hear, the breath of my infant,
There in the room, as I wake from sleep, this vision presses upon me:
The engagement opens there and then, in my busy brain unreal;
The skirmishers begin—they crawl cautiously ahead—
I hear the irregular snap! snap!
I hear the sounds of the different missiles—the short *t-h-t! t-h-t!* of the rifle balls;
I see the shells exploding, leaving small white clouds—
I hear the great shells shrieking as they pass;
The grape, like the hum and whirr of wind through the trees, (quick, tumultuous,
 now the contest rages!)
All the scenes at the batteries themselves rise in detail before me again;
The crashing and smoking—the pride of the men in their pieces;
The chief gunner ranges and sights his piece, and selects a fuse of the right time;
After firing, I see him lean aside, and look eagerly off to note the effect;
—Elsewhere I hear the cry of a regiment charging—(the young colonel leads
 himself this time, with brandish'd sword;)
I see the gaps cut by the enemy's volleys, (quickly fill'd up—no delay;)
I breathe the suffocating smoke—then the flat clouds hover low, concealing all;
Now a strange lull comes for a few seconds, not a shot fired on either side;
Then resumed, the chaos louder than ever, with eager calls, and orders of officers;
While from some distant part of the field the wind wafts to my ears a shout
 of applause, (some special success;)
And ever the sound of the cannon, far or near, (rousing, even in dreams, a devilish
 exultation, and all the old mad joy, in the depths of my soul;)
And ever the hastening of infantry shifting positions—batteries, cavalry,
 moving hither and thither;
(The falling, dying, I heed not—the wounded, dripping and red, I heed not—
 some to the rear are hobbling;)

Grime, heat, rush—aid-de-camps galloping by, or on a full run;
With the patter of small arms, the warning *s-s-t* of the rifles, (these in my vision I
hear or see,)
And bombs bursting in air, and at night the vari-color'd rockets.

Folsom Commentary

In an 1863 notebook, Whitman recorded his experiences at Fredericksburg, Virginia, where he came in search of his wounded brother George, and he jotted down many battle and camp stories that he heard from the soldiers he came to know during his stay there. A number of his war poems emerge from these notes, and on one page he records a list of "scenes, sounds, &c" of "a battle." It is hard to tell if Whitman is recording memories of one or more soldiers or if he is imagining these sounds himself, based on what he has heard of battle. But he eventually employs much of this catalog of battle sounds in his haunting poem "A Veteran's Vision," where the sounds never leave the former soldier's head, even as he lies half-awake in his home, with his wife sleeping at his side and his infant asleep nearby. In a brilliant framing of these battle sounds, Whitman gives us a narrator years after the war, safe in a happy domestic setting, where every night he relives the horror of a battle. We have commented before on Whitman's oxymoronic experience of the war, the way that love and death, beauty and horror, affection and violence, meld and flow into each other continually. In this poem, we see how two apparently distinct and separate realms—the domestic home and the battlefield—encroach on each other as well, insisting on mixing horrifying war memories with the comforting postwar reality of a home and family. In the space of this poem, we discover how that comforting present can never be fully experienced, because it is continually merging with the sounds and excitement and terror of battles past.

In a poem so devoted to sound, it is fitting that Whitman draws our attention to the ways that words, too, slip from one meaning to another, from one realm of experience to another. In his half-sleep, the first sound the veteran hears in the "stillness" and "dark" is "the breath of my infant," and that reassuring sound—the very sound of the hope of his new postwar life—generates a cascade of other sounds: the infant's quick, repetitive, rhythmical breaths become "the short *t-h-t! t-h-t!* of the rifle-balls," and perhaps the happy thought of the infant learning to crawl morphs into the "skirmishers" in the battle who "crawl cautiously ahead." Even the word "infant" generates thoughts of "the hastening of infantry" (the words come from the same roots and both mean "beginners," since the infantry tended to be made up of the youngest and most inexperienced soldiers). The diction of the veteran's memory is oddly linked again and again to the diction of childhood—the "strange lull" in the battle echoes the lullaby that probably put the infant to sleep; the "patter of small arms" might well echo the pitter-patter sounds of the infant crawling on small arms; "the cry of a regiment charging" echoes the crying of the infant that the veteran now experiences daily. We realize that the competing realms that the veteran inhabits—the *martial* and the *marital*—seem so distinct from each other but are in sound and orthography separated only by the reversal of two small letters. The veteran, unlike his wife and infant, lives in both realms simultaneously; he tells us that "the wars are over long," but the distorted syntax ("over long" instead of "long over") lets us know that, while the war may have been over for years, it is nonetheless "overlong," lasting far beyond the formal cessation of hostilities and signing of the Confederate surrender at Appomattox, enduring in fact as long as the veteran lives.

This poem is another of Whitman's extended single-sentence structures, where the opening scene of domestic comfort moves inexorably into the brutal memory, where a few parenthetical interruptions work to repress parts of the memory the veteran has to work hard *not* to heed, not to register, parts that he needs to repress in order to continue to live: he sees "the gaps cut by the enemy's volleys, (quickly fill'd up, no delay)," and we realize that "gaps" here serves as a kind of euphemism, a protective linguistic gesture, to keep away the image of shattered bodies that those "gaps" represent, gaps that are "quickly fill'd up" with other soldiers' bodies (even the elided *e* in "fill'd" is a small orthographical gap). Only late in the poem, protectively distanced in another set of parentheses, does the veteran allow himself to glimpse what those "gaps" really are ("the wounded dripping and red"), even as he reminds himself to "heed [them] not."

Amidst the "chaos louder than ever" of this battle memory, the veteran realizes (in another parenthetical aside) that he is at some level aroused by "the sound of the cannon" and feels a "devilish exultation" and even an "old mad joy in the depths of my soul." He realizes, in other words, that his war experience has left him unsure, in his new home with his wife and infant, whether he can ever be fully at home there, since, night after night, in his marital bed, the sounds of domestic bliss get transmuted into the martial sounds of battle, calling him to another home, one more dangerous and risky and exciting than anything he could find in his postwar life. And so the poem ends with an echo of Francis Scott Key's "Star-Spangled Banner" (which did not become the official national anthem until 1931 but was a popular unofficial anthem from the 1820s on), a reminder that, like the veteran in this poem, Americans today continue in their daily domestic lives, far from scenes of battle, at baseball games and the Super Bowl, to join together to conjure up the buried aural memory of "bombs bursting in air" and the visual flash of "the vari-color'd rockets," their "red glare."

Merrill Commentary

The Italian writer Primo Levi believed that survivors of the Nazi concentration camps fell into two groups: those who could put the terrible events they witnessed and suffered out of their minds, and those who could not. Levi's acclaimed writings about his imprisonment in Auschwitz, including *If This Is a Man, The Drowned and the Saved*, and *The Black Hole of Auschwitz*, testify to his continuing attempt to describe the Nazi cruelty, which he could not forget—and which perhaps contributed to his suicide in 1987. Soldiers and diplomats, journalists and humanitarians—all recall their wartime experiences in the same complicated fashion; hence the fabled strength of the bonds forged in war, which unite combatants and citizens alike long after the last shot is fired. "The Veteran's Vision," Whitman's dramatic monologue from an artilleryman's perspective, is a vivid reconstruction of war's horrors as well as a form of exorcism on behalf of those who inflict death and suffering on their enemies. His ventriloquism thus serves not only a poetic purpose but also a therapeutic one: ridding the imagination of demons is a lifelong project.

In bed one night the artilleryman is wakened by a vision of the war that presses on him—the sounds and sights of battle, which as his wife sleeps beside him he catalogs:

I hear the irregular snap! snap!
I hear the sounds of the different missiles—the short *t-h-t! t-h-t!* of the rifle balls;
I see the shells exploding, leaving small white clouds—
I hear the great shells shrieking as they pass;
The grape, like the hum and whirr of wind through the trees, (quick, tumultuous,
now the contest rages!)

These are the kinds of sensory details that lodge forever in the memory; likewise "the suffocating smoke" that he breathes again and the "strange lull" that comes over the battlefield, the momentary peace that makes the resumption of fighting all the worse. It is common to say that war is a matter of long spells of boredom punctuated by moments of terror, and Whitman brings this idea to life now with the introduction of applause, cannon, and small-arms fire. We do not learn whether the battle is won or lost, only that it persists in his memory like a waking dream.

Note that the monologue consists of a single sentence—hundreds of words spread over twenty-seven lines, delineating an engagement that "begins there and then" in the veteran's "busy brain" and does not end. Which is, of course, how war haunts the minds of those condemned to remember until their dying breath what they saw, did, and suffered. Hundreds of thousands of such men returned to civilian life after the Battle of Appomattox Court House, and among Whitman's many poetic virtues was his determination to find words to heal them, one reader at a time.

25

Walt Whitman to His Mother, Louisa Van Velsor Whitman, March 29, 1864

Washington
Tuesday afternoon M[arch 29]
Dearest mother
I have written [to] George again to Knox[ville]—things seem to be quiet down there so far—We think here that our forces are going to be made strongest here in Virginia this spring, & every thing bent to take Richmond—Grant is here, he is now down at headquarters in the field, Brandy Station—we expect fighting before long, there are many indications—I believe I told you they had sent up all the sick from front—about four nights ago we [had a] terrible rainy afternoon [& night]—Well in the middle [of the w]orst of the rain at [night? th]ere arrived a train [of sick?] & wounded, over 600 [soldiers], down at the depot—[It w]as one of the same [old] sights, I could not keep the tears out of my eyes—many of the poor young men had to be moved on stretchers, with blankets over them, which soon soaked as wet as water in the rain—Most were sick cases, but some badly wounded—I came up to the nearest hospital & helped—Mother, it was a dreadful night (last Friday night)—pretty dark, the wind gusty, & the rain fell in torrents—One poor boy (this is a sample of one case out of the 6000 he seemed to me quite young, he was quite small, (I looked at his body afterwards)—he groaned some as the stretcher-bearers were carrying him along—& again as they carried him through the hospital gate, they set down the stretcher & examined him, & the poor boy was dead—they took him into the ward, & the doctor came immediately, but it was all of no use—the worst of it is too that he is entirely unknown—there was nothing on his clothes, or any one with him, to identify him—& he is altogether unknown—Mother, it is enough to rack one's heart, such things—very likely his folks will never know in the world what has become of him—poor poor child, for he appeared as though he could be but 18—

I feel lately as though I must have some intermission, I feel well & hearty enough, & was never better, but my feelings are kept in a painful condition a great part of the time—things get worse & worse, as to the amount & sufferings of the sick, & as I have said before, those who have to do with them are getting more & more callous & indifferent—Mother, when I see the common soldiers, what they go through, & how every body seems to try to pick upon them, & what humbug there is over them every how, even the dying soldier's money stolen from his body by some scoundrel attendant, or from some sick ones, even from under his head, which is a common thing—& then the agony I see every day, I get almost frightened at the world—Mother, I will try to write more cheerfully next time—but I see so much—well, good bye for present, dear Mother—

Walt

Mother, I got your letter telling [me you were] better—have you got quite we[ll?—I] wish you would write very so[on again] too—I feel uneasy about [you]—I send my love to Jeff & Mat & all—

Folsom Commentary

Here, three years into the war, a year from its conclusion, Whitman is at the breaking point. In this intimate letter to his mother, Louisa Van Velsor Whitman, Walt expresses his emotions openly. The repressed pain and torment that he so often, in his published Civil War writings, contained in parentheses, flow out in this letter: "I could not keep the tears out of my eyes. . . . Mother, it is enough to rack one's heart, such things. . . . My feelings are kept in a painful condition a great part of the time—things get worse & worse, as to the amount & sufferings of the sick. . . . Mother, I will try to write more cheerfully next time—but I see so much." Whitman's letters to his mother during the war are some of the most affecting documents he wrote; his close relationship with her allowed him to express himself in often remarkably unguarded ways.

We feel in this letter the intense relational responsibilities that Whitman felt—responsibilities to his new family in Washington, D.C., made up of the Civil War dying and wounded soldiers in the hospitals he visited daily and nightly, and responsibilities to his biological family back in Brooklyn, which was suffering its own breakdown and disunion. Just a few months before this letter, Whitman's brother Andrew, who served briefly in the war, died of tuberculosis at his home in Brooklyn, leaving behind two children and a pregnant wife, Nancy, who soon became a prostitute. Walt's older brother Jesse lived in the basement of the Whitman family home with mother Louisa and Walt's younger, mentally deficient brother Eddy; Jesse, who would soon be institutionalized, was becoming increasingly violent and threatening the children and wife of Walt's brother Jeff, who lived upstairs. Walt's other brother George, still a soldier involved in some of the most intense battles of the war and soon to become a prisoner of war, was a constant worry for both Whitman and his mother. And for Walt, Louisa's health was an incessant concern as well; scrawled at the top of this letter is one expression of that worry: "I feel uneasy about [you]—" Like his nation, Whitman's family was coming apart at the seams.

The source of his greatest unease, though, was the increasing population of wounded and dying soldiers in Washington. As was happening more and more with Whitman, he was overwhelmed by the sheer numbers (he once estimated he had visited 100,000 sick and wounded soldiers during the final two years of the war), and, to hold on to his sanity, he kept focusing in—as he does in this letter—from the nameless many to the single individual whom he could come to know, comfort, give gifts to, and write letters for, brief as each relationship might be. He would jot down each of their names and a few details of each of their lives in the notebooks he always carried with him. He offered love and confirmed their identity. But in this letter, what causes him to break is his coming upon a single soldier who dies before he can be known, who dies without a name, without a family that can be written to, without an embrace and kiss from the bearded poet who was quick to become father, brother, comrade, mother, nurse, scribe—whatever it took. On this night, however, as a torrential rain falls and over six hundred maimed soldiers enter the capital and are carried to hospitals, Whitman latches on to "one poor boy," small and slight, who dies before he can identify himself, dies with no evidence of who he is, dies—as Whitman so desolately puts it—"entirely unknown."

We recall "The Million Dead, Too, Summ'd Up," where Whitman tells us, as he surveys the growing number of war cemeteries, about "the significant word Unknown," and how "in some of the cemeteries nearly *all* the dead are unknown." Every young soldier who dies in the war is in a very real sense *unknown*, because he hasn't lived long enough to form a full identity. But some soldiers, like the one Whitman loses to death on this blustery March night, are unknown in an even deeper sense, lost even to the small bit of care and love and remembrance that is all Whitman had to give. And now he feels he is about to give out, like so many around him. He senses a growing callousness on the part of the caregivers themselves, a hardening and indifference to suffering that makes Whitman "almost frightened of the world." As one unnamed soldier drifts into permanent oblivion, his youth and fragility making him seem to Whitman "a poor, poor child," Whitman too embraces his own childhood dependence on his mother and, for the space of this letter, releases his fears and his despair and his tears. The next day he would start again and look for others among the dying that he could embrace and promise to remember and make known; he will absorb their fear and despair and tears just as on this night Louisa absorbs Walt's.

Merrill Commentary

The Tomb of the Unknowns in Arlington National Cemetery has its counterparts in many foreign capitals, commemorating the nameless fallen from conflicts around the world. Whitman's letter to his mother in the last year of the war, which testifies to his despair at the ongoing slaughter and his need for an "intermission" from caring for the wounded, is also an elegy for an unidentified soldier whose parents will likely never know what became of him. Think of his cry from the heart as a hymn to what remains unknowable in war: all the what-ifs of a life cut short on the battlefield. It is more than the poet can bear. (No wonder his health soon gave out.) The sight of a train arriving in a torrential rainstorm with six hundred sick and wounded soldiers on stretchers covered with soaking blankets reduces him to tears, his gaze alighting on the "poor poor child" whose death symbolizes all that has gone wrong in his beloved country. He rightly fears for the world.

A Bosnian writer once told me that he had lost track of all the wounds he had suffered during the wars of succession in the former Yugoslavia—though he clearly remembered the day a piece of shrapnel lodged in his tongue, leaving him with a mild speech impediment. "He's lost the plot," a fellow writer said of him—a plot he hoped to recover in the novel he was writing about his time at the front. The recent discovery that the memory of trauma can be passed down from generation to generation suggests that his experience of war will not only shape his literary work but perhaps the lives of his offspring, too. Scientists devised a study of children of Holocaust survivors to mark the epigenetic changes governing their responses to stress, confirming the theory that environmental factors, including war, can alter the genetic makeup of some individuals. War changes everyone in its path—soldiers, survivors, victims and their families, doctors and nurses, diplomats and observers—as well as those who come after. Whitman may have grasped this in the train depot, registering and recording in his body and soul the wounds of a nation.

"The wound and the wasteland are the same thing," one painter tells another in Pat Barker's novel *Toby's Room*, the second part of a trilogy set in World War I. How should artists represent the gruesome facts of war? Barker's various articulations of this question point to the deep human need to make sense of tragedy, as Whitman's confession of despair to his mother makes clear. His feeling for the sick and dying was the opposite of "some scoundrel attendant" preying on them in their time of need—one reason why his war writings continue to resonate. He looked into the abyss, promising his mother "to write more cheerfully next time." What else could he do?

26

"Hymn of Dead Soldiers"

ONE breath, O my silent soul,
A perfum'd thought—no more I ask, for the sake of all dead soldiers.

Buglers off in my armies!
At present I ask not you to sound;
Not at the head of my cavalry, all on their spirited horses,
With their sabres drawn and glist'ning, and carbines clanking by their thighs—
    (ah, my brave horse-men!
My handsome, tan-faced horsemen! what life, what joy and pride,
With all the perils, were yours!)

Nor you drummers—neither at reveille, at dawn,
Nor the long roll alarming the camp—nor even the muffled beat for a burial;
Nothing from you, this time, O drummers, bearing my warlike drums.

But aside from these, and the crowd's hurrahs, and the land's congratulations,
Admitting around me comrades close, unseen by the rest, and voiceless,
I chant this chant of my silent soul, in the name of all dead soldiers.

Faces so pale, with wondrous eyes, very dear, gather closer yet;
Draw close, but speak not.
Phantoms, welcome, divine and tender!
Invisible to the rest, henceforth become my companions;
Follow me ever! desert me not, while I live.

Sweet are the blooming cheeks of the living! sweet are the musical voices sounding!
But sweet, ah sweet, are the dead, with their silent eyes.

Dearest comrades! all now is over;
But love is not over—and what love, O comrades!
Perfume from battle-fields rising—up from fœtor arising.

Perfume therefore my chant, O love! immortal Love!
Give me to bathe the memories of all dead soldiers.

Perfume all! make all wholesome!
O love! O chant! solve all with the last chemistry.

Give me exhaustless—make me a fountain,
That I exhale love from me wherever I go,
For the sake of all dead soldiers.

Folsom Commentary

During the Civil War, Whitman was already preparing to carry out what the critic M. Wynn Thomas has called "the pains and obligations of memory." As the war ground on with its devastating and ever-increasing human toll, Whitman knew that he and the nation would never be able to put the horror behind them. As he said in "A Million Dead, Too, Summ'd Up," America would from now on feed on the endless thousands of dead soldiers who "leaven Southern soil" and "crumble today in Northern earth," and who lend their decayed atoms to "every future grain of wheat and ear of corn, and every flower that grows, and every breath we draw." As the nation sought to make a future out of that mass death, to be sustained by it, its obligation of memory would become ever more demanding. "Hymn of Dead Soldiers" is Whitman's first attempt to begin that painful and arduous task of remembering the dead, many of them unknown (as we saw in his letter to his mother about his despair over a nameless soldier), and to begin the difficult work of *not forgetting.* To do this, the poet demands silence to match his "silent soul." While at the beginning of the war Whitman was entranced by the beating drums and the blowing bugles that were part of the preparations for battle, he now asks the "buglers" and "drummers" to make no sound—he does not want to hear "even the muffled beat for a burial," the "Taps" of death. ("Taps" was originally played on the drums, and the title of Whitman's book of war poems, *Drum-Taps,* thus captures both the loud sounds of entering battles and the muffled sounds of burying the dead after the battles.)

Now, in the resultant silence, "aside . . . from the crowd's hurrahs," the poet summons the dead to gather around him—those "faces so pale" of his "comrades close, unseen by the rest, and voiceless." This silent throng clusters "closer yet" around the poet's "silent soul" and "speak[s] not." The "divine and tender," mute "phantoms" now "become my companions," as Whitman undertakes his obligation never to forget. The poet knows the "blooming cheeks of the living" with their "musical voices sounding" are "sweet," but he insists that "the dead" are just as sweet, "with their silent eyes." These "silent eyes" of all the dead soldiers evoke the "silent I's" that now surround and haunt him, all those emptied identities of the unknown dead, a generation of young men rendered voiceless, many of them nameless. In the years and decades after the war, these voiceless and unnamed phantoms increasingly become Whitman's "comrades."

The poem begins with the surprising image of the poet's "perfum'd thought," an image that toward the end of the poem becomes even more unsettling as he uses "perfume" to characterize the odor arising from the battle-fields, "up from the fœtor arising." We don't normally associate a fetid smell with perfume, but the etymology of "perfume" is "through smoke," and originally the word referred to fumes from something burning. For Whitman, the "ashes of soldiers" (as he would later rename this poem) never stop burning in his memory, and the fumes from their smoke fuel his poetry in the years after the Civil War. They are, as some perfumes indeed were, medicinal for him, and inhaling their burning scent prompts him to "exhale love from me wherever I go." He ends with the image of himself and his poetry as a "fountain" pouring forth "dew," as if his newly articulated words for the silent dead help put out the smoldering flames and begin to fertilize the soil that has been leavened with all those dead bodies.

When he revised the poem years later and retitled it "Ashes of Soldiers," Whitman added at both the opening and closing the reminder that his words were for "ashes of all dead soldiers South or North." Whitman makes it clear that he is mourning all the dead soldiers, whether the ashes derived from Northern or Southern men. His concern in this poem, as he reworked it heavily in the late 1860s and 1870s, was with the way that the reunited nation was all too quickly trying to put the war behind it, forgetting the sacrifice of its soldiers, no matter where they were from. The silence of all the dead soldiers became more and more a key element in the revised versions of the poem, and Whitman increasingly contrasts that silence with the noise of the living. After the war is over, the dead gather around the poet in silence, while the living gather on the "crowded promenade" in the "marts of wealth." Those mute phantoms of soldiers are a stark contrast to the capitalistic world of postwar America that was noisily spending its way into forgetfulness about the massive sacrifice of the war whose ghosts stand silently and invisibly all around them. Only Whitman seems able to give that silence voice.

Merrill Commentary

Against Forgetting: Twentieth Century Poetry of Witness was the title of an influential anthology, edited by Carolyn Forché and published in 1993, which in her words collected "the work of poets from all over the world who endured conditions of social and historical extremity during the twentieth century—those who suffered wars, imprisonment, military occupation, house arrest, forced exile, and political repression." North American poets, Forché argued, had been spared the trauma endemic to authoritarian rule, and so to come to terms with the relationship between politics and poetry, "to understand the impress of such extremity upon the poetic imagination," she sought "the solace of poetic camaraderie" in the writings of Anna Akhmatova, Yannis Ritsos, Paul Celan, Federico García Lorca, Nazim Hikmet, and Miklós Radnóti, who belong to a tradition inaugurated by Whitman. For he played a central role in the development of what Forché calls the poetry of witness, nowhere more poignantly than in his "Hymn of Dead Soldiers."

"Give me exhaustless—make me a fountain," he writes in the last stanza, "That I exhale love from me wherever I go, / For the sake of all dead soldiers." His breath is mingled forever with the stench of rotten flesh rising from the battlefield, transformed by love into perfume, "the last chemistry" of the body and soul enacted in the poetic imagination. This takes place in silence, his love extending into eternity, charging the air with "Phantoms, divine and tender," who circulate whenever a reader takes these lines into his or her heart. "A perfum'd thought"—that is, a poem—preserves the memory of the fallen, Whitman's voiceless comrades, whose last words, recorded or not, inform his, and our, understanding of the war. This wound at the heart of American history must be remembered in all its tragic dimensions. Whitman refuses to forget. "Perfume therefore my chant, O love! immortal Love! / Give me to bathe the memories of all dead soldiers."

27

"Pioneers! O Pioneers!"

1

COME, my tan-faced children,
Follow well in order, get your weapons ready;
Have you your pistols? have you your sharp edged axes?
Pioneers! O pioneers!

2

For we cannot tarry here,
We must march my darlings, we must bear the brunt of danger,
We, the youthful sinewy races, all the rest on us depend,
Pioneers! O pioneers!

3

O you youths, western youths,
So impatient, full of action, full of manly pride and friendship,
Plain I see you, western youths, see you tramping with the foremost,
Pioneers! O pioneers!

4

Have the elder races halted?
Do they droop and end their lesson, wearied, over there beyond the seas?
We take up the task eternal, and the burden, and the lesson,
Pioneers! O pioneers!

5

All the past we leave behind;
We debouch upon a newer, mightier world, varied world;
Fresh and strong the world we seize, world of labor and the march,
Pioneers! O pioneers!

6

We detachments steady throwing,
Down the edges, through the passes, up the mountains steep,
Conquering, holding, daring, venturing, as we go, the unknown ways,
Pioneers! O pioneers!

7

We primeval forests felling,
We the rivers stemming, vexing we, and piercing deep the mines within;
We the surface broad surveying, and the virgin soil up-heaving,
Pioneers! O pioneers!

8

Colorado men are we,
From the peaks gigantic, from the great sierras and the high plateaus,
From the mine and from the gully, from the hunting trail we come,
Pioneers! O pioneers!

9

From Nebraska, from Arkansas,
Central inland race are we, from Missouri, with the continental blood intervein'd;
All the hands of comrades clasping, all the Southern, all the Northern,
Pioneers! O pioneers!

10

O resistless, restless race!
O beloved race in all! O my breast aches with tender love for all!
O I mourn and yet exult—I am rapt with love for all,
Pioneers! O pioneers!

11

Raise the mighty mother mistress,
Waving high the delicate mistress, over all the starry mistress, (bend your heads all,)
Raise the fang'd and warlike mistress, stern, impassive, weapon'd mistress,
Pioneers! O pioneers!

12

See, my children, resolute children,
By those swarms upon our rear, we must never yield or falter,
Ages back in ghostly millions, frowning there behind us urging,
Pioneers! O pioneers!

13

On and on, the compact ranks,
With accessions ever waiting, with the places of the dead quickly fill'd,
Through the battle, through defeat, moving yet and never stopping,
Pioneers! O pioneers!

14

O to die advancing on!
Are there some of us to droop and die? has the hour come?
Then upon the march we fittest die, soon and sure the gap is fill'd,
Pioneers! O pioneers!

15

All the pulses of the world,
Falling in, they beat for us, with the western movement beat;
Holding single or together, steady moving, to the front, all for us,
Pioneers! O pioneers!

16

Life's involv'd and varied pageants,
All the forms and shows, all the workmen at their work,
All the seamen and the landsmen, all the masters with their slaves,
Pioneers! O pioneers!

17

All the hapless silent lovers,
All the prisoners in the prisons, all the righteous and the wicked,
All the joyous, all the sorrowing, all the living, all the dying,
Pioneers! O pioneers!

18

I too with my soul and body,
We, a curious trio, picking, wandering on our way,
Through these shores, amid the shadows, with the apparitions pressing,
Pioneers! O pioneers!

19

Lo! the darting bowling orb!
Lo! the brother orbs around! all the clustering suns and planets;
All the dazzling days, all the mystic nights with dreams,
Pioneers! O pioneers!

20

These are of us, they are with us,
All for primal needed work, while the followers there in embryo wait behind,
We to-day's procession heading, we the route for travel clearing,
Pioneers! O pioneers!

21

O you daughters of the west!
O you young and elder daughters! O you mothers and you wives!
Never must you be divided, in our ranks you move united,
Pioneers! O pioneers!

22

Minstrels latent on the prairies!
(Shrouded bards of other lands! you may sleep—you have done your work;)
Soon I hear you coming warbling, soon you rise and tramp amid us,
Pioneers! O pioneers!

23

Not for delectations sweet;
Not the cushion and the slipper, not the peaceful and the studious;
Not the riches safe and palling, not for us the tame enjoyment,
Pioneers! O pioneers!

24

Do the feasters gluttonous feast?
Do the corpulent sleepers sleep? have they lock'd and bolted doors?
Still be ours the diet hard, and the blanket on the ground,
Pioneers! O pioneers!

25

Has the night descended?
Was the road of late so toilsome? did we stop discouraged, nodding on our way?
Yet a passing hour I yield you, in your tracks to pause oblivious,
Pioneers! O pioneers!

26

Till with sound of trumpet,
Far, far off the day-break call—hark! how loud and clear I hear it wind;
Swift! to the head of the army!—swift! spring to your places,
Pioneers! O pioneers!

Folsom Commentary

In 1872, a little-known Prussian-born artist named John Gast, then living in Brooklyn, painted an image, *American Progress*, that became famous in the following decades in the United States, as the destructive energies of the Civil War were funneled into what was then considered the much more constructive efforts of Manifest Destiny—America's westward movement and its determination to occupy and dominate the entire breadth of the continent, from the Atlantic to the Pacific. Gast's painting, which was quickly reproduced in a series of popular lithographs, portrayed a giant image of Columbia or Freedom (or maybe America herself) leading the western advance of civilization, bringing eastern light to the western darkness as American Indians and the buffalo vanished into the darkness, while the evolving lines of American technology, including trains and telegraph lines, followed the horses, covered wagons, and carriages into the expansive and expanding frontier. The painting could almost be an illustration for Whitman's "Pioneers! O Pioneers!," a hymn that seems to be an equally spirited paean to the American domination of the continent: "We primeval forests felling, / We the rivers stemming, vexing we, and piercing deep the mines within; / We the surface broad surveying, and the virgin soil upheaving, / Pioneers! O Pioneers!" Today, many of us hear such rousing language as a kind of ecological/genocidal nightmare, the optimistic and unexamined cheering on of a postwar capitalistic fervor raping the "virgin" land and claiming Indian territory—all presented to us in a strong, relentless (and uncharacteristic) Whitman trochaic beat, a marching song calling America's pioneers to action.

In the context of the Civil War, though, the poem might be viewed a little more sympathetically. Whitman, like many in the wounded and divided nation at the time, worried a great deal about what would happen when hundreds of thousands of soldiers, Union and Confederate, returned home, carrying with them their rifles, their experiences of bloodshed, and their lingering enmity. It was one of the great challenges for the tenuously reunited nation: how to turn soldiers back into citizens; how to make the warring armies of a fractured country a single unified army

John Gast, *American Progress* (1872). Chromolithograph by George A. Crofutt (1873). Library of Congress Prints and Photographs Division, Washington, D.C.

dedicated to building a civilization; how to turn bloody fields of battle into productive and fertile fields of crops. In 1876, at the end of Reconstruction, Whitman wrote: "In all History, antique or modern, the grandest achievement yet for political Humanity—grander even than the triumph of THIS UNION over Secession—was the return, disbanding, and peaceful disintegration from compact military organization, back into agricultural and civil employments, of the vast Armies, the two millions of embattled men of America." He published these words as the headnote to his poem "The Return of the Heroes," a poem that confronted what was, for Whitman, always a double-edged problem: the "heroes" who died and "returned" to the land ("the dead . . . fit very well in the landscape under the trees and grass") needed to be always remembered, absorbed into the nation's future, while the "heroes" who lived and returned to civilized life needed to *create* that future.

"O Pioneers!," then, provides an outlet, an opportunity for the demobilized troops to remobilize as an ardent civilian population—the equal of heroic Civil War soldiers—to now take on the task of building, out of the rubble, a perfect democracy. Whitman saw the war finally as having been fought for the West, the area of the country most associated with its future, where the "tan-faced" "Western youths"—who had been some of his favorite soldiers—with their "sharp-edged axes" would shape the nation's destiny. This new "central inland race" would finally, Whitman believed, resolve all the nation's old enmities: "All the hands of comrades clasping, all the Southern, all the Northern," and even "all the masters with their slaves" would join together in one national body with a blended "continental blood intervein'd."

Buried in this unyielding march of progress ("we must never yield or falter") are "the apparitions pressing," "those swarms upon our rear." In one sense, these "swarms" are the civilizations of the past that are now giving way to the democracy of the future, but in another sense, they are the countless Civil War dead that continue to haunt Whitman, the "ghostly millions frowning there behind us urging"; *they* are the invisible force that pushes us on, that urges us to make a worthy future out of their sacrifice. So, while Whitman celebrates the "resistless restless race" that Americans have become, still his "breast aches with tender love for all": "I mourn and yet exult," he says, always expressing the conflicted obligations he feels to both the living and the dead—those who make the future, and those out of whose deaths the future is made. Amidst the stirring march, then, remains a warning: we are moving into this future, Whitman sternly reminds us, "Not for delectations sweet, / . . . Not the riches safe and palling," not for the "gluttonous feast."

When he looked around the nation in the 1870s, as it entered what would come to be called the Gilded Age, Whitman was appalled to see a growing worship of money, wealth, ease; a growing divide in income distribution; and a growing forgetfulness of the awful sacrifice that had been made so that the nation might have a united, slave-free, democratic future. His ultimate fear was that the nation would give itself over to the "corpulent sleepers" with their "lock'd and bolted doors," becoming a fat land of easy comfort for some, a parched land of poverty for others. If this antidemocratic nightmare happened, Whitman knew, the Civil War dead would remain lost, forgotten, mere ashes, their heroic deaths reduced to useless and meaningless butchery.

Merrill Commentary

"Note to future historians," Charles Simic writes: "Don't read old issues of *The New York Times.* Read the poets." If the true history of a people can be discovered in its poetry, then what I heard in a car driving across northern Afghanistan, from the fabled birthplace of the poet Rumi in Balkh to the capital of the province, Mazar-e-Sharif, may prove to be more enduring than whatever comes of the fitful peace process designed to bring an end to the conflict: four older men reciting ghazals, one of which concluded with this couplet: "I'm tired, stressed out, depressed—do you know why? / The history of yesterday is repeated again." This made sense to me, for I had gazed in fascination on another drive at the burnt hulks of more than a dozen Soviet tanks: informal shrines arranged in a landscape that in some places is lined with unexploded ordnance.

How to rebuild a country torn apart by civil war? The work of poets may seem negligible. But a poem can contain a nation's history as well as some of its possible futures. And Whitman's "Pioneers! O Pioneers!" is a fine example of a poem in the form of a rallying cry. Dispensing with the lyric "I," which in "Song of Myself" represents the entire cosmos, the poet adopts the voice of the collective "we," summoning his countrymen to a new vision of their body politic, one rooted in westward expansion. This is how he proposes to bind the country together, healing the wounds of war with a call to action; hence in twenty-six numbered quatrains, each ending with the title as a refrain, he issues orders to the convalescing masses, urging them to convert the passion they once reserved for war against their brethren to commence a long march across the continent: "We to-day's procession heading, we the route for travel clearing, / Pioneers! O pioneers!"

The distinctly militaristic aspect of this poem, not to say jingoistic, is part and parcel of the dark history of westward expansion, which among other things resulted in the Indian removals and widespread destruction of native habitats. This is not to blame Whitman for that—this dynamic was in place long before he was born—but to note some of the consequences of his enthusiasm for the conquering of the West. Recall Simic's observation from his essay on the Balkan wars: "Sooner or later our tribe always comes to ask us to agree to murder." The Afghan poets escorting me around their province knew this well. By the time we reached Qala-e-Jangi, a castle on the outskirts of Mazar-e-Sharif, my translation of one ghazal was complete: "You said it was the last time—yet again. / The history of yesterday is repeated again." And so it was: not long after the U.S. invasion of Afghanistan in 2001, this castle was the site of a prison uprising, during which a CIA officer named Johnny "Mike" Spann became the first American killed in action. "You knew it was wrong," the Afghan poet said, "and you did it again."

28

"Abraham Lincoln," "Murder of President Lincoln," and "No Good Portrait of Lincoln"

"Abraham Lincoln"

Aug. 12.—I see the President almost every day, as I happen to live where he passes to or from his lodgings out of town. He never sleeps at the White House during the hot season, but has quarters at a healthy location, some three miles north of the city, the Soldiers' Home, a United States military establishment. I saw him this morning about 8½ coming in to business, riding on Vermont avenue, near L street. The sight is a significant one, (and different enough from how and where I first saw him). He always has a company of twenty-five or thirty cavalry, with sabres drawn, and held upright over their shoulders. The party makes no great show in uniforms or horses. Mr. Lincoln, on the saddle, generally rides a good-sized easy-going gray horse, is dress'd in plain black, somewhat rusty and dusty; wears a black stiff hat, and looks about as ordinary in attire, &c., as the commonest man. A Lieutenant, with yellow straps, rides at his left, and following behind, two by two, come the cavalry men in their yellow-striped jackets. They are generally going at a slow trot, as that is the pace set them by the One they wait upon. The sabres and accoutrements clank, and the entirely unornamental *cortege* as it trots towards Lafayette square, arouses no sensation, only some curious stranger stops and gazes. I see very plainly ABRAHAM LINCOLN'S dark brown face, with the deep cut lines, the eyes, &c., always to me with a deep latent sadness in the expression. We have got so that we always exchange bows, and very cordial ones.

Sometimes the President goes and comes in an open barouche. The cavalry always accompany him, with drawn sabres. Often I notice as he goes out evenings—and sometimes in the morning, when he returns early—he turns off and halts at the large and handsome residence of the Secretary of War, on K street, and holds conference there. If in his barouche, I can see from my window he does not alight, but sits in the vehicle, and Mr. Stanton comes out to attend him. Sometimes one of his sons, a boy of ten or twelve, accompanies him, riding at his right on a pony.

Earlier in the summer I occasionally saw the President and his wife, toward the latter part of the afternoon, out in a barouche, on a pleasure ride through the city. Mrs. Lincoln was dress'd in complete black, with a long crape veil. The equipage is of the plainest kind, only two horses, and they nothing extra. They pass'd me once very close, and I saw the President in the face fully, as they were moving slow, and his look, though abstracted, happen'd to be directed steadily in my eye. He bow'd and smiled, but far beneath his smile I noticed well the expression I have alluded to. None of the artists or pictures have caught the deep, though subtle and indirect expression of this man's face. There is something else there. One of the great portrait painters of two or three centuries ago is needed.

"Murder of President Lincoln"

The day, April 14, 1865, seems to have been a pleasant one throughout the whole land—the moral atmosphere pleasant too—the long storm, so dark, so fratricidal, full of blood and doubt and gloom, over and ended at last by the sun-rise of such an absolute National victory, and utter breaking-down of Secessionism—we almost doubted our own senses! Lee had capitulated beneath the apple-tree of Appomattax [*sic*]. The other armies, the flanges of the revolt, swiftly follow'd........And could it really be, then? Out of all the affairs of this world of woe and passion, of failure and disorder and dismay, was there really come the confirm'd, unerring sign of plan, like a shaft of pure light—of rightful rule—of God?........So the day, as I say, was propitious. Early herbage, early flowers, were out. (I remember where I was stopping at the time, the season being advanced, there were many lilacs in full bloom. By one of those caprices that enter and give tinge to events without being at all a part of them, I find myself always reminded of the great tragedy of that day by the sight and odor of these blossoms. It never fails.)

But I must not dwell on accessories. The deed hastens. The popular afternoon paper of Washington, the little *Evening Star*, had spatter'd all over its third page, divided among the advertisements in a sensational manner in a hundred different places, *The President and his Lady will be at the Theatre this evening*.......(Lincoln was fond of the theatre. I have myself seen him there several times. I remember thinking how funny it was that He, in some respects, the leading actor in the greatest and stormiest drama known to real history's stage, through centuries, should sit there and be so completely interested and absorb'd in those human jack-straws, moving about with their silly little gestures, foreign spirit, and flatulent text.)

On this occasion the theatre was crowded, many ladies in rich and gay costumes, officers in their uniforms, many well known citizens, young folks, the usual clusters of gaslights, the usual magnetism of so many people, cheerful, with perfumes, music of violins and flutes—(and over all, and saturating all, that vast vague wonder, *Victory*, the Nation's Victory, the triumph of the Union, filling the air, the thought, the sense, with exhilaration more than all perfumes.)

The President came betimes, and, with his wife, witness'd the play, from the large stage-boxes of the second tier, two thrown into one, and profusely draped with the National flag. The acts and scenes of the piece—one of those singularly written compositions which have at least the merit of giving entire relief to an audience engaged in mental action or business excitements and cares during the day, as it makes not the slightest call on either the moral, emotional, esthetic, or spiritual nature—a piece, ("Our American Cousin,") in which, among other characters, so call'd, a Yankee, certainly such a one as was never seen, or the least like it ever seen, in North America, is introduced in England, with a varied fol-de-rol of talk, plot, scenery, and such phantasmagoria as goes to make up a modern popular drama—had progress'd through perhaps a couple of its acts, when in the midst of this comedy, or tragedy, or non-such, or whatever it is to be call'd, and to off-set it or finish it out, as if in Nature's and the Great Muse's mockery of those poor mimes, comes interpolated that Scene, not really or exactly to be described at all, (for on the many hundreds who were there it seems to this hour to have left little but a passing blur, a dream, a blotch)—and yet partially to be described as I now proceed to give it.......There is a scene in the play representing a modern parlor, in which two unprecedented English ladies are inform'd by the unprecedented and impossible Yankee that he is not a man of fortune, and therefore undesirable for marriage-catching purposes; after which, the comments being finish'd, the dramatic trio make exit, leaving the stage clear for a moment. There was a pause, a hush as it were. At this period came the murder of Abraham Lincoln. Great as that was, with all its manifold train, circling round it, and stretching into the future for many a century, in the politics, history, art, &c., of the New World, in point of fact the main thing, the actual murder, transpired with the quiet and simplicity of any commonest occurrence—the bursting of a bud or pod in the growth of vegetation, for instance. Through the general hum following the stage pause, with the change of positions, &c., came the muffled sound of a pistol shot, which not one hundredth part of the audience heard at the time—and yet a moment's hush—somehow, surely a vague startled thrill—and then, through the ornamented, draperied, starr'd and striped space-way of the President's box, a sudden figure, a man raises himself with hands and feet, stands a moment on the railing, leaps below to the stage, (a distance of perhaps fourteen or fifteen feet,) falls out of position, catching his boot-heel in the copious drapery, (the American flag,) falls on one knee, quickly recovers himself, rises as if nothing had happen'd, (he really sprains his ankle, but unfelt then,)—and so the figure, Booth, the murderer, dress'd in plain black broadcloth, bare-headed, with a full head of glossy, raven hair, and his eyes like some mad animal's flashing with light and resolution, yet with a certain strange calmness, holds aloft in one hand a large knife—walks along not much back from the footlights—turns fully toward the audience his face of statuesque beauty, lit by those basilisk eyes, flashing with desperation, perhaps insanity—launches out in a firm and steady voice the words, *Sic semper tyrannis*—and then walks with neither slow nor very rapid pace diagonally across to the back of the stage, and disappears.......(Had not all this terrible scene—making the mimic ones preposterous—had it not all been rehears'd, in blank, by Booth, beforehand?)

A moment's hush, incredulous—a scream—the cry of *Murder*—Mrs. Lincoln leaning out of the box, with ashy cheeks and lips, with involuntary cry, pointing to the retreating figure, *He has kill'd the President*.......And still a moment's strange, incredulous suspense—and then the deluge!—then that mixture of horror, noises, uncertainty—(the sound, somewhere back, of a horse's hoofs clattering with speed)—the people burst through chairs and railings, and break them up—that noise adds to the queerness of the scene—there is inextricable confusion and terror—women faint—quite feeble persons fall, and are trampled on—many cries of agony are heard—the broad stage suddenly fills to suffocation with a dense and motley crowd, like some horrible carnival—the audience rush generally upon it—at least the strong men do—the actors and actresses are all there in their play-costumes and painted faces, with mortal fright showing through the rouge, some trembling—some in tears—the screams and calls, confused talk—redoubled, trebled—two or three manage to pass up water from the stage to the President's box—others try to clamber up—&c., &c., &c.

In the midst of all this, the soldiers of the President's Guard, with others, suddenly drawn to the scene, burst in—(some two hundred altogether)—they storm the house, through all the tiers, especially the upper ones, inflamed with fury, literally charging the audience with fix'd bayonets, muskets and pistols, shouting *Clear out! clear out! you sons of*—.......Such the wild scene, or a suggestion of it rather, inside the play-house that night.

Outside, too, in the atmosphere of shock and craze, crowds of people, fill'd with frenzy, ready to seize any outlet for it, come near committing murder several times on innocent individuals. One such case was especially exciting. The infuriated crowd, through some chance, got started against one man, either for words he utter'd, or perhaps without any cause at all, and were proceeding at once to actually hang him on a neighboring lamp post, when he was rescued by a few heroic policemen, who placed him in their midst and fought their way slowly and amid great peril toward the Station House.......It was a fitting episode of the whole affair. The crowd rushing and eddying to and fro—the night, the yells, the pale faces, many frighten'd people trying in vain to extricate themselves—the attack'd man, not yet freed from the jaws of death, looking like a corpse—the silent resolute half-dozen policemen, with no weapons but their little clubs, yet stern and steady through all those eddying swarms—made indeed a fitting side-scene to the grand tragedy of the murder.......They gain'd the Station House with the protected man, whom they placed in security for the night, and discharged him in the morning.

And in the midst of that night-pandemonium of senseless hate, infuriated soldiers, the audience and the crowd—the stage, and all its actors and actresses, its paint-pots, spangles, and gas-lights—the life-blood from those veins, the best and sweetest of the land, drips slowly down, and death's ooze already begins its little bubbles on the lips.......Such, hurriedly sketch'd, were the accompaniments of the death of President Lincoln. So suddenly and in murder and horror unsurpass'd he was taken from us. But his death was painless.

[He leaves for America's History and Biography, so far, not only its most dramatic reminiscence—he leaves, in my opinion, the greatest, best, most characteristic, artistic, Personality. Not but that he had faults, and show'd them in the Presidency; but honesty, goodness, shrewdness, conscience, and (a new virtue, unknown to other lands, and hardly yet really known here, but the foundation and tie of all, as the future will grandly develop,) Unionism, in its truest and amplest sense, form'd the hard-pan of his character. These he seal'd with his life. The tragic splendor of his death, purging, illuminating all, throws round his form, his head, an aureole that will remain and will grow brighter through time, while History lives, and love of Country lasts. By many has *this Union* been conserv'd and help'd; but if one name, one man, must be pick'd out, he, most of all, is the Conservator of it, to the future. He was assassinated—but the Union is not assassinated—*ça ira!* One falls, and another falls. The soldier drops, sinks like a wave—but the ranks of the ocean eternally press on. Death does its work, obliterates a hundred, a thousand—President, general, captain, private—but the Nation is immortal.]

"No Good Portrait of Lincoln"

Probably the reader has seen physiognomies (often old farmers, sea-captains, and such) that, behind their homeliness, or even ugliness, held superior points so subtle, yet so palpable, defying the lines of art, making the real life of their faces almost as impossible to depict as a wild perfume or fruit-taste, or a passionate tone of the living voice.....and such was Lincoln's face, the peculiar color, the lines of it, the eyes, mouth, expression, &c. Of technical *beauty* it had nothing—but to the eye of a great artist it furnished a rare study, a feast and fascination.......The current portraits are all failures—most of them caricatures.

Folsom Commentary

"Abraham Lincoln," Whitman's concise little recollection of some of his encounters with the president during the war years in Washington, D.C., was written shortly before the assassination. It gives us an idea of just how different citizens' encounters with their president were in the mid-nineteenth century, as Whitman recounts the numerous (often daily) encounters he had with Lincoln on the streets of the capital. There was always a military cortege accompanying him, but still the president and Whitman exchanged glances and "very cordial" bows as they passed. What strikes Whitman most about Lincoln is how "ordinary" he always looked—like "the commonest man." And yet what haunts him is the president's "dark brown face, with the deep cut lines, the eyes, &c., always to me with a deep latent sadness in the expression"—a face, he says here (and he would repeat it many times), that escapes all the best efforts of photographers and painters to capture it. Lincoln's face has a "deep, though subtle and indirect expression": "There is something else there." That "something else" was as undefinable as Whitman's vague phrase. He tries to name it in "No Good Portrait of Lincoln" but again comes up short: "the peculiar color, the lines of it, the eyes, mouth, expression, &c." That "peculiar color" in the president's "dark brown face" suggested, perhaps, a racial darkening of the nation that Whitman was experiencing and often commented on during the last year of the war as thousands of emancipated slaves made their way to the capital, turning it into a truly biracial city. It's as if American racial history was somehow inscribing itself on Lincoln's face. The poet and biographer Daniel Mark Epstein describes what he calls "the very peculiar matter of the president's skin" as Lincoln's funeral cortege passed through Pennsylvania coal country, where his face surprisingly turned black, requiring morticians to apply a white chalky paste to it so that the face would not appear black to those who viewed the open casket in New York. Whitman sensed that Lincoln's face embodied, almost mysteriously, the nation's turmoil and its transformation.

Whitman did not start out as a great supporter of Lincoln, and the poet's only mention of the 1863 Emancipation Proclamation is an offhand comment about how the proclamation was greeted with indifference in Washington, D.C. But as Whitman saw the president more frequently and traced the way the national trauma impressed itself into the president's face and body, he gradually came to admire him and associate him fully with the preservation of the Union. Whitman acknowledges that Lincoln "had faults, and show'd them in the Presidency; but honesty, goodness, shrewdness, conscience, and (a new virtue, unknown to other lands, and hardly yet really known here, but the foundation and tie of all, as the future will grandly develop,) Unionism, in its truest and amplest sense, form'd the hard-pan of his character." *That* is what Whitman saw in Lincoln that he believed no artist could capture, no photograph record: "hard-pan," after all, is the impervious layer of soil just below the surface, which cannot be seen and yet is what prevents the rains from soaking in. This quality of "Unionism"—this stalwart dedication to keeping the United States whole, to containing the nation's contradictions, to not giving in to fracture and fragmentation—was the unbending quality just below the surface of Lincoln's darkening face, the quality that made him, in Whitman's mind, "the greatest, best, most characteristic, artistic, Personality."

Whitman's comments on Lincoln's "unionism" appear in "Murder of President Lincoln," the poet's first attempt to capture the drama of the assassination and assess its significance for the country's future. These notes would become the heart of Whitman's famous "Lincoln Lecture," that he gave numerous times from 1879 through the 1880s, most famously at Madison Square Theatre in New York on April 14, 1887, when Mark Twain, Andrew Carnegie, John Hay, William Tecumseh Sherman, James Russell Lowell, Mary Mapes Dodge, and many other celebrities filled the auditorium (William Dean Howells was pressed into service to collect tickets). Whitman, aged and infirm, with "deep cut lines" now in his own face, presented his talk and guided the rapt audience back through the drama of the assassination, emphasizing how appropriate it was that the killing took place in a theatre, with an actor as the assassin, with the real national drama not being played out on the stage of Ford's Theatre but in the balcony, as the entire nation served as the continental stage for the playing out of a stormy drama that Lincoln, the main actor, led us safely through, before, inevitably it seemed, dying in the final scenes, just as the war ended. Whitman was in New York when the assassination occurred, but he pieced together his firsthand account from discussions with his young lover/companion, Peter Doyle, a former Confederate soldier, who was at Ford's Theatre that fateful night.

In Springfield, Illinois, on the same day that Whitman gave his lecture, exactly twenty-two years after John Wilkes Booth fired his fatal shot, the Lincoln Guard of Honor and numerous friends of the president gathered to witness the opening of Lincoln's coffin. They reported that the corpse was in excellent condition but that the white paste on Lincoln's face had turned to dust, leaving the president's face black.

Merrill Commentary

William Matthews concludes his poem from the tumultuous 1960s, "Why We Are Truly a Nation," with a startling image: "Because grief unites us, / like the locked antlers of moose / who die on their knees in pairs." After the assassinations of John

F. Kennedy, Martin Luther King, Jr., and Robert Kennedy, American poets searched for a language adequate to the national tragedies that would shape the future, and what Matthews discovered was an image, drawn from the natural world, to instruct readers on the ways in which economic, political, and social divisions may have suicidal consequences: the legacy of the Civil War lives on in this land.

This is why Whitman's identification of Unionism as Lincoln's "new virtue, unknown to other lands, and hardly yet really known here, but the foundation and tie of all, as the future will grandly develop," is crucial to understanding the relationship of his poetics to American politics. In grief the poet grasps the fact that history will record the president's life and death as integral to the American experiment, which he will continue to sing and celebrate, explore and lament, until he can no longer hold a pen. From "Song of Myself" to "When Lilacs Last in the Door-Yard Bloom'd" and *Democratic Vistas* he will link his writings to the fate of his country; for in the years leading up to the war he fashioned an individual poetic self—"Walt Whitman, an American, one of the roughs, a kosmos"—that in the wake of Lincoln's assassination would summon new energy to preserving the nation, which otherwise might tear itself apart again.

Lincoln concluded his first Inaugural Address with a powerful appeal to those who would secede from the Union:

> We are not enemies, but friends. We must not be enemies. Though passion may have strained it must not break our bonds of affection. The mystic chords of memory, stretching from every battlefield and patriot grave to every living heart and hearthstone all over this broad land, will yet swell the chorus of the Union, when again touched, as surely they will be, by the better angels of our nature.

But in the aftermath of the war a sizable portion of the Confederacy refused to heed those better angels. Lincoln's death laid bare the wounds of the blood-soaked nation, threatening to sunder it at the very moment that healing might begin. Whitman observed that no good portrait existed of the president—the "peculiar color" of his face, "the lines of it, the eyes, mouth, expression, &c."—though he recognized that for "a great artist it furnished a rare study, a feast and fascination." He was such an artist. And these notes serve as preliminary sketches for his portrait of Lincoln in his poem "When Lilacs Last in the Door-Yard Bloom'd." Soon he would transform his sorrow into a search for "a passionate tone of the living voice," a healing sound that would reverberate down through the ages, calling us to join "the chorus of the Union."

29

"Hush'd Be the Camps To-Day"

A. L. BURIED APRIL 19, 1865.

HUSH'D be the camps to-day;
And, soldiers, let us drape our war-worn weapons;
And each, with musing soul retire, to celebrate,
Our dear commander's death.

No more for him life's stormy conflicts;
Nor victory, nor defeat—No more time's dark events,
Charging like ceaseless clouds across the sky.

But sing, poet, in our name;
Sing of the love we bore him—because you, dweller in camps, know it truly.

Sing, to the lower'd coffin there;
Sing, with the shovel'd clods that fill the grave—a verse,
For the heavy hearts of soldiers.

Folsom Commentary

After languishing in Confederate prisoner-of-war camps for months, Whitman's brother George was finally released and made his way home to New York; Whitman, after receiving word of George's return, quickly took leave from his clerk's job in Washington and headed to New York. Arriving at his mother's home in late March of 1865, he began to make arrangements for the printing of *Drum-Taps*, his book of Civil War poems, and on April 1 he signed a contract with Brooklyn printer Peter Eckler. The war was not yet quite over, but President Lincoln was already discussing Reconstruction with his generals, and, in the following few days, the Confederates would abandon their capital, Richmond, and Jefferson Davis and his cabinet would flee to Danville, Virginia. The end was near enough for Whitman to get his book printed and ready for sale by the official conclusion of hostilities.

As had been the case with the first two editions of *Leaves of Grass*, Whitman was self-publishing (and paying for) his book, and his timing could hardly have been worse. The war had pushed paper prices to record levels, and as critic Ted Genoways has shown, Whitman immediately began scaling back his original plans for a 120-page book and worked to rearrange his poems to take advantage of all the available space on each valuable page, turning it into a 72-page book with virtually no blank space. Amidst much shuffling of texts and type design in order to make everything fit, as well as last-minute revisions to acknowledge that the war had in fact ended (General Lee surrendered at Appomattox Court House on April 9), he faced his greatest challenge when, with the book set to be printed, Abraham Lincoln was shot on the night of April 14 and died the next morning. Whitman now knew his book of war poetry would immediately be an anachronism if he did not somehow acknowledge this momentous event that punctuated the war in a way few could have imagined.

So Whitman told Eckler to delay the printing while he quickly wrote the short "Hush'd Be the Camps To-Day." He had Eckler remove a poem of similar length and substitute this one, which Whitman had unfortunately subtitled "A. L. buried April 19, 1865." Trying to keep abreast of fast-moving events in Washington, he relied on false initial reports that Lincoln would be buried in the capital, and so Whitman's subtitle remained an embarrassing error, since Lincoln would not be buried until May 4, in Springfield, Illinois, after the long railroad journey that allowed much of the nation to see his coffin and to honor him. And the poem was in error, too, about the way Lincoln was buried: there was no "lower'd coffin" and no "shovel'd clods" filling "the grave," since the president's body was instead put into a vault in Springfield. In the 1871 printing of this poem in *Leaves of Grass*, Whitman corrected the subtitle to "(May 4, 1865)" and altered the final stanza: "As they invault the coffin there, / Sing—as they close the doors of earth upon him—one verse, / For the heavy hearts of soldiers."

Eckler printed the book, but Whitman, already aware that *Drum-Taps* would now need additional work, kept the printing small and the number of bound copies even smaller. He would immediately begin working on more accurate and fitting tributes to Lincoln, and his *Sequel to Drum-Taps* (with "O Captain! My Captain!" and "When Lilacs Last in the Door-Yard Bloom'd") would be printed six months later and would be bound together with *Drum-Taps*.

For all the problems Whitman faced in getting his book of war poems into print in the form that he wanted, and for all the haste with which he wrote "Hush'd Be the Camps," this quiet little poem is nonetheless quite moving. Whitman immediately locates the scene of mourning not among the populace in the streets but among the soldiers in their camps, who have fallen silent, have draped their weapons, and now "retire . . . to celebrate" their "dear commander's death." The poem lets us experience not the death of a president so much as the death of the civilian commander-in-chief of the armed forces. The soldiers' "celebration" is of course akin to a religious celebration—"celebrate" in its etymological sense of keeping solemn, gathering to honor and sing praises. Then, in the suggestive third stanza, the soldiers movingly look up from their own makeshift rituals of mourning and loss, and they beseech Whitman himself, the "poet," to write something "in our name," to "sing of the love we bore him." And they look to *this* poet, to Whitman, because they know him—he was after all a "dweller in camps," not to mention a comrade in hospitals—and he is therefore the only poet they trust to sing for them. And so Whitman offers a small "verse" here, but in the months to come, he would embrace their imagined request and compose a song of national loss and healing, not only for the dead president but also for "the debris and debris of all dead soldiers." While recalling the aroma of the early-blooming lilacs that he inhaled in his mother's dooryard the day that he heard the news of Lincoln's death, he would in fact sing one of the most powerful odes ever written.

Merrill Commentary

Necessity is the mother of invention. I like to think the unknown author of this proverb was a poet, since poetry depends for some of its effects on the limitations it sets for itself, whether it is written in traditional or open forms. And there is no better example of a poet inventing on the nonce than Whitman's "Hushed Be the Camps To-Day," the inspiration for which, as Ed Folsom notes, was the fact that his collection of Civil War poems, *Drum-Taps,* was about to go to press when Lincoln was assassinated. How to address the most important casualty of the war in twelve lines—the space that became available with the removal of another poem? Impossible, of course. Which is why this late addition, poignant as it is, cannot compare to his forthcoming magisterial elegy, "When Lilacs Last in the Door-Yard Bloom'd." Think of it as a stop-gap measure, which acquired a certain beauty from its setting among soldiers stunned by the loss of their commander-in-chief. Whitman's larger poetic problem—finding the right words to reconcile North and South, on the page if not in the body politic—would exact from him considerably more toil.

In its very modesty the poem speaks volumes not only to the grief of the soldiers, who were well acquainted with death and doubtless grasped what this might presage for the cause of peace, but also to the necessity of poetry in a time of national crisis: how it can clarify, if not transfigure, emotions triggered by the event. Lincoln's death would complicate the work of reconciliation and reconstruction, jeopardizing the Union, the preservation of which had already demanded too much from the soldiers, the heavy-hearted young men who trust Whitman to give voice to the pain they feel in the harsh light of this ultimate sacrifice.

The poet who competes with historical events, the meaning of which will inevitably change over time, is bound to make mistakes, especially in war—where, as it is often said, the first casualty is the truth. This Whitman discovered when the details of Lincoln's burial became clear—after his book had been printed. One imagines that the language, by which all poets live, forgave him for that slip, and in any case he corrected it in the next edition of *Leaves of Grass*. What matters here is that as a "dweller in the camps" he knew how to sing truly to his comrades, and so he did.

30

"When Lilacs Last in the Door-Yard Bloom'd," Sections 1–13

1

WHEN lilacs last in the door-yard bloom'd,
And the great star early droop'd in the western sky in the night,
I mourn'd ... and yet shall mourn with ever-returning spring.

O ever-returning spring! trinity sure to me you bring;
Lilac blooming perennial, and drooping star in the west,
And thought of him I love.

2

O powerful, western, fallen star!
O shades of night! O moody, tearful night!
O great star disappear'd! O the blank murk that hides the star!
O cruel hands that hold me powerless! O helpless soul of me!
O harsh surrounding cloud that will not free my soul!

3

In the door-yard fronting an old farm-house, near the white-wash'd palings,
Stands the lilac bush, tall-growing, with heart-shaped leaves of rich green,
With many a pointed blossom, rising, delicate, with the perfume strong I love,
With every leaf a miracle ...... and from this bush in the door-yard,
With its delicate-color'd blossoms, and heart-shaped leaves of rich green,
A sprig, with its flower, I break.

4

In the swamp, in secluded recesses,
A shy and hidden bird is warbling a song.

Solitary, the thrush,

The hermit, withdrawn to himself, avoiding the settlements,
Sings by himself a song.

Song of the bleeding throat!
Death's outlet song of life—(for well, dear brother, I know,
If thou wast not gifted to sing, thou would'st surely die.)

5

Over the breast of the spring, the land, amid cities,
Amid lanes, and through old woods, (where lately the violets peep'd from the ground,
 spotting the gray debris;)
Amid the grass in the fields each side of the lanes—passing the endless grass;
Passing the yellow-spear'd wheat, every grain from its shroud in the dark-brown
 fields uprising;
Passing the apple-tree blows of white and pink in the orchards;
Carrying a corpse to where it shall rest in the grave,
Night and day journeys a coffin.

6

Coffin that passes through lanes and streets,
Through day and night, with the great cloud darkening the land,
With the pomp of the inloop'd flags, with the cities draped in black,
With the show of the States themselves, as of crape-veil'd women, standing,
With processions long and winding, and the flambeaus of the night,
With the countless torches lit—with the silent sea of faces, and the unbared heads,
With the waiting depot, the arriving coffin, and the sombre faces,
With dirges through the night, with the thousand voices rising strong and solemn;
With all the mournful voices of the dirges, pour'd around the coffin,
The dim-lit churches and the shuddering organs—Where amid these you journey,
With the tolling, tolling bells' perpetual clang;
Here! coffin that slowly passes.
I give you my sprig of lilac.

7

(Nor for you, for one, alone;
Blossoms and branches green to coffins all I bring:

For fresh as the morning—thus would I chant a song for you, O sane and sacred death.

All over bouquets of roses,
O death! I cover you over with roses and early lilies;
But mostly and now the lilac that blooms the first,
Copious, I break, I break the sprigs from the bushes:
With loaded arms I come, pouring for you,
For you and the coffins all of you, O death.)

8

O western orb, sailing the heaven!
Now I know what you must have meant, as a month since we walk'd,
As we walk'd up and down in the dark blue so mystic,
As we walk'd in silence the transparent shadowy night,
As I saw you had something to tell, as you bent to me night after night,
As you droop'd from the sky low down, as if to my side, (while the other stars all look'd on;)
As we wander'd together the solemn night, (for something
I know not what, kept me from sleep;)
As the night advanced, and I saw on the rim of the west, ere you went, how full you were of woe;
As I stood on the rising ground in the breeze, in the cool transparent night,
As I watch'd where you pass'd and was lost in the netherward black of the night,
As my soul, in its trouble, dissatisfied, sank, as where you, sad orb,
Concluded, dropt in the night, and was gone.

9

Sing on, there in the swamp!
O singer bashful and tender! I hear your notes—I hear your call;
I hear—I come presently—I understand you;
But a moment I linger—for the lustrous star has detain'd me;
The star, my comrade, departing, holds and detains me.

10

O how shall I warble myself for the dead one there I loved?

And how shall I deck my song for the large sweet soul that has gone?
And what shall my perfume be, for the grave of him I love?

Sea-winds, blown from east and west,
Blown from the eastern sea, and blown from the western sea, till there on
    the prairies meeting:
These, and with these, and the breath of my chant,
I perfume the grave of him I love.

11

O what shall I hang on the chamber walls?
And what shall the pictures be that I hang on the walls,
To adorn the burial-house of him I love?

Pictures of growing spring, and farms, and homes,
With the Fourth-month eve at sundown, and the gray-smoke lucid and bright,
With floods of the yellow gold of the gorgeous, indolent, sinking sun, burning,
    expanding the air;
With the fresh sweet herbage under foot, and the pale green leaves of the trees
    prolific;
In the distance the flowing glaze, the breast of the river, with a wind-dapple here
    and there;
With ranging hills on the banks, with many a line against the sky, and shadows;
And the city at hand, with dwellings so dense, and stacks of chimneys,
And all the scenes of life, and the workshops, and the workmen homeward returning.

12

Lo! body and soul! this land!
Mighty Manhattan, with spires, and the sparkling and hurrying tides, and the ships;
The varied and ample land—the South and the North in the light—Ohio's shores,
    and flashing Missouri,
And ever the far-spreading prairies, cover'd with grass and corn.

Lo! the most excellent sun, so calm and haughty;
The violet and purple morn, with just-felt breezes:
The gentle, soft-born, measureless light;
The miracle, spreading, bathing all—the fulfill'd noon;

The coming eve, delicious—the welcome night, and the stars,
Over my cities shining all, enveloping man and land.

13

Sing on! sing on, you gray-brown bird!
Sing from the swamps, the recesses—pour your chant from the bushes;
Limitless out of the dusk, out of the cedars and pines.

Sing on, dearest brother—warble your reedy song;
Loud human song, with voice of uttermost woe.

O liquid, and free, and tender!
O wild and loose to my soul! O wondrous singer!
You only I hear ...... yet the star holds me, (but will soon depart;)
Yet the lilac, with mastering odor, holds me.

Folsom Commentary

Having printed *Drum-Taps* just after Abraham Lincoln's assassination, Whitman knew immediately that he would have to revise or add to the book so that he could explore more deeply the significance of the loss of the president. He worked during the summer of 1865 to write what became his best-known poem, "O Captain! My Captain!," in which he imagines a sailor processing the loss of his "captain," the commander-in-chief of the ship of state, "fallen cold and dead" on "the deck." But the poem he most fully devoted himself to was "When Lilacs Last in the Door-Yard Bloom'd." He published both poems along with a handful of others in a supplement or "sequel" to *Drum-Taps,* which he bound into the back of the copies of *Drum-Taps* that he had held back from distribution when it was originally supposed to be issued back in April of 1865. He published the new book in October and entitled his sequel *When Lilacs Last in the Door-Yard Bloom'd and Other Pieces,* using a specially designed font of type in which the very letters of the title are created out of splintered and broken staffs, indicating visually what the poem itself enacts—its creation out of shattered pieces. Pieces—the result of massive fragmentation, amputations, deaths beyond retrieval—were all that the people of America had left, and the hope, such as it was, was that someone would begin to compose something, *make* something, out of the broken pieces of what was once a unified whole, a Union. "Lilacs" is a poem about loss and death and the sense of the world coming to a stasis. Lincoln was assassinated in April. Whitman, who lived at the time in Washington, D.C., was visiting his mother in New York, and he heard the news from a newsboy shouting it in the street. Standing up and walking out to his mother's dooryard, he stood where the lilacs were blooming early that year, and in the inhalation of his grief, a kind of bodily merger occurred: the horrifying news of Lincoln's death was in that moment fused with the aroma of lilacs, a smell that until then had signaled for the poet new birth, hope; but now, in an unsettling synesthetic melding, lilacs would be forever associated with death and loss.

And yet we should note that the poem begins with the sound of hope buried in the diction—the ringing *-ing* rhyme of participial endings, indicating the desire to continue on: "spring / returning / bring / blooming / drooping." What does not rhyme or ring with the recurring *-ing* in the opening lines of the poem is the "thought of him I love"—because now "ever-returning spring," instead of bringing freshness and new beginnings, brings a mix of memory and desire, a "thought of him I love," the one who is no more. How can spring ever again contain the promise of a new beginning, when its annual return will from now on insist on bringing instead the thought of the dead one who was loved, and the thought of the hundreds of thousands dead who fought for and against the Union that Lincoln stood for? The poem will gradually work its way to trying to restore the progressive and ongoing sense of the participles that begin the poem, even as the poet's first act is to "break" a "sprig" of lilac to put on Lincoln's passing coffin. Not only is the breaking of that sprig a breaking off of the life of that spring's lilac blossoms; we realize too that the word "sprig" is itself a kind of broken "spring"—a "spring" that, minus the *n*, is now without life, without the sense of continuity and future that is built into the *-ing* forms of present participles (which themselves are words that store action, awaiting conjugation to bring that action into being). The poem wrestles, then, with conflicting senses: Is this the spring that stops all springs, that ends renewal (a broken sprig), or will the "ever-returning spring," by the sheer force of its cycling, eventually tease out hope again?

"Lilacs" may remind us of another famous American poem, written sixty years later, also in the aftermath of a bloody and catastrophic war that tested the resolve of the poet to continue writing poetry. By the time T. S. Eliot published *The Waste Land* in the 1920s, he had worked hard to distance himself from Whitman, calling his poetry "clap-trap" and finding Whitman himself a "pathetic creature." And yet, Eliot made one striking exception: "When Whitman speaks of the lilacs," Eliot said, "his theories and beliefs drop away like a needless pretext." And we can indeed hear the impact Whitman's lilacs had on Eliot when we recall the iconic opening lines of *The Waste Land*: "April is the cruelest month, breeding / Lilacs out of the dead land, mixing / Memory with desire, stirring / Dull roots with spring rain." The direct echoes of Whitman are undeniable, not just in the way that

April becomes cruel with its reminders of memory and desire, but in the same use of the insistent participles ("breeding," "mixing," "stirring") that nearly rhyme with "spring" in the fourth line, except that "spring" is oddly out of place, buried in the penultimate position, not allowed to attach to the participles that hang at the ends of the lines, reaching and yearning for conjugation.

Both these poems, with their elegiac tones, never name the person being mourned. Most readers assumed Whitman was writing about Lincoln, but Whitman's great elegy is in part remarkable because we never hear the name of "him I loved": the loss is detached from specificity and bleeds out into a vaster, even more unnameable loss that eventually in the poem will yield "armies" of loss, "battle-corpses, myriads of them." The subject of Eliot's elegy is even more deeply buried: he had a secretive loving relationship with Jean Verdenal, a young medical officer in World War I who was killed during the Gallipoli landing, which began in April of 1915, exactly fifty years after Lincoln's assassination. In his one published memory of Verdenal, Eliot recalls their last meeting in Paris, and it is tinged with lilacs: "My own retrospect is touched by a sentimental sunset, the memory of a friend coming across the Luxembourg Gardens in the late afternoon, waving a branch of lilac, a friend who was later (so far as I can tell) to be mixed with the mud of Gallipoli." Like Lincoln, Verdenal was shot in the head, and like Lincoln's death for Whitman, Verdenal's death for Eliot reified the vast mass death of the war into a single beloved person, whose loss would forever mix memory and desire in the cruelty of ever-returning spring, and whose death left the world in pieces. Whitman's title page for "Lilacs" used images of broken pieces of wood to compose the poem's words, and Eliot's poem ends with the poet "shoring these fragments against my ruins." April is the cruelest month . . .

Merrill Commentary

Synesthesia, the mingling of sense perceptions at the heart of "When Lilacs Last in the Door-Yard Bloom'd," is for certain artists an essential element of their work. Thus Proust tasted a madeleine, and a vanished world came flooding back to him, which he chronicled in the seven volumes of *In Search of Lost Time*; Kandinsky assigned colors to particular notes of music, which governed how he painted; and composers such as Liszt, Messiaen, Rimsky-Korsakov, and Sibelius saw colors when they composed. Art, literature, and music can be multisensory experiences, which engage the full range of the imagination, and the mysterious currents that carry one from the familiar to the strange depend to some extent upon the joining of different senses—which is why it is sometimes difficult to explain one's response to poems like "When Lilacs Last in the Door-Yard Bloom'd." Heartache summoned Whitman to his best writing, and with Lincoln's assassination, which stood in his mind for all the needless deaths of the war, he recalls the fragrance of the lilac by the door to his mother's house, a blooming perennial that each spring had heretofore signaled new life for him, its "every leaf a miracle." Henceforth it would be a symbol of his bereavement.

How to transfigure such pain into poetry? In the third section, Whitman describes the lilac, its "heart-shaped leaves of rich green" (a phrase repeated three lines later), and the flowering sprig, the breaking of which forms the prelude to his introduction, in the next section, of a thrush warbling in "secluded recesses" of the swamp, a solitary gray-brown bird that chants "a song for you, O sane and sacred death." The drab bird's "reedy song" follows the coffin bearing Lincoln through the streets and lanes, cities and states, to his final resting place, accompanied by the dirges of his mourners; with sea-winds blowing from east and west to meet in the prairie and "the breath of my chant," the poet will "perfume the grave of him I love." This song, the evening star "sailing the heaven," and the "mastering odor" of lilacs hold him in a fierce embrace: a "trinity sure," which is designed to rival the Christian Trinity of Father, Son, and Holy Spirit.

Researchers understand that trauma can live on in the body and memory long after the event—which may explain the prevalence of war literature the world over: poets and journalists, soldiers and survivors—they reckon up the costs of war, physical, psychic, and spiritual. Just as Coleridge's Ancient Mariner is condemned to tell the story of the tragedy he set in motion with his thoughtless act, killing the albatross that followed his ship across the sea, so the sight or smell of lilacs triggers Whitman's memory of the shock he experienced at the news of Lincoln's death. The lilac sprig he imagines placing on the coffin is a token of his elegy, the thrush's song, and with that gesture we, too, linger, gazing at the star that fell too soon.

31

"When Lilacs Last in the Door-Yard Bloom'd," Sections 14–21

14

Now while I sat in the day, and look'd forth,
In the close of the day, with its light, and the fields of spring, and the farmer preparing his crops,
In the large unconscious scenery of my land, with its lakes and forests,
In the heavenly aerial beauty, (after the perturb'd winds, and the storms;)
Under the arching heavens of the afternoon swift passing, and the voices of children and women,
The many-moving sea-tides,—and I saw the ships how they sail'd,
And the summer approaching with richness, and the fields all busy with labor,
And the infinite separate houses, how they all went on, each with its meals and minutia of daily usages;
And the streets, how their throbbings throbb'd, and the cities pent,—lo! then and there,
Falling among them all, and upon them all, enveloping me with the rest,
Appear'd the cloud, appear'd the long black trail;
And I knew Death, its thought, and the sacred knowledge of death.

15

Then with the knowledge of death as walking one side of me,
And the thought of death close-walking the other side of me,
And I in the middle, as with companions, and as holding the hands of companions,
I fled forth to the hiding receiving night, that talks not,
Down to the shores of the water, the path by the swamp in the dimness,
To the solemn shadowy cedars, and ghostly pines so still.

And the singer so shy to the rest receiv'd me;
The gray-brown bird I know, receiv'd us comrades three;
And he sang what seem'd the song of death, and a verse for him I love.

From deep secluded recesses,
From the fragrant cedars, and the ghostly pines so still,
Came the singing of the bird.

And the charm of the singing rapt me,
As I held, as if by their hands, my comrades in the night;
And the voice of my spirit tallied the song of the bird.

16

Come, lovely and soothing Death,
Undulate round the world, serenely arriving, arriving,
In the day, in the night, to all, to each,
Sooner or later, delicate Death.

Prais'd be the fathomless universe,
For life and joy, and for objects and knowledge curious;
And for love, sweet love—But praise! O praise and praise,
For the sure-enwinding arms of cool-enfolding Death.

Dark Mother, always gliding near, with soft feet,
Have none chanted for thee a chant of fullest welcome?
Then I chant it for thee—I glorify thee above all;
I bring thee a song that when thou must indeed come, come unfalteringly.

Approach, encompassing Death—strong Deliveress!
When it is so—when thou hast taken them, I joyously sing the dead,
Lost in the loving, floating ocean of thee,
Laved in the flood of thy bliss, O Death.

From me to thee glad serenades,
Dances for thee I propose, saluting thee—adornments and feastings for thee;
And the sights of the open landscape, and the high-spread sky, are fitting,
And life and the fields, and the huge and thoughtful night.

The night, in silence, under many a star;
The ocean shore, and the husky whispering wave, whose voice I know;
And the soul turning to thee, O vast and well-veil'd Death,
And the body gratefully nestling close to thee.

Over the tree-tops I float thee a song!

Over the rising and sinking waves—over the myriad fields, and the prairies wide;
Over the dense-pack'd cities all, and the teeming wharves and ways,
I float this carol with joy, with joy to thee, O Death!

17

To the tally of my soul,
Loud and strong kept up the gray-brown bird,
With pure, deliberate notes, spreading, filling the night.

Loud in the pines and cedars dim,
Clear in the freshness moist, and the swamp-perfume;
And I with my comrades there in the night.

While my sight that was bound in my eyes unclosed,
As to long panoramas of visions.

18

I saw the vision of armies;
And I saw, as in noiseless dreams, hundreds of battle-flags;
Borne through the smoke of the battles, and pierc'd with missiles, I saw them,
And carried hither and yon through the smoke, and torn and bloody;
And at last but a few shreds of the flags left on the staffs, (and all in silence,)
And the staffs all splinter'd and broken.

I saw battle-corpses, myriads of them,
And the white skeletons of young men—I saw them;
I saw the debris and debris of all dead soldiers;
But I saw they were not as was thought;
They themselves were fully at rest—they suffer'd not;
The living remain'd and suffer'd—the mother suffer'd,
And the wife and the child, and the musing comrade suffer'd,
And the armies that remain'd suffer'd.

19

Passing the visions, passing the night;
Passing, unloosing the hold of my comrades' hands;
Passing the song of the hermit bird, and the tallying song of my soul,

Victorious song, death's outlet song, (yet varying, ever-altering song,
As low and wailing, yet clear the notes, rising and falling, flooding the night,
Sadly sinking and fainting, as warning and warning, and yet again bursting with joy,)
Covering the earth, and filling the spread of the heaven,
As that powerful psalm in the night I heard from recesses.

20

Must I leave thee, lilac with heart-shaped leaves?
Must I leave thee there in the door-yard, blooming, returning with spring?
Must I pass from my song for thee;
From my gaze on thee in the west, fronting the west, communing with thee,
O comrade lustrous, with silver face in the night?

21

Yet each I keep, and all;
The song, the wondrous chant of the gray-brown bird, I keep,
And the tallying chant, the echo arous'd in my soul, I keep,
With the lustrous and drooping star, with the countenance
full of woe;
With the lilac tall, and its blossoms of mastering odor;
Comrades mine, and I in the midst, and their memory ever
I keep—for the dead I loved so well;
For the sweetest, wisest soul of all my days and lands ...
and this for his dear sake;
Lilac and star and bird, twined with the chant of my soul,
With the holders holding my hand, nearing the call of the
bird,
There in the fragrant pines, and the cedars dusk and dim.

Folsom Commentary

Much of "When Lilacs Last in the Door-Yard Bloom'd" records the search of the poet for a way to sing appropriately of the president's death and the massive death of the war. He listens to a solitary unseen bird—a hermit thrush—that sings loudly what the poet hears as "death's outlet song of life." He is desperate to translate that bird's "warble" into a "human song" and to use it as his own as he too seeks an "outlet" from the war's carnage that seems to surround him. So he follows the bird's call into "the swamps, the recesses," where he finds himself walking with two spectral companions on either side of him—"the knowledge of death" and "the thought of death." The swamp is the ultimate site of composting—the place where the liquid and the solid merge and meld, where the decay of death is at its most fertile, continually producing new life out of the muck, a landscape that embodies "death's outlet song of life." We all live continually with the "thought of death"—it walks with us during all the moments of our life—but none of us has the "knowledge of death." If there is "knowledge" to be had, it can only come after death has occurred. So all of us walk suspended between the thought and knowledge of death. In the swamp, though, the poet begins translating the song of the solitary singer, the thrush's song that is at once assuring and unsettling: death will come "sooner or later" "to all, to each," but it is "lovely and soothing" and "cool-enfolding." Death's song is finally a "carol" sung "with joy."

So, surrounded by the "swamp-perfume" and held close by the thought and knowledge of death, the poet for the first time allows himself to open his eyes fully to the horror of the Civil War he has experienced over the previous couple of years. In a remarkable unbinding of his sight, he allows his experiences of caring for a hundred thousand sick, wounded, and dying young soldiers to tumble from his eyes deep into his brain, imagination, and perception. Up to now, he has kept his "sight . . . bound in my eyes," but now the carnage flows into his mind unchecked, and his world shatters into fragments—we see "the staffs all splinter'd and broken," like the broken staffs that make up the title page of his *Drum-Taps* sequel. And, as his sight opens up to the "battle-corpses, myriads of them, / And the white skeletons of young men," he absorbs "the debris and debris of all the slain soldiers of the war." These are, as we saw earlier, the "million dead" that he can "sum up" but not "summon up": they are already "debris," part of the same landscape that Lincoln's death train traveled through on its way to Springfield, Illinois, that Whitman described in section 5 of the poem: "Amid lanes and through old woods, where lately the violets peep'd from the ground, spotting the gray debris." America's lands are melded now with this "debris and debris" (even Whitman's repetition of the word emphasizes its root meaning of "breaking apart," as if simply saying the word leads to another breaking off of more debris).

The comfort for Whitman is that he now carries with him the knowledge from the thrush's solitary song that one thing death is *not* is suffering: he knows that the dead "themselves were fully at rest, they suffer'd not." It is "the living" who remain and suffer. The dead are beyond that concern—they *know* the "soothing" peace of death; we the living are the ones who carry the burden of suffering.

So the poem ends with the return of the participles (those verbs of continuing action) in a long chain of repetitions of the word "passing" (with its buried "sing") as the poet now finds he can take the first steps of leaving behind all the things he has been occupied with in the poem—he passes the vision of the dead, the night, the song of the hermit thrush, the lilacs themselves. While other ongoing participles record persistent mourning ("falling," "flooding," "sinking," "fainting," "warning," "bursting"), he can nonetheless begin to sense the "blooming, returning with spring," the spring as faint sign of hope instead of reminder of immense loss.

But the poem does not end there. Like T. S. Eliot sixty years later in *The Waste Land*, Whitman leaves us with fragments that he is trying to shore against his ruin. For Whitman, those fragments are what he calls "retrievements out of the night," the bits and pieces of the debris that he is able to hold on to for guidance and to shape into this poem—the evening star (Venus) that seemed so bright and low in those nights before the assassination of Lincoln, the bird that sang death's outlet song, the aromatic lilac, the "comrades" that accompanied him in the swamp, the mass of "the dead I loved so well," and the unnamed Lincoln himself ("the sweetest, wisest soul of all my days and lands").

In 1865, the final verse paragraph of the poem began "Yet each I keep, and all." Whitman would later revise that opening to "Yet each to keep and all." It's a tiny change—from "I" to "to"—but it makes all the difference. As he imagines shoring up those precious "retrievements from the night," pulling the fragments together to begin to create a future out of the debris, we realize with a sudden shock that Whitman's delicate revision has transformed the final nine-line verse paragraph into a sentence fragment. He has removed the subject/actor (the "I") and left the act of "retrievement" an infinitive verb ("to keep"), held forever in suspended animation, something hoped for but never achieved, never activated in time. A fragment.

Merrill Commentary

To the "trinity sure" in the opening section of "When Lilacs Last in the Door-Yard Bloom'd," consisting of the lilac, the star, and "ever-returning spring" (soon to be replaced by the song of the thrush), Whitman adds a third triad: the speaker walking in the swamp with his boon companions, the thought of death and the knowledge of death, one whom he knows well and one he cannot know until he dies. The altar of his civic religion, we learn at the start of the last third of the poem, lies in "the hiding receiving night," where the thrush "receiv'd us comrades three; / And he sang what seem'd the song of death, and a verse for him I love." Mortality is the key in which Whitman wrote from the first version of "Song of Myself" through the deathbed edition of *Leaves of Grass*, and nowhere is this more apparent than in his elegy for Lincoln, when "the voice of [his] spirit tallied the song of the bird," tally in this instance meaning both to correspond and to calculate. The losses he tallied among the "ghostly pines," personal and political, were enormous.

This song, which in the poet's imagination has crossed the country as part of the president's funeral procession, now brings him visions of the war—armies, shredded flags, broken staffs. And more: "I saw battle-corpses, myriads of them, / And the white skeletons of young men—I saw them; / I saw the debris and debris of all dead soldiers." Their suffering is over, their knowledge of death complete, and so it falls to the living—mothers, wives and children, "the musing comrade" (the poet, that is)—to deal with their losses. Impossible, of course. Which is why he is haunted by "the ever-altering song" of the thrush, a psalm rising from the swamp to flood the night, cover the earth, and fill the heavens: "death's outlet song." It changes key with each and every death.

Among the usages cited in Merriam-Webster's definition of the word *keep*, which appears four times in the final ten-line section of the poem, are: to keep a promise, to keep the Sabbath, to keep time, to keep us from harm, to keep a garden, to keep watch, and to keep a diary, all of which must have figured in Whitman's thinking. (See his list of words relating to the thrush.) To have, to continue, to protect, to provide for, to honor or fulfill—these meanings no doubt echoed in his memory of his fallen comrades and Lincoln, "the sweetest, wisest soul of all my days and lands." The last word is a surprise (we expect to hear *nights*), as death so often is. This death in particular would shape the lands anew, as the war itself had already done. In the dictionary we learn that the keep was the strongest part of a medieval castle. The same holds for Whitman's poem.

32

"Chanting the Square Deific"

1

CHANTING the square deific, out of the One advancing, out of the sides;
Out of the old and new—out of the square entirely divine,
Solid, four-sided, (all the sides needed) ... from this side JEHOVAH am I,
Old Brahm I, and I Saturnius am;
Not Time affects me—I am Time, modern as any;
Unpersuadable, relentless, executing righteous judgments;
As the Earth, the Father, the brown old Kronos, with laws,
Aged beyond computation—yet ever new—ever with those mighty laws rolling,
Relentless, I forgive no man—whoever sins, dies—I will have that man's life;
Therefore let none expect mercy—Have the seasons, gravitation, the appointed
days, mercy?—No more have I;
But as the seasons, and gravitation—and as all the appointed days, that forgive not,
I dispense from this side judgments inexorable, without the least remorse.

2

Consolator most mild, the promis'd one advancing,
With gentle hand extended, the mightier God am I,
Foretold by prophets and poets, in their most rapt prophecies and poems;
From this side, lo! the Lord CHRIST gazes—lo! Hermes I—lo! mine is Hercules' face;
All sorrow, labor, suffering, I, tallying it, absorb in myself;
Many times have I been rejected, taunted, put in prison, and crucified—and many
times shall be again;
All the world have I given up for my dear brothers' and sisters' sake—for the soul's
sake;
Wending my way through the homes of men, rich or poor, with the kiss of affection;
For I am affection—I am the cheer-bringing God, with hope, and all-enclosing
Charity;

(Conqueror yet—for before me all the armies and soldiers of the earth shall yet
bow—and all the weapons of war become impotent:)
With indulgent words, as to children—with fresh and sane words, mine only;
Young and strong I pass, knowing well I am destin'd myself to an early death:
But my Charity has no death—my Wisdom dies not, neither early nor late,
And my sweet Love, bequeath'd here and elsewhere, never dies.

3

Aloof, dissatisfied, plotting revolt,
Comrade of criminals, brother of slaves,
Crafty, despised, a drudge, ignorant,
With sudra face and worn brow—black, but in the depths of my heart, proud as any;
Lifted, now and always, against whoever, scorning, assumes to rule me;
Morose, full of guile, full of reminiscences, brooding, with many wiles,
(Though it was thought I was baffled and dispell'd, and my wiles done—but that
will never be;)
Defiant, I, SATAN, still live—still utter words—in new lands duly appearing,
(and old ones also;)
Permanent here, from my side, warlike, equal with any, real as any,
Nor time, nor change, shall ever change me or my words.

4

Santa SPIRITA, breather, life,
Beyond the light, lighter than light,
Beyond the flames of hell—joyous, leaping easily above hell;
Beyond Paradise—perfumed solely with mine own perfume;
Including all life on earth—touching, including God—including Saviour and Satan;
Ethereal, pervading all, (for without me, what were all? what were God?)
Essence of forms—life of the real identities, permanent, positive, (namely the
unseen,)
Life of the great round world, the sun and stars, and of man—I, the general Soul,
Here the square finishing, the solid, I the most solid,
Breathe my breath also through these little songs.

Folsom Commentary

There are a number of poems in *Drum-Taps and Sequel* that may initially seem like odd inclusions in a book of Civil War poems, and "Chanting the Square Deific" is one of them. What does this strange theological poem about a four-sided God have to do with the war? And what are we to make of its grammatically inchoate title, with a participle followed by a definite article and two hanging adjectives? Whitman had been thinking about this poem throughout the war, and in his working copy of the 1860 edition of *Leaves of Grass* he made notes to himself about adding the poem to his next edition—at the time, he was considering calling it "Quadriune" or "Deus Quadriune" (he also invented other possible names for this four-person god, including "Quatuor," "Quatruna," and "Quadrel"). When he decided on "Square Deific," he turned an adjective—meaning "making divine"—into a noun, an act of making divine. What is being "chanted" in this poem is a god-making *act*, a poetic performance of a new and ever-shifting divinity. And in typical Whitman participial fashion, this act is an ongoing one—a never-ending chanting of an always active and conflicted and shape-shifting god. Americans, Whitman suggests, will forever be in the act of *making* a god but never settling on one.

And that new, morphing divinity, we come to realize, is a god carefully constructed for a nation that had nearly broken in two, a god for a reunified America that contains within itself the continual urge for rebellion, the continual testing of any set limits. This necessary satanic urge to rebel is something Whitman had been exploring from the beginning of *Leaves of Grass* (he named the rebellious slave in "The Sleepers" *Lucifer*), but it became even more crucial to explore during the war, when the Confederacy used the same rationale for its revolutionary secession from the Union that the original colonies had used for their revolutionary secession from Britain.

Late in his life, Whitman struggled to explain the significance of the poem: "It would be hard to give the idea mathematical expression: the idea of spiritual equity—of spiritual substance: the four-square entity—the north, south, east, west of the constituted universe (even the soul universe)—the four sides as sustaining the universe (the supernatural something): this is not the poem but the idea back of the poem or below the poem." Whitman's turn to geography here—a god that brings "spiritual equity" to "north, south, east, and west"—is revealing because those are the regions of the country—the North, the South, the East, and the West—that Whitman was continually trying to unite and blend after the war (think of "O Pioneers!").

But this fourfold god—a nervous expansion of the Trinity—was evocative of American history, as the critic Kerry Larson has proposed. The first side of the new godhead is the lawgiver—Jehovah, Brahma, Saturnius, the "father" with "those mighty laws rolling," the Old Testament God dispensing "judgments inexorable without the least remorse." In a political sense, this god is the United States Constitution, the legal document that defines how the nation must govern itself. But that Constitution was of course written by revolutionaries, by the side of the godhead that is always "plotting revolt" and appears "full of guile," "proud," "defiant," and "warlike." The Confederacy represented the most obvious and dangerous example in American history of this always-present satanic force, but Whitman also associates this "comrade of criminals" with the "brother of slaves," and gives him a "sudra" and "black" face. Slave revolts in antebellum America were often justified (by abolitionists and by slaves themselves) with an appeal to the nation's revolutionary founding, to its Declaration of Independence, to its belief in the right of those who felt oppressed to revolt against their oppressors. Built deep into American history, then, is the tension Whitman later defined as "personalism," the endless struggle between individual rights and communal responsibility, between each state's autonomy and federal control. When the Revolution was constituted into a governing document, the Constitution itself soon came to seem oppressive to some, and American history became a ceaseless battle over how the nation, its member states, and its individual citizens interpreted the Constitution's protection of diverse individual rights versus its fostering of a common social bond.

So America, Whitman decided, needed a wound-dresser built into the godhead, a "consolator" like Christ or Hermes (or like Whitman the visitor of hospitals), who is "the cheer-bringing God, with hope and all-enclosing charity," bequeathing "sweet love" to all the wayward and unsatisfied children of the nation who came to feel dispossessed. Whitman's "Square Deific" is a godhead, then, that contains the law-giving Union, the rebellious Confederacy, and the loving and forgiving spirit of healing that mends the inevitable fractures that occur when law gets tested by revolt and when law then gets amended to absorb that revolt (as the Constitution was amended to abolish slavery and invest the rights of citizenship in former slaves, in women—even in former Confederates). Whitman's "square" god embodies the Satan-aspect *within* the godhead, making this peculiarly American god a self-challenger, a god that inevitably tests its own authority, pushes at the boundaries of the set law, amends and expands what had previously been considered to be the limits.

The fourth side of this godhead, then, is "Santa Spirita," the "breather, life," the "general soul" that is at once "ethereal" and "the most solid." This aspect of the godhead is the spirit of reconciliation itself, the joiner of God and Satan who proves that each needs the other to define itself (without revolt, the limits of law are invisible; without the limits of law, there is no arena of revolt). Transgression needs limits in order to be seen as transgression; limits need transgression in order to indicate what the limits are. The sustaining and uniting "breath" of the "Santa Spirita" is the very inspiration and respiration of the nation's history, as it continues its wild, unending fluctuation between celebrating the rights of the individual and celebrating the rights of the diverse multitude, between favoring the strong and favoring the weak, between turning "red" and turning "blue" (as our current electoral maps visualize the conflict). As this national breathing in and breathing out goes on, the tensed "spirit" of the country takes on solidity in the very history that we live. What we are as a nation is what the breathing of the "general soul" produces. That solid reality may, at times, be ugly and violent, but ultimately, Whitman believes, the Union holds, new limits are set, and reconciliation occurs, even as rebellion sows its seeds again, always in surprising and revolutionary ways. America keeps chanting its god-making song, and its spirit is the very breath of this poem on its rectangular page—four sides containing incessantly tensed and warring and healing and reconciling parts.

Merrill Commentary

God-making is integral to religious poetry, from the Psalms and Song of Solomon to the Ramayana and Rumi's ecstatic verses. Ferdowsi's *Shahnameh*, Dante's *Divine Comedy*, Milton's *Paradise Lost* and *Paradise Regained*, Basho's *Narrow Road to the Interior*, Sor Juana Inés de la Cruz's *Dream*, William Blake's prophetic books, Czesław Miłosz's *Second Space*—all seek the divine, describing in physical or metaphorical terms what inevitably remains beyond our comprehension. What these and other works from different faith traditions suggest is that the pursuit of spiritual meaning lies at the core of the human condition. It was thus fitting that in the aftermath of the Civil War, Whitman revised his understanding of cosmology to account for, and attempt to heal, the rift between the North and South. To paraphrase a line from Auden's elegy for Yeats: the madness of war hurt Whitman into a new vision of poetry, which in the case of "Chanting the Square Deific" posits a godhead that embodies the tension at the heart of American experience: the twin urges to revolt and reconcile that from the founding of the republic have shaped its history.

The voices he adopts, salvific and satanic, represent different aspects of being, different ways of apprehending reality, "foretold by prophets and poets, in their most rapt prophesies and poems." Key words from "When Lilacs Last in the

Door-Yard Bloom'd" and "Song of Myself" appear in a single line in the second section: "All sorrow, labor, suffering, I tallying it, absorb in myself." To the herculean task of absorbing all, which preoccupied Whitman before the war, must now be added the tallying of pain and loss—prerequisites for his construction of "the general Soul, / Here the square finishing, the solid, I the most solid." Here is the largest version of the soul, which will suffice for the rest of his journey: "Breathe my breath also through these little songs."

Whitman's fourfold god brings to mind not only the four points of the compass, the four seasons of the year, the four elements, and the four phases of life, but also Blake's fourfold vision, which he spelled out in a letter to Thomas Butts on November 22, 1802:

Now I a fourfold vision see,
And a fourfold vision is given to me;
'Tis fourfold in my supreme delight,
And threefold in soft Beulah's night,
And twofold always. May God us keep
From single vision & Newton's sleep.

Beaulah was Blake's figure for the subconscious, the source of poetry and dreams, without which it is impossible to grasp the whole. Not for him the trap of single, Manichean, or mechanical visions of the world. His is an argument for multiple perspectives, which is of course the "supreme delight" of reading Whitman before and after the Civil War.

33

"I Heard You, Solemn-Sweet Pipes of the Organ"

I HEARD you, solemn-sweet pipes of the organ, as last Sunday morn I pass'd the church;
Winds of autumn!—as I walk'd the woods at dusk, I heard your long-stretch'd sighs, up above, so mournful;
I heard the perfect Italian tenor, singing at the opera—I heard the soprano in the midst of the quartet singing;
...Heart of my love!—you too I heard, murmuring low, through one of the wrists around my head;
Heard the pulse of you, when all was still, ringing little bells last night under my ear.

Folsom Commentary

Like the poem we looked at previously ("Chanting the Square Deific"), this quiet little poem initially strikes us as an odd inclusion in a book of Civil War poems. When it originally appeared in the *New York Leader* in October 1861, however, it was much more obviously a war poem—it opened with three lines that Whitman later removed before including the poem in his *Sequel to Drum-Taps*: "War-suggesting trumpets, I heard you; / And you I heard beating, you chorus of small and large drums; / You round-lipp'd cannons!—you I heard, thunder-cracking, saluting the frigate from France." The poem as originally published, then, began very much in the tone of "Beat! Beat! Drums!," which had appeared in *Harper's* just weeks earlier. But what makes this poem so powerful is the way that it moves from the beating drums and thunderous cannons and "war-suggesting trumpets" to a much different set of sounds, sounds that persisted during the war even if they were often drowned out by the noise and news of incessant battle. By the time Whitman included it in his *Sequel to Drum-Taps*, this poem was just five lines, with each of the first four offering a distinct new sound before the final line dwells on the sound that appears in line four and then rests there.

The poet James Wright called this a great poem because of "the almost perfect delicacy of its form." Five lines, four sounds, as the "I" moves from the church to the lover's bed via the woods and the opera house, from the sound of the "solemn-sweet pipes of the organ" of the church to the much quieter but more riveting sounds of another organ—the "heart of my love!"—that can be heard in the pulsing of the blood through the pipes of the lover's arteries out to the wrist, which carries the "little bells" of the heartbeat to yet another organ—"my ear"—which rests on the lover's wrist. The repeated "I heard" (echoing five times in the first four lines) gives way to the near-identity of the words "Heart" and "Heard" which open the final two lines as the "I" disappears in the final line into the act of hearing the heart of the lover. And at the heart of both words—"Heart," "Heard"—is the word "ear," the core of the poem's sensual evocation, the little word that ends the poem and reminds us (in the orthographic accident of one word being contained in another) how the "ear" is so intimately attached to the lover's "heart." Even the exclamation—"Heart of my love!" (which initially sounds like a romantic metaphor, evoking the common association of "heart" and "love")—captures the excited moment of realization that this little "murmuring" in the ear is in fact the *actual* beating heart of my love.

Coming, as it does, immediately after "Chanting the Square Deific," this poem underscores the necessity of the intimacy of reconciliation that becomes, in Whitman's formulation, the Holy Spirit of America's always-forming godhead. As the sounds of war recede (or, as happens in the revision of this poem, simply vanish), what is left behind are the sounds of devotion, the sounds of nature, the sounds of voices soaring ("the quartet" is "singing," perhaps the North, South, East, and West discovering a new harmony), the sounds of intimacy. The poems of *Sequel to Drum-Taps* turn more and more now toward reconciliation, toward a call for intense renewed camaraderie across what had been deep and seemingly irreconcilable regional and ideological divides.

Merrill Commentary

Fitted with hearing aids, a writer noted in a recent Facebook post that after a few days she realized "there are definitely things (people) I don't care about hearing, but the most wonderful thing I can now hear ringing loud and clear and pure: bird song!" She wrote this during a contentious political season, which may explain both her scorn for humankind and her delight in the sounds of nature. What she celebrates is the fact that she has adjusted her hearing, just as in the poem "I Heard You, Solemn-Sweet Pipes of the Organ" Whitman registers his surroundings as if with new ears—music in the church he passes, the autumn wind in the woods at dusk, the singing of a tenor and a soprano, the heartbeat of his lover "ringing little bells last night under my ear." After witnessing so much pain and suffering in the war, which surely blunted his senses and left him in despair, he found to his astonishment that he was capable of experiencing the world afresh.

The back history of this poem, the martial imagery and cacophony that Whitman cut from the original version ("War-suggesting trumpets," a chorus of drums, "round-lipp'd cannons!"), is a study in the growth of the poet's mind. For once the guns stopped firing he could hear what had always been there: the music of time, to which he was largely oblivious during his ministry to sick and wounded soldiers. In the silence after the signing of the armistice, though, he recognized that the true subject of his little poem was—had always been—love. What happens in the heat of battle and its immediate aftermath may be difficult, if not impossible, to gauge. What is certain is that the shock will reverberate for generations. Poetry can restore, however momentarily, a sense of proportion, first to the writer and then to the reader: "Heart of my love!"

Love and loss: these eternal themes of literature reveal new complexities in wartime, when social conventions are suspended and bloodletting rules the day. Exhausted as Whitman was from documenting the carnage and caring for the fallen, he nevertheless discovered within himself the spring that from time immemorial has nourished humankind: the touch of another. Whitman's lover takes his head in his hands and, "murmuring low," brings the poet back to himself. "He who has ears to hear," Jesus said to his disciples, "let him hear." Love conquers all.

34

"Two Brothers, One South, One North"

Two Brothers, one South, one North —*May* 28–9.—I staid tonight a long time by the bed-side of a new patient, a young Baltimorean, aged about 19 years, W. S. P., (2nd Md. Southern,) very feeble, right leg amputated, can't sleep hardly at all—has taken a great deal of morphine, which, as usual, is costing more than it comes to. Evidently very intelligent and well bred—very affectionate—held on to my hand, and put it by his face, not willing to let me leave. As I was lingering, soothing him in his pain, he says to me suddenly, "I hardly think you know who am—I don't wish to impose upon you—I am a rebel soldier." I said I did not know that, but it made no difference.......Visiting him daily for about two weeks after that, while he lived, (death had mark'd him, and he was quite alone,) I loved him much, always kiss'd him, and he did me.

In an adjoining Ward I found his brother, an officer of rank, a Union soldier, a brave and religious man, (Col. Clifton K. Prentiss, Sixth Md. Infantry, Sixth Corps, wounded in one of the engagements at Petersburgh, April 2—linger'd, suffer'd much, died in Brooklyn, Aug. 20, '65.) It was in the same battle both were hit. One was a strong Unionist, the other Secesh; both fought on their respective sides, both badly wounded, and both brought together here after absence of four years. Each died for his cause.

Folsom Commentary

Just as he was doing in his poetry at the end of the Civil War, so in his prose was Whitman recording images of reunification, of reconciliation between countrymen who had become enemies but who needed, now that the war was ending, to once again become comrades. And, like the "Consolator" in "Chanting the Square Deific," Whitman, the caregiver to both Union and Confederate soldiers in the Washington hospitals, modeled for his readers the unifying gestures of healing love needed to mend the national fracture. In this entry in *Memoranda During the War*, which he copied out of one of his hospital notebooks from May of 1865 (just after final hostilities had ended and just as President Andrew Johnson issued a proclamation giving general amnesty to most of those who had taken part in the rebellion), the poet records a fairly common encounter—a meeting of brothers, one who had fought for the Union, the other for the Confederacy. Such instances of fraternal bonds splintering into fratricidal hatred were particularly common in the border states like Maryland, where many families were divided in their loyalties to North and South.

The month before, General Grant had ordered an all-out Union assault on Confederate forces that had long been dug in south of Petersburg, Virginia. Major Clifton Prentiss of the 6th Maryland Union Volunteers personally led the attack and penetrated the enemy fortifications, only to be shot in the lung. Prentiss's younger brother, William, was one of the Confederate soldiers defending the fortification, and in the same battle he received a shell fragment in his knee. Some of the Maryland Union soldiers, after their victory, were tending to the wounded on the battlefield when they came upon William Prentiss, who told them that he had a brother in the 6th Maryland. The soldiers realized that Prentiss's brother was in fact their major, who was lying gravely wounded not far away. William said he wanted to see his brother. When word was brought to Clifton, however, the Union soldier refused to see his Confederate brother, whom he now considered a traitor. The Union commanding officer begged Clifton to relent and ordered William to be brought over beside his brother. Clifton glared at William, but William smiled back, and then both men, who hadn't seen each other since the war began, broke into tears and were briefly reunited. Soon after, William had his leg amputated, and Clifton's lung became infected.

Clifton and William then ended up in Armory Square hospital together, where Whitman cared for both of them. But his notebook entry lingers on his warm encounters with the Confederate William, with whom Whitman could enact the affection across the regional divide that he believed was the only hope for the country's future. When William tells the poet he is "a rebel soldier," Whitman replies that "it made no difference." In Whitman's quiet response, we can hear the erasure of "difference," the hoped-for fading away of distinction between Union and Confederate, as the nation began its long process of healing. Clifton and William had fought each other fiercely through four years, but here at the end of the war they were "both brought together" in Armory Square "after a separation of four years." Neither would survive the wounds they received in the same battle. The entire country, it seemed to Whitman, had been hospitalized for the duration of the war: as Whitman wandered the wards of the hospitals that had colonized and taken over the nation's capital, he encountered young men from the North and South and West, black youth and white youth, immigrants and native-born, a microcosm of the young, vast, and expanding nation battered, torn, suffering, and dying. William would never leave Armory Square, dying there in June. Clifton managed to get to his home in Brooklyn but died soon after in August. They became part of Whitman's "million dead." But increasingly, for Whitman and the rest of America that emerged from the war hospital to face and build a future, the question now was how to carry on the democratic experiment that had just passed through its most dire test. America may have been in its "fair youth" when it was brought to the hospital of the war, but the country that was released from that hospital was now, as it faced its own massive Reconstruction, forced to quickly mature.

Merrill Commentary

Displayed on the mantelpiece of my grandparents' living room, in northern Maryland, was a blood-stained bullet chiseled from a tree on the battlefield at Gettysburg—a symbol, I knew from an early age, of the fratricide at the core of American history. My grandfather was a country doctor who treated everyone in the community, rich and poor, black and white, and after he died it came out that he had forgiven thousands of dollars in debts owed by indigent patients. His oldest son, an Episcopal priest and my godfather, hailed this as evidence of the ways in which faith had informed his practice. My grandmother, a nurse and the church organist, heartily agreed. But his death also led to a breach in the family, when my mother objected to her brother serving as executor of the estate, in fulfillment of their father's wishes. This complicated my relationship to both my mother and my uncle. Nor did they reconcile before my mother slipped into dementia.

Differences of opinion, which are integral to family life, escalate when money and beliefs collide, as happens in every civil war. For example, a Serbian poet married to a Muslim writer in Sarajevo found himself estranged during the siege from his father and brothers, who took to the surrounding hills to rain down terror on the civilians trapped in the city without water, electricity, or gas. One night in his unheated flat the poet told me that whenever he published an article in the daily newspaper a shot was fired through his roof, presumably by someone in his family. He added ruefully that if he were more prolific his place would resemble a gingerbread house!

Whitman's small sketch of two brothers fighting on opposing sides and dying from wounds suffered in the same battle reveals the costs of war. It is significant that the younger brother, a rebel soldier struck by shrapnel, is the one who asks to see his older brother, a religious man who cannot summon the faith to overcome his anger, despite the bullet in his lung. "Every word is a doorway to a meeting, / one often canceled," wrote the Greek poet Yannis Ritsos, "and that's when a word is true: / when it insists on the meeting." William Prentiss insisted on meeting his brother, and that made all the difference to Whitman, who saw no difference between the warriors from the North and South. Peace would endure only if the victors and the defeated made gestures, large and small, to overcome their hostility—and their grief. Then the poet's word would ring true.

35

"Convulsiveness" and "Three Years Summ'd Up"

"Convulsiveness"

As I have look'd over the proof-sheets of the preceding Memoranda, I have once or twice fear'd that my little tract would prove, at best, but a batch of convulsively written reminiscences. Well, be it so. They are but items, parts of the actual distraction, heat, smoke and excitement of those times—of the qualities that then and there took shape. The War itself with the temper of society preceding it, can indeed be best described by that very word, *Convulsiveness.*

"Three Years Summ'd Up"

During my past three years in Hospital, camp, or field, I made over 600 visits or tours, and went, as I estimate, among from 80,000 to 100,000 of the wounded and sick, as sustainer of spirit and body in some degree, in time of need. These visits varied from an hour or two, to all day or night; for with dear or critical cases I always watch'd all night. Sometimes I took up my quarters in the Hospital, and slept or watch'd there several nights in succession. Those three years I consider the greatest privilege and satisfaction, (with all their feverish excitements and physical deprivations and lamentable sights,) and, of course, the most profound lesson and reminiscence, of my life. I can say that in my ministerings I comprehended all, whoever came in my way, Northern or Southern, and slighted none. It afforded me, too, the perusal of those subtlest, rarest, divinest volumes of Humanity, laid bare in its inmost recesses, and of actual life and death, better than the finest, most labor'd narratives, histories, poems in the libraries. It arous'd and brought out and decided undream'd-of depths of emotion. It has given me my plainest and most fervent views of the true *ensemble* and extent of The States. While I was with wounded and sick in thousands of cases from the New England States, and from New York, New Jersey, and Pennsylvania, and from Michigan, Wisconsin, Ohio, Indiana, Illinois, and all the Western States, I was with more or less from all the States, North and South, without exception. I was with many from the Border States, especially from Maryland and Virginia; and found, during those lurid years 1862–65, far more Union Southerners, especially Tennesseans, than is supposed. I was with many rebel officers and men among our wounded, and gave them always what I had, and tried to cheer them the same as any. I was among the army teamsters considerably, and, indeed, always found myself drawn to them. Among the black soldiers, wounded or sick, and in the contraband camps, I also took my way whenever in their neighborhood, and did what I could for them.

Folsom Commentary

Originally, Whitman concluded his *Memoranda During the War* with the section called "The Million Dead, Too, Summ'd Up—The Unknown." But then he appended a long series of "Notes," the first of which was a brief statement called "Convulsiveness." He feared, he said, that his Civil War notes "would prove . . . but a batch of convulsively written reminiscences," but that was fine, he decided, since "the War itself with the temper of society preceding it" could "be best described by that very word, *Convulsiveness*." It is telling that Whitman chose this unfamiliar form of the word instead of the more commonly used "convulsion": rather than indicating a single violent social and political upheaval, "convulsiveness" captured the ongoing nature of the turmoil. The word has a fascinating etymology, containing in its Latin roots two contradictory motions—a movement together (*com*) and a violent pulling apart (*vellere*). That continually pulling together and pulling apart was, of course, at the very heart of Whitman's poetics and of his conception of the self (an entity that kept expanding out into the world, threatening dispersion into the vast variety of experience, and then contracting back in, holding the contradictory materials in one single identity), and he came to see this convulsiveness as built into the very fabric of the American national experience—endless cycles of revolution and constitution. In another note appended to *Memoranda*, he explained how convulsiveness in fact defined the United States: "And now I have myself, in my thought, deliberately come to unite the whole conflict, both sides, the South and North, really into One, and to view it as a struggle going on within One Identity. Like any of Nature's great convulsions, wars going on within herself—not from separated sets of laws and influences, but the same—really, efforts, conflicts, most violent ones, for deeper harmony, freer and larger scope, completer homogeneousness and power. What is any Nation, after all—and what is a human being—but a struggle between conflicting, paradoxical, opposing elements—and they themselves and their most violent contests, important parts of that One Identity, and of its development?"

It is what we saw in Whitman's construction of an American deity in "Chanting the Square Deific," his effort to build ongoing revolt and ever-renewing reconciliation into the guiding spirit of the nation. A nation, like every individual, is a set of tensely "united" states, containing warring contradictions that need continually to be negotiated and contained in order to maintain Union. This idea became so central to Whitman that, when he revised *Memoranda* and incorporated it within his autobiography called *Specimen Days*, he moved the "Convulsiveness" note directly into the text and left it there as a central defining concept of the country—the nation's remarkable ability to continually pull itself apart and then blend itself back together, to privilege the individual over the community, then to privilege the community over the individual; to give precedence to states' rights, then to give precedence to federal power; to protect the weak and impoverished, then to protect the rich and powerful. There is an endless convulsiveness to America's history, and the Civil War was but one particularly violent convulsion in that ongoing history. We are always and inevitably experiencing convulsions.

In his many hospital visits—which Whitman tallies in his section called "Three Years Summ'd Up" and estimates at up to 100,000—he often encountered soldiers undergoing convulsions: he recalls one soldier, a "perfect specimen of physique," who experienced "convulsive spasms and working of muscles, mouth, and throat," and he describes how, often, "some youngster holds on to me convulsively, and I do what I can for him." Convulsions were all around Whitman—on the battlefields, in the hospitals, in the political debates—and so it is no surprise that, when he thought of the nation's dramatic history up through Abraham Lincoln's assassination, the word he used to describe the drama "of this America of ours" was "convulsionary."

Those "three years summ'd up" evoke the same odd contraction that he used in "The Million Dead, Too, Summ'd Up"—a *summing* and a *summoning*. Now, in his convulsive, start-and-stop notes, he was adding it all up but also *calling* it all up, reliving the convulsions that he saw wounded soldiers go through and reexperiencing the convulsions of the long fratricidal war, even perhaps recognizing the convulsions within himself that he tried so desperately to suppress during his extraordinary service in the war's hospitals, where a nation torn apart by regional and racial convulsions came, and where Whitman experienced for the first time the fullness and unified diversity of his always convulsive nation, where he cared for the "wounded and sick . . . from all the states, North and South, without exception"—and from "all the Western States" as well, "rebel" and Union, white and black. The nation had come to hospital, and there is where it found Walt Whitman and where Whitman found it, convulsive and desperate for healing.

Merrill Commentary

In times of spiritual aridity I often turn to the wisdom of the Desert Fathers and Mothers, those brave Christians who retreated into the Egyptian desert in the fourth century to draw closer to God, fasting and praying, singing hymns and reading Scripture. They emptied themselves of worldly ambitions, concerns, and pleasures to become vessels for the divine and taste eternity. "Give me a word, *abba* (father)" or "Give me a way of life, *amma* (mother)," visitors would petition the desert dwellers; collections of their replies have nourished readers, religious and secular, for 1,500 years. One favorite from *The Heart of the Desert*, a compendium assembled by John Chryssavgis—"A certain brother asked Abba Pimenion, saying, 'What is faith?' And the old man said, 'To live ever in loving kindness and in humbleness, and to do good to one's neighbors.'"—reads like a gloss on Whitman's "Three Years Summ'd Up." For the poet's ministry to sick and wounded soldiers, which lasted about as long as Christ's ministry in the Galilee, schooled him in loving-kindness, if not necessarily humility; for his efforts to do right by his neighbors, on both sides of the war, he was vouchsafed a healing vision of literature—which governed his writing during and after the convulsions through which he and his compatriots lived.

He described the "convulsively written reminiscences" in *Memoranda During the War* as being "part of the actual distraction, heat, smoke and excitement of those times—of the qualities that then and there took shape." Writing constantly, bearing witness to the birth of a new political order, he produced the first draft of a history that continues to unfold in an unpredictable manner. In his determination to sustain in body and spirit upwards of 100,000 warriors in their time of need, "in Hospital, camp, or field," he claims to have "comprehended all, whoever came in my way." The largeness of spirit that characterized his writing during and after the war was a function of his caring for men in their final hours, which allowed him to peruse "those subtlest, rarest, divinest volumes of Humanity, laid bare in its inmost recesses, and of actual life and death, better than the finest, most labor'd narratives, histories, poems in the libraries." The exigencies of writing on the fly, taking testimony minute by minute, inspired him to a new way of writing, capturing the essence of an individual at a stroke, distilling salient details from his life in order to account for what was heretofore too awful to contemplate: death on an industrial scale.

In the crucible of war Whitman did what he could do—and that made all the difference.

36

"Reconciliation"

WORD over all, beautiful as the sky!
Beautiful that war, and all its deeds of carnage, must in time be utterly lost;
That the hands of the sisters Death and Night, incessantly softly wash again, and
ever again, this soil'd world:
... For my enemy is dead—a man divine as myself is dead;
I look where he lies, white-faced and still, in the coffin—I draw near;
I bend down and touch lightly with my lips the white face in the coffin.

Folsom Commentary

One of the most remarkable poems to appear in Whitman's *Sequel to Drum-Taps* is this little poem with its evocative title, "Reconciliation." Whitman, in a manuscript note probably written before the war began, was already thinking through what he called "the idea of reconciliation": "that what has been done, is consumed—Ever, out of its ashes, let new, sweeter, more amicable fruits ripen." Etymologically, the word means "to bring together again" or, more precisely, "to make friendly again." It is as if, even before the war broke out, Whitman realized that what lay ahead for his country was an entire era of the difficult work of turning enemies back into friends, turning disunion back into union. And buried deep in the idea of "reconciliation" for Whitman was his old notion of "compost": out of the ashes of the war's conflagration would grow "sweeter, more amicable fruits," the fruits of a new and intensified camaraderie emerging from the consuming fires of four years of fratricide.

The poem's hauntingly beautiful opening lines mythologize the process of composting, as we get "Death and Night" turned into "sisters" who, like the wound-dresser, are now making their rounds and washing the hundreds of thousands of ruined bodies that lie upon "this soil'd world" (the world, as always for Whitman, is "soil'd," covered with a layer of death, and after the war, that layer is thick with "carnage" and desperately needs those sisters' hands to "wash" it away and make the soil fertile for the "amicable fruits" of a postwar reconciliation to grow and ripen). The speaker hauntingly verbalizes the "chemistry" that we saw in "The Million Dead, Too, Summ'd Up"—the composting power of nature that turns death to life again, that heals the "deeds of carnage" in a way Whitman captured in the closing words of *Memoranda During the War*, as he looked back a decade later on the Civil War battlefields and cemeteries: "From ten years' rain and snow, in their seasons—grass, clover, pine trees, orchards, forests—from all the noiseless miracles of soil and sun and running streams—how peaceful and how beautiful appear to-day even the Battle-Trenches, and the many hundred thousand Cemetery mounds!" In "Reconciliation," this realization is put in the voice of a speaker who seems to be experiencing "this soil'd world" up close. The speaker looks at the dead body of his "enemy" and approaches it, bends down, and kisses its "white face." Again, we can hear the faint echoes of the wound-dresser and of Whitman himself, holding and kissing the dying soldiers in the hospitals.

But just who *is* the speaker of this poem? Twice, a "white face" of the "enemy" appears, and the insistence seems odd: "he lies white-faced and still in the coffin" and the speaker "touch[es] lightly with my lips the white face in the coffin." Many readers will read through the whiteness here, finding nothing remarkable in the description and perhaps hearing it only as a reference to the pallid complexion of the corpse (or even as the white skull itself). But the double reference in the final two lines draws attention to itself, and it is difficult not to hear some racial edge to the description. Some readers have heard the insistence as the sign of Whitman's affirming a racial bond with his white Southern enemies, the explicit reference to "white" becoming an exclusionary statement, as white racial solidarity finally trumps sectional enmity to bond the South to the North again. The historian David Blight, for example, sees the poem as underscoring Whitman's "virtual kinship" with "all the 'white-faced' dead brothers," thus enacting "the ultimate betrayal of the dark-faced folk whom the dead had shared in liberating." Similarly, the poet Natasha Trethewey hears Whitman's emphasis on the "white face" in this poem as an indication that he "leaves out the reality of so many dead soldiers whose faces were not white."

The opposite may be the case, however. Whitman records in *Memoranda* that some of the last soldiers in the hospitals that he was talking to were African Americans. And what would he have been hearing from them? If he was jotting down their experiences, as he had with other soldiers over the previous two years, he would have been recording the main duty of black soldiers at the end of the war—burying the corpses left on America's battlefields. If Whitman is again speaking in the voice of a soldier-persona, and if that persona was originally conceived of by Whitman as a black soldier, then the "I" of this poem might be heard as another of Whitman's excursions into black subjectivity, and the speaker's peculiar insistence on the white face makes sense, for *this* reconciliation promises now to transcend race, to bring black and white together, as the war produces (if only temporarily) a previously unimaginable reconciliation between the races.

"Reconciliation" is, after all, an outdoor poem, taking place under the sky and on the "soil'd world" (we're certainly not in a funeral parlor). If the narrator is heard, then, as one of the black soldiers who so often placed the white dead in coffins and buried them, he now finds that his labors of gathering death from the "soil'd world" of shallow graves strewn across the Southern landscape provides him a moment to express affection in a charged kiss on the lips of "the white face in the coffin," and the double emphasis on *white* captures the amazement of the former slave at this newfound liberty to kiss and honor the dead white soldier. Whether that dead white soldier was a Union or a Confederate corpse, it would have been—for most of American history—the black's "enemy," but now, in this moment of intimate confrontation with the corpse, the experience of being a soldier unites rather than separates the black speaker from his dead white enemy, allowing this powerful (if macabre) experience of reconciliation. This is one Whitman poem for which we have no manuscripts, so it is impossible to determine (as we can, for example, in "The Sleepers" manuscripts) if there is an erased black presence, even an erased black speaker, here. But the manuscript evidence for other such charged passages is strong enough to allow us to entertain the possibility of a ghost–black speaker in "Reconciliation" and to imagine this poem as another of the ways Whitman transformed his notes of what soldiers told him into a haunting and lasting poem. In this case, those soldiers would have been black soldiers who had been on grave detail, burying white soldiers and finding themselves again and again in the position of the speaker in this poem, drawing near to the coffin with the dead "enemy," all too familiar now with what it feels like to touch a white-faced corpse with affection.

Merrill Commentary

"In the beginning was the Word," according to the Gospel of John, "and the Word was with God, and the Word was God." Now at the end of the war Whitman renders this sentence as "Word over all," translating a statement about the nature of divinity into a secular call for reconciliation, which must shape a new covenant between the North and South. Men and women, blacks and whites, slaves and slave masters, all must be reconciled to keep at bay the ever-present forces of division. Stitching together the Union and the Confederacy will be the task of generations, taking its cue on the battlefield from one man kissing another—possibly a black soldier on a burial detail bending over a fallen white man to bid him adieu.

Tender and taboo, this shocking image offers proof that what transpires in any confrontation—in politics or war, at table or in the bedroom—may in the fullness of time acquire other meanings. Death dissolves differences, reminding us that even before the dust settles we ought to honor one "Word over all": reconciliation.

We have seen how Whitman thought another word—convulsiveness—best described the war, "the temper of society preceding it," and the tenor of his reminiscences in *Memoranda During the War.* Writers are cautioned to avoid what the critic Yvor Winters called the fallacy of imitative form: "To say that a poet is justified in employing a disintegrating form in order to express a feeling of disintegration, is merely a sophistical justification for bad poetry, akin to the Whitmanian notion that one must write loose and sprawling poetry to 'express' the loose and sprawling American continent." But the convulsive aspect of Whitman's wartime writings was a function not only of his determination to create a vibrant mosaic of historical events but of his mastery of the tools of reportage—sketch, anecdote, testimony, reflection, digression, and surmise. Out of carnage and chaos he created an American form of literary journalism, which fed his poetry.

The intimate moment recorded in "Reconciliation" represents the sort of loving-kindness that for Whitman was a prerequisite for healing the rift between the North and South, a virtue to be practiced soul by soul. The poem neatly divides in two, the first half praising the ways in which time and death and night wash clean the horrors of war, the second half adopting the viewpoint and voice of the speaker, who recognizes that he shares with the dead man lying before him the same spark of divinity, and must be treated with the same dignity that he himself hopes will guide the hands of those who will usher him to his final resting place: a perfectly balanced representation of forces, passive and active, dead and alive, joined in a kiss.

We, too, are living in convulsive times—I am writing this during the pandemic of the novel coronavirus, which has killed hundreds of thousands of people around the world, left tens of millions of Americans unemployed, and introduced into the global systems of finance and politics a level of uncertainty not seen since the Great Depression and World War II. Mindful of the continued fighting in Afghanistan, the refugee crisis in Greece, and the threat of climate change, not to mention the profound divisions on display in nearly every arena of American society, I look to Whitman's writings to discern ways to capture the essence of this moment, hoping that we, too, may discover how to reconcile ourselves to "this soil'd world"—how to carry on.

37

"To the Leaven'd Soil They Trod"

To the leaven'd soil they trod, calling, I sing, for the last;
(Not cities, nor man alone, nor war, nor the dead,
But forth from my tent emerging for good—loosing, untying the tent-ropes;)
In the freshness, the forenoon air, in the far-stretching circuits and vistas,
again to peace restored,
To the fiery fields emanative, and the endless vistas beyond—to the south and
the north;
To the leaven'd soil of the general western world, to attest my songs,
(To the average earth, the wordless earth, witness of war and peace,)
To the Alleghanian hills, and the tireless Mississippi,
To the rocks I, calling, sing, and all the trees in the woods,
To the plain of the poems of heroes, to the prairie spreading wide,
To the far-off sea, and the unseen winds, and the sane impalpable air;
... And responding, they answer all, (but not in words.)
The average earth, the witness of war and peace, acknowledges mutely;
The prairie draws me close, as the father, to bosom broad, the son;
The Northern ice and rain, that began me, nourish me to the end;
But the hot sun of the South is to ripen my songs.

FINIS.

Folsom Commentary

Whitman decided to conclude his *Sequel to Drum-Taps* with this poem about the demobilization of the troops. Imagining himself again as a soldier, Whitman creates a speaker who comes "forth from my tent emerging for good—loosing, untying the tent-ropes," an image of the final soldier putting away the accoutrements and implements of war to begin a postwar life. The haziness of the nation's future at this moment can be felt in the almost inchoate syntax of the poem's opening line: "To the leaven'd soil they trod, calling, I sing, for the last" (later Whitman would remove the commas in the line, creating even more of a syntactic mess). There are double or triple inversions, and it's unclear who is "calling"—"they" who "trod," or the "I" who "sings," or the "soil" that "they trod"? It is difficult to undo the inversions and make a clear sentence emerge from the syntactical fog: I sing, calling to the leaven'd soil they trod, for the last [the last time? the last of the dead?]."

Whatever meaning we extract from the convoluted opening, one thing is clear. Whether we hear the "they" as the dead soldiers of the war who "leaven" the soil with their decaying bodies, or whether we hear the "they" as the living soldiers who now trod a soil they know has already been leavened with the corpses of their comrades and enemies, it is now a "leaven'd" soil that forms "the average earth, the wordless earth, witness of war and peace." Leavening is a fermenting agent in dough that makes it rise, or more generally, any agent introduced into something to initiate a change or transformation. The word comes from Latin roots meaning "to lift or to raise." "Leavening" acquired the figurative meaning of a powerful, invisible influence or force. As we have seen throughout Whitman's Civil War writings, the invisible agent working through the soil of the war-torn earth was death itself, eternally composting through invisible and magical forces into new life, into the food that sustains us and the air we breathe. "The million dead" are now the leavening of a new nation, a new life: the postwar world must experience the literal raising of the dead.

Buried deep in "leaven'd," too, is Whitman's old play on one of his favorite words, "leaves." Nature puts forth new leaves but always and only does so out of what Whitman calls the "leavings of many deaths." His characteristic apostrophe turns the word "leaven'd" into both "leave" and "end." Whitman's preferred word of renewal—"leaves"—is conflated with the word of stoppage and conclusion. The horrors of the Civil War provide the ultimate test of the "leavings of many deaths": can they once again (so *many* leavings) be turned into new leaves (new pages of the history of an emerging democracy), or do they mark the end of the democratic experiment that had barely gotten a start? This is why the speaker "sings" and "calls"—to find out if there's a future.

The poem is a kind of call-and-response. It opens with the survivors calling to the leaven'd land, from North to South to West, from forests to prairies to mountains to the sea. The call goes to the Alleghenies and the "tireless Mississippi," mountains and a river that join the North to the South, natural formations that refused to fracture when the South seceded from the North but instead served as geological reminders of union. The call reaches far and wide over the entire mourning, fragile, healing nation, over the injured landscape. And in the final five lines, the landscape answers the soldier's call, "but not in words." Instead, "the average earth"—the democratic land that now works to smooth away distinctions and discriminations and differences—responds by embracing, nourishing, and ripening, and the nourishment and ripening now come equally from the formerly divided North and South, drawing the soldiers close, like a father holding a son to his bosom. The "fiery fields" of the battles become "emanative" again, emanating now not destruction and endings but "endless vistas beyond"—what Whitman would a couple of years later call "Democratic Vistas," the always hazy borders and boundaries that the democratizing nation would test and cross and reset and violate again over and over (it was built into America's "Square Deific").

And so Whitman ends his volume with a Latin word, "Finis," appearing in open space at the end of the poem. In English, *finis* is an unfinished "finish," a conclusion that does not conclude. It's an ancient word for boundaries, borders, things that divide. It sits there at the end of Whitman's book, with the punctuating mark of conclusion—a period—and with two borderlines above and below. Much is finished—now, certainly, the *war* is finished, as is Whitman's book of the war—but the nation is not. Those borders above and below "Finis" are, after all, small (as if they are shrinking), easily crossed, and surrounded by space—a place for words yet to be written, words without end.

Merrill Commentary

"Poets to come! orators, singers, musicians to come!" Whitman wrote in the 1872 edition of *Leaves of Grass*, invoking the future to justify his poetry, which in the wake of the Civil War had acquired graver tones. Song was as important a trope in his work as the grass under which his artistic heirs were advised to look for him. These unknown figures from the future would balance all the unknown dead decomposing in the earth; hence it is fitting that *Drum-Taps* concludes with a song of creation for a new America, "To the Leaven'd Soil They Trod," which calls into being a people and a body politic suited to this bloody, "emanative" land.

No small task.

A dark coda to "Song of Myself," this poem is a leave-taking in sixteen disjointed lines, a song to accompany soldiers on their homeward journey, a benediction for the fallen who lie buried in "the average earth, the wordless earth, witness of war and peace," a summons to peace and reconciliation, and a map to "the far-stretching circuits and vistas" that mark the boundaries of this westward-expanding country, all ripened by "the hot sun of the South" into the bitter fruits of a conflict that will henceforth define the character of its citizenry. As in the myth of Orpheus, he sings to rocks and trees, calling "the unseen winds and the sane impalpable air" to charm Creation; like Orpheus, he wants to lead his compatriots, his Eurydice, back from the underworld to which the war consigned them. We know how that worked out for Eurydice.

What Whitman achieved was closer to the ideal that Rainer Maria Rilke sang into being in the first of his *Sonnets to Orpheus*, an astonishing cycle of fifty-five poems composed in just three weeks in the aftermath of World War I, in what he called a "savage creative storm":

A tree ascended there. Oh, pure transcendence!
Oh Orpheus sings! Oh tall tree in the ear!
And all things hushed. Yet even in that silence
a new beginning, beckoning, change appeared.

Animals gather in Rilke's poem to listen to the music of the Greek poet and prophet, who "built a temple deep inside their hearing." Whitman built such a temple for his readers, drawing on the tragic knowledge he acquired during his journey to the underworld of Civil War hospitals, where all too many of his companions perished. His singing will rise like bread from "the leaven'd soil of the general western world" to nourish those in need, who will attest to them.

38

"Results South—Now and Hence"

Results South—Now and Hence.—The present condition of things (1875) in South Carolina, Mississippi, Louisiana, and other parts of the former Slave States—the utter change and overthrow of their whole social, and the greatest coloring feature of their political institutions—a horror and dismay, as of limitless sea and fire, sweeping over them, and substituting the confusion, chaos, and measureless degradation and insult of the present—the black domination, but little above the beasts—viewed as a temporary, deserv'd punishment for their Slavery and Secession sins, may perhaps be admissible; but as a permanency of course is not to be consider'd for a moment. (Did the vast mass of the blacks, in Slavery in the United States, present a terrible and deeply complicated problem through the just ending century? But how if the mass of the blacks in freedom in the U. S. all through the ensuing century, should present a yet more terrible and more deeply complicated problem?)

The conquest of England eight centuries ago, by the Franco-Normans—the obliteration of the old, (in many respects so needing obliteration)—the Domesday Book, and the repartition of the land—the old impedimenta removed, even by blood and ruthless violence, and a new, progressive genesis establish'd, new seeds sown—Time has proved plain enough that, bitter as they were, all these were the most salutary series of revolutions that could possibly have happen'd. Out of them, and by them mainly, have come, out of Albic, Roman and Saxon England—and without them could not have come—not only the England of the 500 years down to the present, and of the present—but These States. Nor, except for that terrible dislocation and overturn, would These States, as they are, exist to-day.

Extricating one's-self from the temporary gaucheries of the hour, can there be anything more certain than the rehabilitated prosperity of the Southern States, all and several, if their growing generations, refusing to be dismay'd by present embarrassments and darkness, accept their position in the Union as an immutable fact, and like the Middle and Western States, "fly the flag of practical industry and business, and adopting the great ideas of America with faith and courage, developing their resources, providing for education, abandoning old fictions, leave the Secession war and its bygones behind, and resolutely draw a curtain over the past"?

I want to see the Southern States, in a better sense than ever, and under the new dispensation, again take a leading part in what is emphatically *their* Nationality as much as anybody's. Soon, soon, it will begin to be realized that out of the War, after all, *they* have gained a more substantial victory than anybody.

Folsom Commentary

Memoranda During the War has always been read as one of Whitman's great Civil War documents, and rightfully so, but it was not published until—as Whitman dated it on the title page—1875–76, at the end of Reconstruction. Even though it reprints many of Whitman's Civil War articles and journal entries, *Memoranda* can and should be read as a Reconstruction document. Whitman appended to the original version of *Memoranda* a set of notes, which he removed when he reprinted most of the book in *Specimen Days* in 1882. Those *Memoranda* notes, gathered from his various jottings during the Reconstruction years (and now rarely mentioned), can be read as a kind of expansion and historicizing of the airy conclusion to Whitman's 1870 essay *Democratic Vistas*, where he strains his sight to glimpse America's hazy future: "I say my eyes are fain to behold, though with straining sight—and my spirit to prophecy—far down the vistas of These States, that Order, Class, superber, far more efficient than any hitherto, arising." The notes at the end of *Memoranda* likewise deal with the nation's hazy future, one where he vaguely sees great things emerging from the war's debris, but it is also a future now haunted by the racial realities that surrounded him. Perhaps most remarkable of all these notes is this one called "Results South—Now and Hence." What he gives us here is an unsettling mix of the reactionary and the prophetic, and, unlike most of the other notes in *Memoranda*, Whitman never reprinted it. Since most readers have encountered *Memoranda* in the context of *Specimen Days*, the note is seldom read today.

Here Whitman, at the end of Reconstruction, throws up his hands at any solution to the problem of freed blacks remaining in the country and becoming citizens in a biracial democracy; what he here calls "black domination" consisted, of course, of the first attempts to have black representation at state and national levels, and such lasting change to a shared democratic representation is simply, by his lights, "not to be consider'd for a moment." At the end of Reconstruction, then, all Whitman can offer is a parenthetical prophecy that racial relations would become "a yet more terrible and deeply complicated problem" in America's future than it had been in the past, even in times of slavery. The fact that this turned out to be true may well point to one of Whitman's greatest failures, and even more, to one of the tragic failures of our literary democracy. Back in the early 1970s, just after the United States had celebrated the centennial of the end of the Civil War, Daniel Aaron published an important book called *The Unwritten War* that was making everyone rethink the odd lacuna in American literature, where, with precious few exceptions, our major writers did not do much to help the nation understand the war and certainly did not produce the needed magisterial books about the nation's trauma that would help the country process and understand the carnage. While some of the anomalies of our literary history that Aaron pointed out *do* in fact remain, it is safe to say the Civil War does not continue to seem quite as unwritten in our literature as it did forty years ago, when Aaron's book appeared. And as Aaron made clear, Whitman *was* one of the writers we were able to turn to in order to think through the implications of that national rupture.

But that's where the failure comes in, because what is powerfully *absent* in Whitman's voluminous writings about the war and its aftermath is any real engagement with the defining issue of the war—the issue of race—and what is even more powerfully and oddly *unwritten*—by Whitman or any of our other major writers, with the exception of Frederick Douglass—is Reconstruction. The "unwritten Reconstruction"—the way canonical nineteenth-century U.S. white writers failed to imagine, articulate, and nurture its attempts to build a truly biracial nation—is a major failing of this country's literature as we have both constructed and inherited it. We experience today the still unresolved issues that plagued this split nation in the Reconstruction years, when the American writers we have studied over the past century tended to agree with Whitman that regional reconciliation trumped racial reconciliation, that it was more important to heal the rift between Southern whites and Northern whites than to heal the divide between Black America and White America. Whitman leaves us with the "yet more terrible and deeply complicated problem" but without even a hint of a solution.

Had black lives begun to matter at that juncture in American history, had America's social history—its educational systems, its voting systems, its employment practices, its justice system, its housing patterns—followed the promising enactment of the Fourteenth and Fifteenth Amendments to the Constitution, and had Whitman and other white writers helped the nation imagine, in those years of egalitarian promise, how racial reconciliation might take precedence over regional reconciliation, there might now be no Confederate statues to pull down and little lingering reverence for the Confederate flag. There might have been less need for nationwide protests to undo the systemic racism that Reconstruction's ultimate failure allowed to take hold in American culture and fester for the next 150 years. America might now be much farther along the road toward its founding goals of equality of opportunity and of justice.

For all his failures after the war to even consider the possibilities of a biracial democracy, though, Whitman did give us a voice in his poetry that no other writer was able to create, a voice that celebrated American diversity and embraced the nation's vast variety, a voice that loved us all. That voice has been vital for writers ever since—Black and white and Asian American and American Indian. That absorptive poetic voice was so much better and more inspiring than the more cautious and occasionally racist voice of the nineteenth-century historical figure named Walt Whitman. It was that voice that prompted Langston Hughes in 1925 to write his poem, "I, Too," which takes up Whitman's invitation to join him in singing America's "varied carols": "I, too, sing America. / I am the darker brother." By the end of the poem, Hughes has assumed Whitman's position as the American poet: "I, too, am America." The Black poet, Hughes demonstrates, can voice the nation every bit as powerfully and fully as the white poet.

In 1953, when Hughes's own positive comments about Whitman were challenged by a critic pointing out Whitman's racism, Hughes responded: "Many great writers, artists, worldly and spiritual leaders, have not always been great men and women in their every day thoughts, speech or ways of living. But they have left, at their flaming best, a great light for others, burning even brighter perhaps from the embers of their own personal failures. . . . [I]f we let temporary human failings destroy for us the timeless values of the best of their work, we will have only their sins to contemplate. . . . Out of the best of his love, Whitman created the best of his poems."

Merrill Commentary

What writer has not responded to "the temporary gaucheries of the hour" and later regretted what they wrote in anger? Intemperate writings may reveal our darkest impulses, which in subsequent drafts of a work or editions of a book may be modified or abandoned. Whitman's exasperation over the state of race relations during Reconstruction, recorded in a note titled "Results South—Now and Hence" and appended to *Memoranda During the War*, is thus comprehensible and unsettling, even unforgivable—which may be why he chose to excise it from *Specimen Days*. D. H. Lawrence rued anything derived from what he called "the voice of [his] education"—acts rooted in fear, writings that skimmed the surface of the subject. Whitman seems to have fallen into the same trap, dashing off a diatribe that would not survive closer scrutiny. Better to explore your fears, continually seeking a language adequate to what you most wish to evade, as Lawrence did in his best work, rewriting some novels many times over, than to expunge an ill-considered judgment. For the sentiment that inspires our severest judgments rarely vanishes without a serious attempt to examine our motives, biases, and blind spots.

Whitman's blind spots are on full display from the first breathless sentence of this note, which includes a racially charged aside—"the black domination, but little above the beasts"—that occupies a singular place in the history of American literary racism. His decision to invoke the Norman conquest of England as the first in "the most salutary series of revolutions," with the implicit suggestion that we must take the long view of "the old impedimenta removed," only makes matters worse. This was not the time for the poet to throw up his hands; even if it seemed that race relations were doomed to become "a yet more terrible and deeply complicated problem," the poet was obliged to address this state of affairs with the same determination to plumb its depths that he had shown in the writing of "Song of Myself." The die was not cast to make permanent the divisions between North and South, black and white, as the poet who advised his future readers to "look for me under your boot-soles" should have known. "First thought, best thought," said Allen Ginsberg, Whitman's poetic heir. Not this time.

39

"Ethiopia Saluting the Colors"

(*A REMINISCENCE OF* 1864.)

1

WHO are you, dusky woman, so ancient, hardly human,
With your woolly-white and turban'd head, and bare bony feet?
Why, rising by the roadside here, do you the colors greet?

2

('Tis while our army lines Carolina's sand and pines,
Forth from thy hovel door, thou, Ethiopia, com'st to me,
As, under doughty Sherman, I march toward the sea.)

3

Me, master, years a hundred, since from my parents sunder'd,
A little child, they caught me as the savage beast is caught;
Then hither me, across the sea, the cruel slaver brought.

4

No further does she say, but lingering all the day,
Her high-borne turban'd head she wags, and rolls her darkling eye,
And curtseys to the regiments, the guidons moving by.

5

What is it, fateful woman—so blear, hardly human?
Why wag your head, with turban bound—yellow, red and green?
Are the things so strange and marvelous, you see or have seen?

Folsom Commentary

For Whitman, the Civil War was fought for the vital goal to preserve the Union, and, while the first three editions of *Leaves of Grass* portrayed slaves sympathetically and showed empathetic concern for African Americans, he in fact had little to say about emancipated slaves or the Emancipation Proclamation itself. His one recorded comment on the Emancipation Proclamation is a manuscript note that appears to be the beginning of an intended newspaper piece; in it, he notes "the phlegmatic coolness all through Washington, under the new emancipation document," and he hears "little allusion made to it in the public places of the city." Whitman is complicit in this cool silence: the issues of slavery and emancipation never enter his Civil War poems, *Drum-Taps and Sequel to Drum-Taps*, nor are they mentioned in his *Memoranda During the War*. The Civil War was a vital, defining event for Whitman, but there is little evidence in his writing during or after the war that he considered race or slavery a key element in the war's importance. We saw in our examination of "Reconciliation" that race and slavery may have a kind of hidden presence in the poem, but it was only after the war that he decided to amend *Drum-Taps* by adding a poem that specifically addresses the issue of race and slavery. It was added to the 1871 edition of *Leaves of Grass* in a cluster of poems called "Bathed in War's Perfume," and then in 1881 it took its place in the final arrangement of the "Drum-Taps" cluster.

"Ethiopia Saluting the Colors" has always been a puzzling poem to confront. Often read as betraying Whitman's racism, the poem has nonetheless been revered by many African American writers over the past century. Langston Hughes called it "one of the most beautiful poems in our language concerning a Negro subject," and the great African American composer H. T. Burleigh set it to music; it was often sung at Harlem Renaissance gatherings. It has always seemed that African American writers and critics see and hear something in the poem that most white readers do not.

It is another poem that Whitman writes based on his notes of what soldiers told him. Whitman writes this poem from the perspective of a white Union soldier who is marching with General Sherman across Georgia and into the Carolinas in 1864, a march that resulted in the liberation of many slaves, who often—to the irritation of the Northern army—tried to latch on to the soldiers for protection and guidance. In Whitman's poem, a hundred-plus-year-old slave woman, dismissively named "Ethiopia" by the soldier-narrator, comes out of her hovel and salutes the American flag, to the consternation of the white soldier, who wonders who this "dusky woman, so ancient hardly human" is, and why she should care about the

American colors. The old slave woman, who was torn from her parents in Africa by slavers a century before and has experienced the brutal Middle Passage and witnessed the American Revolution, the founding of the country, and its development as a slave republic, is now experiencing something she could not have imagined: white soldiers liberating her and her people. The white soldier-narrator, however, can't see it from her perspective and can only ask, dismissively, "Are the things so strange and marvelous you see or have seen?" But of course the things she has seen *are* indeed strange and marvelous, none more so than what she is seeing at that moment, when the nation's flag, for the first time, seems suddenly to symbolize something positive and is even beginning to include this ancient and "fateful" woman. (At the end of the Civil War, when abolitionists came to Charleston harbor to raise the Union flag over Fort Sumter, a ship in the harbor was filled with celebrating African Americans—many with their children along. They heard a white officer say, as the flag was raised, "Now for the first time it is the black man's as well as the white man's flag.")

The old slave woman is given voice in this poem, but only briefly. And what is perhaps most striking about her words is that she literally cannot speak an "I": her voice is all object instead of subject—"*Me master years a hundred since from my parents sunder'd*"—and her self is defined by its being acted upon rather than acting. Her grammar—restricted to the passive voice—echoes a long lifetime that has been out of her control. In this poem, as she approaches the soldier, she is perhaps taking her first step into active identity, after a lifetime of being "sundered," "caught," "brought," and "bought." Ethiopia now looks to the confused soldier-narrator as the next person to guide her out of her objecthood and into her selfhood.

On election night in 2008, Barack Obama stood before 250,000 people in Chicago's Grant Park and spoke to the nation of its history and how its citizens were now experiencing the nation doing something, responding to something, that they could barely begin to register. Obama evoked a hundred-plus-year-old black woman to guide us through the moment. This woman was 106-year-old Ann Nixon Cooper, who cast her ballot that day in Atlanta. It's one of "many stories that will be told for generations" about this election, Obama said, and it's the "one that's on my mind tonight": "She was born just a generation past slavery; a time when there were no cars on the road or planes in the sky; when someone like her couldn't vote for two reasons—because she was a woman and because of the color of her skin." Obama then took us through our history, from the "time when women's voices were silenced and their hopes dismissed," to the "despair in the dust bowl and depression across the land," to the bombs falling "on our harbor and tyranny threatening the world," to "the buses in Montgomery, the hoses in Birmingham, a bridge in Selma, and a preacher from Atlanta who told a people that 'We Shall Overcome,'" to a man touching down on the moon, a wall coming down in Berlin, to a moment when Ann Nixon Cooper "touched her finger to a screen, and cast her vote, because after 106 years in America, through the best of times and the darkest of hours, she knows how America can change." It was during that catalog of the past century's history that Obama began to intone his campaign chant, but somberly now and with quiet conviction: "Yes we can."

He ended his amazing address by saying, just as the old slave woman of "Ethiopia" had indicated, "America, we have come so far. We have seen so much. But there is so much more to do." Another 100-plus-year-old black woman had looked at what America had become and was, like Whitman's slave woman 150 years earlier, shaking her head at what she had seen. Many white Americans, like the befuddled Union soldier in Whitman's poem, were wondering what was so "strange and marvelous" about what Ann Nixon Cooper had seen. But Obama helped the nation see what those Harlem Renaissance writers had found in Whitman's poem, how they had felt that "fateful" ancient slave woman's wonderment at what the American flag could come to mean, had felt how its shape-shifting symbolism actually could change, had felt how far the nation had come, and, because of that, of how far it might still go.

Merrill Commentary

Not long after the events of 9/11, on a panel discussion about the challenges facing policymakers in the war on terror, a security expert lamented the inability of her colleagues in the intelligence community to foresee what havoc men armed only with box-cutters might wreak. This represented in her view a failure of imagination, the analysts having proved themselves unable or unwilling to synthesize various strands of information collected about Al-Qaeda and imagine the unimaginable. A useful list of credible threats must include the most outlandish plots—which prompted me to suggest that it might be wise to call on writers adept at the art of connecting disparate images and ideas, people and places. They think outside the box, dreaming up storylines, creating characters whose motives must be discerned. Inasmuch as they find points of correspondence in incidents that may be far removed from their experience, they provide ways of understanding what may otherwise be incomprehensible. An encounter with a work of art can provide insights unavailable to logical thought processes. How else shall we prepare ourselves for the surprises that define our lives?

The old slave woman in Whitman's "Ethiopia Saluting the Colors" was surely surprised to find herself freed near the end of a long life spent in chains, literal and figurative. She speaks only three lines, at the center of the poem, and yet her words haunt us still: "*Me, master, years a hundred, since from my parents sunder'd, / A little child, they caught me as the savage beast is caught; / Then thither me, across the sea, the cruel slaver brought.*" Note how the blues-like internal rhymes in the first line—hundred/sunder'd—are balanced by perfect end rhymes in the two lines that close the stanza—caught/brought. Whitman's virtue in this poem is to reproduce a snatch of music from the slave songs that gave rise to the blues and jazz: the signal American contribution to music.

Left unsung in this poem is the trail of destruction blazed by troops under the command of General William Tecumseh Sherman—houses, barns, and cities burned to the ground during his 1864 march to the sea, undertaken not only to defeat the Confederate forces but to demoralize the citizens backing the insurrection. The Union soldier narrating this poem marvels at what the "fateful woman" curtseying to the passing regiments must have seen in her life, including, perhaps, the destruction of Columbia, the state capital of South Carolina, in February 1865. On April 26, 1865, twelve days after Lincoln's assassination, nearly ninety thousand men from the Army of the South surrendered to Sherman at a farmhouse near Durham, North Carolina, bringing the war to an end. Now the difficult task of reconciliation between those divided by geography, culture, politics, class, and race would begin, helped or hurt by writers connecting the dots, for good or ill.

40

"The Real War Will Never Get in the Books"

DURING the Union War I commenced at the close of 1862, and continued steadily through '63, '64 and '65, to visit the sick and wounded of the Army, both on the field and in the Hospitals in and around Washington city. From the first I kept little note-books for impromptu jottings in pencil to refresh my memory of names and circumstances, and what was specially wanted, &c. In these I brief'd cases, persons, sights, occurrences in camp, by the bedside, and not seldom by the corpses of the dead. Of the present Volume most of its pages are *verbatim* renderings from such pencillings on the spot. Some were scratch'd down from narratives I heard and itemized while watching, or waiting, or tending somebody amid those scenes. I have perhaps forty such little note-books left, forming a special history of those years, for myself alone, full of associations never to be possibly said or sung. I wish I could convey to the reader the associations that attach to these soil'd and creas'd little livraisons, each composed of a sheet or two of paper, folded small to carry in the pocket, and fasten'd with a pin. I leave them just as I threw them by during the War, blotch'd here and there with more than one blood-stain, hurriedly written, sometimes at the clinique, not seldom amid the excitement of uncertainty, or defeat, or of action, or getting ready for it, or a march. Even these days, at the lapse of many years, I can never turn their tiny leaves, or even take one in my hand, without the actual army sights and hot emotions of the time rushing like a river in full tide through me. Each line, each scrawl, each memorandum, has its history. Some pang of anguish—some tragedy, profounder than ever poet wrote. Out of them arise active and breathing forms. They summon up, even in this silent and vacant room as I write, not only the sinewy regiments and brigades, marching or in camp, but the countless phantoms of those who fell and were hastily buried by wholesale in the battle-pits, or whose dust and bones have been since removed to the National Cemeteries of the land, especially through Virginia and Tennessee. (Not Northern soldiers only—many indeed the Carolinian, Georgian, Alabamian, Louisianian, Virginian—many a Southern face and form, pale, emaciated, with that strange tie of confidence and love between us, welded by sickness, pain of wounds, and little daily, nightly offices of nursing and friendly words and visits, comes up amid the rest, and does not mar, but rounds and gives a finish to the meditation.) Vivid as life, they recall and identify the long Hospital Wards, with their myriad-varied scenes of day or night—the graphic incidents of field or camp—the night before the battle, with many solemn yet cool preparations—the changeful exaltations and depressions of those four years, North and South—the convulsive memories, (let but a word, a broken sentence, serve to recall them)—the clues already quite vanish'd, like some old dream, and yet the list significant enough to soldiers—the scrawl'd, worn slips of paper that came up by bushels from the Southern prisons, Salisbury or Andersonville, by the hands of exchanged prisoners—the clank of crutches on the pavements or floors of Washington, or up and down the stairs of the Paymasters' offices—the Grand Review of homebound veterans at the close of the War, cheerily marching day after day by the President's house, one brigade succeeding another until it seem'd as if they would never end—the strange squads of Southern deserters, (*escapees*, I call'd them;)—that little *genre* group, unreck'd amid the mighty whirl, I remember passing in a hospital corner, of a dying Irish boy, a Catholic priest, and an improvised altar—Four years compressing centuries of native passion, first-class pictures, tempests of life and death—an inexhaustible mine for the Histories, Drama, Romance and even Philosophy of centuries to come—indeed the Verteber of Poetry and Art, (of personal character too,) for all future America, (far more grand, in my opinion, to the hands capable of it, than Homer's siege of Troy, or the French wars to Shakspere;)—and looking over all, in my remembrance, the tall form of President Lincoln, with his face of deep-cut lines, with the large, kind, canny eyes, the complexion of dark brown, and the tinge of wierd melancholy saturating all.

More and more, in my recollections of that period, and through its varied, multitudinous oceans and murky whirls, appear the central resolution and sternness of the bulk of the average American People, animated in Soul by a definite purpose, though sweeping and fluid as some great storm—the Common People, emblemised in thousands of specimens of first-class Heroism, steadily accumulating, (no regiment, no company, hardly a file of men, North or South, the last three years, without such first-class specimens.)

I know not how it may have been, or may be, to others—to me the main interest of the War, I found, (and still, on recollection, find,) in those specimens, and in the ambulance, the Hospital, and even the dead on the field. To me, the points illustrating the latent Personal Character and eligibilities of These States, in the two or three millions of American young and middle-aged men, North and South, embodied in the armies—and especially the one-third or one-fourth of their number, stricken by wounds or disease at some time in the course of the contest—were of more significance even than the Political interests involved. (As so much of a Race depends on what it thinks of death, and how it stands personal anguish and sickness. As, in the glints of emotions under emergencies, and the indirect traits and asides in Plutarch, &c., we get far profounder clues to the antique world than all its more formal history.)

Future years will never know the seething hell and the black infernal background of countless minor scenes and interiors, (not the few great battles) of the Secession War; and it is best they should not. In the mushy influences of current times the fervid atmosphere and typical events of those years are in danger of being totally forgotten. I have at night watch'd by the side of a sick man in the hospital, one who could not live many hours. I have seen his eyes flash and burn as he recurr'd to the cruelties on his surrender'd brother, and mutilations of the corpse afterward. . . .

Such was the War. It was not a quadrille in a ball-room. Its interior history will not only never be written, its practicality, minutia of deeds and passions, will never be even suggested. The actual Soldier of 1862–'65, North and South, with all his ways, his incredible dauntlessness, habits, practices, tastes, language, his appetite, rankness, his superb strength and animality, lawless gait, and a hundred unnamed lights and shades of camp—I say, will never be written—perhaps must not and should not be.

The present Memoranda may furnish a few stray glimpses into that life, and into those lurid interiors of the period, never to be fully convey'd to the future. For that purpose, and for what goes along with it, the Hospital part of the drama from '61 to '65, deserves indeed to be recorded—(I but suggest it.) Of that many-threaded drama, with its sudden and strange surprises, its confounding of prophecies, its moments of despair, the dread of foreign interference, the interminable campaigns, the bloody battles, the mighty and cumbrous and green armies, the drafts and bounties—the immense money expenditure, like a heavy pouring constant rain—with, over the whole land, the last three years of the struggle, an unending, universal mourning-wail of women, parents, orphans—the marrow of the tragedy concentrated in those Hospitals—(it seem'd sometimes as if the whole interest of the land, North and South, was one vast central Hospital, and all the rest of the affair but flanges)—those forming the Untold and Unwritten History of the War—in-finitely greater (like Life's) than the few scraps and distortions that are ever told or written. Think how much, and of importance, will be—how much, civic and military, has already been—buried in the grave, in eternal darkness !........But to my Memoranda.

Folsom Commentary

We began this book at the end, and we end it with what was originally Whitman's beginning of *Memoranda During the War*, a section that later, when he revised *Memoranda* to include it in his longer autobiographical work *Specimen Days*, became the conclusion. Whitman knew what T. S. Eliot was to express many years later in his poem "Little Gidding": "What we call the beginning is often the end / And to make an end is to make a beginning. / The end is where we start from." Whitman certainly started his book about the Civil War at the end of the war, which, for him, was the beginning of writing a book about the war. But he knew as he began that there could be no ending, because, as he famously said in the conclusion of the Civil War section of *Specimen Days*, "the real war will never get in the books." Whitman already knew that this war would be endlessly written about (he probably would not be surprised to find that the Library of Congress estimates that around seventy-five thousand books about the Civil War have now appeared, and more are always on the way), and he was certain that none of those books (including his own) would capture "the real war." The war—its causes, its battles, its strategies, its horrors, its statistics—would be played and replayed, revised and rethought, argued over and forever debated, written and rewritten. Each new book about the war begins again to narrate it to its end, only for others to begin again. (And as we look around this still-divided nation, we may ask if in fact the Civil War has ever ended, or whether it has simply begun again, and again, in various guises.)

Whitman can only hint at what he means by the "real war": he talks about its "interior history," the way it was experienced by "the actual Soldier of 1862–'65, North and South, with all his ways, his incredible dauntlessness, habits, practices, tastes, language, his appetite, rankness, his superb strength and animality, lawless gait, and a hundred unnamed lights and shades of camp." And what he hopes his book can do is "furnish a few stray glimpses into that life, and into those lurid interiors of the period," even while he knows these lost experiences can "never . . . be fully convey'd to the future." The war experience he knows best—those hundreds of thousands of sick, wounded, and dying soldiers in the hospitals of the nation's capital—is the one, he believes, that has been and always will be least captured by books: "the marrow of the tragedy [is] concentrated in those Hospitals—(it seem'd sometimes as if the whole interest of the land, North and South, was one vast central Hospital, and all the rest of the affair but flanges)." The best we can hope will "ever [be] told or written," Whitman reminds us, are a "few scraps and distortions." "Think how much," Whitman writes, "and of importance, will be—how much, civic and military, has already been—buried in the grave, in eternal darkness."

Like those hundreds of thousands of graves of soldiers—all of whom are now "unknown" because they died too young ever to form the kinds of full identities that we *could* begin to know—the intense and lived experiences of the war are also now in their own unmarked graves, never to be brought to light.

In an earlier section of *Memoranda,* Whitman thought about the wounds and diseases he had seen in the hospitals during and right after the war: "A large majority of the wounds are in the arms and legs. But there is every kind of wound, in every part of the body. I should say of the sick, from my observation, that the prevailing maladies are typhoid fever and the camp fevers generally, diarrhœa, catarrhal affections and bronchitis, rheumatism and pneumonia. These forms of sickness lead; all the rest follow. There are twice as many sick as there are wounded." This, for Whitman, was the key: the war was experienced *in the body, on the body,* and *by the body.* Whitman himself felt it in every fiber of his physical being; we have seen in the previous works we have examined just how intensely the experience affected him, what a physical toll it took. In 1891, Whitman would add a final "concluding note" to *Leaves of Grass,* in which he traces his "late-years palsied old shorn and shell-fish condition" to his Civil War experiences: "the indubitable outcome and growth . . . of too over-zealous, over-continued bodily and emotional excitement and action through the times of 1862, '3, '4, and '5, visiting and waiting on wounded and sick army volunteers, both sides." That "bodily and emotional excitement and action" and strain is what will "never get into the books," because what is missing from any writing is the body itself that experienced what the words can only point to, mutely. "Will the America of the future—will this vast rich Union ever realize what itself cost, back there after all?"

This, of course, is why Whitman wrote about the war, to offer a few scraps that might indicate the physical and emotional cost of those years of fratricide. Even if his own books failed to capture the "real war," he nonetheless created a new way to represent war, one that has had a major impact on Civil War history in recent decades—as he turned his descriptions from a focus on the battlefields to a focus on the end results of those battles, the casualties in the hospitals; as he turned from the generals who designed war strategies to the troops who put their bodies onto and often into the fields. Just as in his prewar poetry Whitman broke down hierarchies and helped us see things democratically, so in his war writing did he break down the traditional ways of narrating war by making us painfully aware of the trials and heroism and horror and courage of the ordinary soldiers from all over the divided nation, whom he tended and loved and remembered. Those often forgotten soldiers who were taken off the battlefield by illness, injury, or death are illuminated in Whitman's books as the war itself becomes re-centered on the hospitals. The people who so often don't get in the books—and the messiness and carnage that they bring with them—*do* get in Whitman's, and they form the very heart of his Civil War writing.

Merrill Commentary

If it is true that "the real war will never get in the books," as Whitman observes in *Specimen Days*, then the question arises: What does appear in the poetry, fiction, essays, reminiscences, histories, journals, and other works about the war, in his time and down through the generations? The Library of Congress calculates that approximately seventy-five thousand books have been published on the Civil War—more than one a day since Appomattox—and if you add films, television shows, and video games, not to mention songs, symphonies, and operas, it becomes clear that there has been, and likely will continue to be, no shortage of works about this defining event of American history, each of which has portrayed something about the war, essential or peripheral, true or false. But the real war—where is it to be found, if not in books, and films, and music?

Some years ago, at a meeting in Nairobi of writers and scholars who were designing a new university for the Agha Khan, a novelist suggested that in addition to gathering books, periodicals, papers, films, sound recordings, and digital archives, the library would collect and catalog smells from around the world, natural and manmade—rose blossoms, car exhaust, pine pitch, smoke and sweat, nectar and silver polish, the tang of the sea, the scent of sautéed onions, the stench of death: a gallery of fragrances, ordered from the rank to the sublime, available to perfumers, pathologists, and anyone seeking to identify a particular aroma. The idea never progressed beyond the drawing board, confirming the wisdom of Robert Hass's insight: "There are limits to imagination." But perhaps the novelist will work this idea into a book, inspiring an enterprising librarian to create an olfactory gallery. In the meantime it may help to explain why the volume of corpses decomposing in the earth convinced Whitman that the real war would lie forever beyond any medium of artistic expression. How to translate the mingled odors of grass and gangrene?

Geoffrey Hill's meditations on the problem of evil include these memorable lines: "Art is impregnable in its claims, / Consoles itself while children curl in flames. / I could not say what registers the shock." Whitman was shocked by the amount of blood spilled in the Civil War; the scale of loss, personal and collective, broke his health and spirits. But what he registered in his writings ensures that the carnage at the heart of American history can still shape the sensibilities of a people who daily register new shocks in their ongoing experiment in liberty.

Walt Whitman and the Civil War

A Selected Annotated Bibliography • Ed Folsom

EDITIONS OF WHITMAN'S CIVIL WAR WRITINGS

The most extensive available collection of Whitman's Civil War writings is at the website of the *Walt Whitman Archive* (whitmanarchive.org); this online resource offers the original editions of *Drum-Taps, Sequel to Drum-Taps,* and *Memoranda During the War,* along with a complete collection of Whitman's Civil War correspondence, his Civil War journalism, his Civil War notebooks, and all known photographs of Whitman taken during the war. Other notable book editions of Whitman's Civil War writings are listed below, from the most recent to the earliest.

Danh, Binh, and Robert Schultz. *War Memoranda: Photography, Walt Whitman, and Memorials.* Roanoke, VA: Taubman Museum of Art, 2019. [Features "chlorophyll prints of [Civil War] soldiers and civilians" as well as daguerreotypes and cyanotypes of Civil War sites by Binh Danh and Robert Schultz, along with essays, selections from Whitman's writings, and poems by Schultz, all evoking in striking ways the relationship of Civil War soldiers to the land they died on.]

Whitman, Walt. *Drum-Taps: The Complete 1865 Edition.* Ed. Lawrence Kramer. New York: NYRB Poets, 2015. [Republication of the original (1865) edition of *Drum-Taps,* with an extensive introduction and annotations by Lawrence Kramer.]

Whitman, Walt. *Drum-Taps: The Complete Civil War Poems.* Kennebunkport, ME: Cider Mill Press, 2015. [Illustrated edition of *Drum-Taps,* along with other Whitman Civil War writings, with an introduction by James M. McPherson.]

Sharp, Kevin. *Bold, Cautious, True: Walt Whitman and American Art of the Civil War Era.* Memphis: The Dixon Gallery, 2009. [Catalog of the art exhibit "Bold, Cautious, True: Walt Whitman and American Art of the Civil War Era," held at the Dixon Gallery in Memphis, Tennessee, July 5 through October 4, 2009, featuring American artwork from the 1860s accompanied by Whitman's Civil War prose and poetry; the catalog offers a detailed history of Whitman and his brother George during the Civil War, viewing the poet's life and work in the context of the art and history of the period, with numerous color reproductions of Civil War artwork; some chapters are co-authored by Adam M. Thomas.]

Whitman, Walt. *Memoranda During the War.* Ed. Peter Coviello. New York: Oxford University Press, 2004. [Reprints Whitman's 1875–76 *Memoranda During the War;*

with an introduction, "Whitman at War" (ix–liv), offering biographical and historical contexts for reading the memoranda; editor's notes (134–41) and appendices reprinting Whitman's "Death of Abraham Lincoln" (144–57); selected Whitman poems (158–64), and one Whitman letter, to the parents of soldier Erastus Haskell (165–69).]

Whitman, Walt. *Specimen Days.* Introduction by Alfred Kazin. Boston: David R. Godine, 1971. [A large-format reprinting of *Specimen Days,* generously illustrated with photographs of Whitman, with a large selection of Civil War photographs of soldiers and Civil War Washington, D.C., to accompany the Civil War section of the book.]

Basler, Roy, ed. *Walt Whitman's Memoranda During the War [&] Death of Abraham Lincoln.* Bloomington: University of Indiana Press, 1962. [Offers a true photo-facsimile of the original edition of *Memoranda During the War* and a transcription of Whitman's lecture on the "Death of Abraham Lincoln," along with photo-facsimiles of related manuscript and printed materials; with an informative introduction by Basler covering the publication history of *Memoranda* and a history of Whitman's oft-repeated lecture on Lincoln.]

Lowenfels, Walter, ed. *Walt Whitman's Civil War.* New York: Knopf, 1961. [Attempts to create "a new book by Whitman" by arranging and melding his various Civil War writings—nonfiction prose, poetry, notebooks, and journalism—into fourteen separate categories.]

Whitman, Walt. *Walt Whitman's Drum-Taps (1865) and Sequel to Drum-Taps (1865–6).* Ed. F. DeWolfe Miller. Gainesville, FL: Scholars' Facsimiles & Reprints, 1959. [Offers a true photo-facsimile of the original *Drum-Taps and Sequel,* with a long and informative introduction by Miller tracking the composition and publication of the book.]

Glicksberg, Charles I., ed. *Walt Whitman and the Civil War: A Collection of Original Articles and Manuscripts.* Philadelphia: University of Pennsylvania Press, 1933 [repr., New York: A. S. Barnes, 1963]. [Collects Whitman's Civil War writings, including his 1862 *City Photographs,* manuscript notes, poem drafts, unpublished letters, other journalism, his diary for 1863, and his notes on various aspects of the war, hospitals, and Lincoln; includes a list of newspaper clippings Whitman made, evidence of "the nature of Whitman's interest and his reactions to many phases of the Civil War" and possible source material for him as well; with an introduction by Glicksberg reviewing Whitman's experiences before and during the war.]

CRITICISM ON WHITMAN AND THE CIVIL WAR

Serious critical work on Whitman and the Civil War did not begin until the centenary of the war in the 1960s. Revisionary work in the late 1980s by critics like M. Wynn Thomas, Kerry Larson, and Betsy Erkkila inspired many others to reconsider Whitman's Civil War writings in the context of new political and historical approaches and discoveries. It has only been in the twenty-first century that the full power and significance of Whitman's war writings have begun to be appreciated. This bibliography moves from the most recent work backwards, so that readers can trace from the present to the past how the interest in Whitman's war writing and the methodologies for reading it have changed. I have attempted to include all books and essays that have contributed in some significant way to the development of our understanding of *Drum-Taps, Memoranda During the War,* and other Civil War work by Whitman, and my annotations specify what each piece contributes. All of the early reviews of *Drum-Taps* published during Whitman's lifetime are available at the *Walt Whitman Archive* (whitmanarchive.org).

Scholnick, Robert J. "Dispatches to Henry Raymond's *New York Times*: Whitman on Trauma in Civil War Washington." *Common-Place: The Journal of Early American Life* 19 (Spring 2019), common-place.org. [Explores how Whitman "made brilliant use of [Henry] Raymond's *Times* during the Civil War to reach a national audience with acute, penetrating analysis of the medical catastrophe that had engulfed the nation, . . . deploy[ing] his considerable skill as a journalist to introduce readers everywhere to the suffering of the hospitalized soldiers, focusing particularly on syndromes that, he claimed, were not well understood: trauma and its intersection with a wide range of disabilities"; shows how the war changed Whitman from the journalist who set out "to inspire and instruct Americans in the search for perfect health" to a writer who sought "to embrace a wounded nation and heal broken spirits."]

Tuggle, Lindsay. *The Afterlives of Specimens: Science, Mourning, and Whitman's Civil War.* Iowa City: University of Iowa Press, 2017. [Examines the significance of "specimens" (and the concept of specimens) in Whitman's Civil War writings, arguing that "Whitman's specimens inhabit the threshold between scientific exploration and melancholic attachment, embodying the intimacy of mourning in the face of anonymity and dismemberment"; analyzes botanical, medical, spiritualist, and sentimental influences on Whitman's work; and probes the nature of Whitman's connections to prominent medical figures such as John H. Brinton and Silas Weir Mitchell.]

Folsom, Ed. "Counting from One to a Million: Whitman's Engagement with Large Numbers." *Walt Whitman Quarterly Review* 34 (Fall 2016): 146–68. [Final part of the essay analyzes how Whitman's exhilaration with large numbers was muted by the Civil War, when we see him "struggling with the impossible arithmetic of the Civil War's mass death"; offers a close reading of "The Million Dead, Too, Summ'd Up," where Whitman "invents a syntax of mass death" and searches for the lost "one" in the generalized million.]

Buinicki, Martin. "Walt Whitman." In Coleman Hutchison, ed., *History of American Civil War Literature* (New York: Cambridge University Press, 2016), 181–94. [Discusses the impact of the Civil War on Whitman's life and career; shows how in 1863 "the poet set about remaking himself as a resident of Washington, DC"; examines "the complicated interplay between the poet's private and public writing about the war and the way that his hospital experiences shaped his subsequent poetry and prose"; and demonstrates how his "writing was forever transformed by the Civil War."]

Price, Kenneth M., and Jacqueline M. Budell. "'Written by Walt Whitman, a friend': Three Letters from Soldiers." *Prologue Magazine* 48 (Summer 2016): 36–45. [Examines the three known cases of Whitman's writing letters for Civil War soldiers and considers "the implications of Whitman's effort to ventriloquize" these soldiers and "his attempt to channel the thoughts, anguish, and love of ordinary people in an extraordinary time"; goes on to provide information about Robert Nelson Jabo, Albion F. Hubbard, and David Ferguson, the soldiers for whom Whitman wrote these letters.]

Marrs, Cody. *Nineteenth-Century American Literature and the Long Civil War.* New York: Cambridge University Press, 2015. [Chapter 1, "Walt Whitman's Dialectics," examines how "Whitman's career . . . bridges the very epochal boundaries and periodic subsets that have long structured American literary studies" and goes on to look at how Whitman "writes prodigiously across the nineteenth century by continually retiming the war in his poems and prose," a retiming that has a profound impact on "his sense of national, authorial, and sexual identity"; shows how, inspired by Hegel, Whitman's work takes a "futural turn" deriving from his "refusal to accept the troubled present as the solid horizon of political possibility" and his decision to make an "investment in deferral," putting his faith in "a capacious timeframe for democracy."]

Bellis, Peter J. "Reconciliation as Sequel and Supplement: *Drum-Taps* and *Battle-Pieces.*" *Leviathan* 17 (October 2015): 79–93. [Begins with the question "Why does *Drum-Taps* require a sequel, and *Battle-Pieces* a supplement?" and goes on to note how Whitman and Herman Melville "could simply have ended their books with the close of Civil War hostilities," but both felt "something more" was needed "to give the war shape and meaning: an additional movement toward reunification and reconciliation," though both supplements brought "formal disruption" as "reconciliation is deferred or displaced into a separate section of the text and marked by an all too visible scar or seam."]

Parsons, Amy. "Desire, Forgetting, and the Future: Walt Whitman's Civil War." *Arizona Quarterly* 71 (Autumn 2015): 85–109. [Asks how "issues of desire, trauma, and memory [were] understood before psychoanalysis" and argues "that Walt Whitman's war writing in *Specimen Days* and *Drum-Taps* offers an alternative landscape for the psyche, one quite distinct from the psychoanalytic emphasis on interiority, privacy, and the priority of the past over the present," instead finding a "solution to the devastation of the war . . . grounded in idiosyncratic notions of desire and forgetting," as he "responds to the overwhelming physical destruction of bodies with a desirous, affectionate care for them," providing a "solace" that is "entirely directed toward having been wounded rather than wounding, dying rather than killing."]

Peck, Garrett. *Walt Whitman in Washington, D.C.: The Civil War and America's Great Poet.* Charleston, SC: History Press, 2015. [Detailed overview, with numerous photographs, of Whitman's decade living in Washington, D.C., written for a general audience.]

Price, Kenneth M. "Walt Whitman and Civil War Washington." In Susan C. Lawrence, ed., *Civil War Washington: History, Place, and Digital Scholarship* (Lincoln: University of Nebraska Press, 2015), 187–206. [Examines Whitman's years in Washington, D.C.—his life, work, associations—and the indelible impact the city had on him and his work.]

Matthews, Joshua. "Walt Whitman's Vision of the Inferno, or Dante in *Drum-Taps*." *Walt Whitman Quarterly Review* 32 (Summer/Fall 2014): 36–69. [Examines Whitman's rereading of Dante's *Inferno* in 1862, analyzes his notes on the poem, and demonstrates how "the *Inferno* offered Whitman a powerful exemplar poem of the historical and sociological interconnections between sociology, theology, civil war, and the politics of union and disunion"; argues that Dante's work "inspired the relationship between the form, content, and tone of much of Whitman's wartime poetry and prose."]

Buinicki, Martin. "The 'need of means additional': Walt Whitman's Civil War Fundraising." *Walt Whitman Quarterly Review* 31 (Spring 2014): 135–57. [Examines the history of fundraising for injured and sick soldiers in D.C.'s Civil War hospitals; raises important questions about Whitman's affiliation with the U.S. Christian Commission; and examines how "in large part because of his brother Jeff's advice, [Whitman's] abilities as a fundraiser improved significantly as the war continued" as he began "to learn the importance of direct solicitation and social networks in large-scale fundraising."]

Folsom, Ed. "'That towering bulge of pure white': Whitman, Melville, the Capitol Dome, and Black America." *Leviathan* 16 (March 2014): 87–120. [Examines Whitman's and Herman Melville's experiences with and writings about the U.S. Capitol dome during its construction, and suggests a "forgotten aspect" of the history of the dome—"the way the statue of Freedom and, in a sense, the Capitol dome itself, was racially tinged and how Whitman and Melville would have experienced it that way"; concludes that "by the end of the war, Whitman and Melville were, oddly, more in line with Jefferson Davis's original conception of what that 'towering bulge of pure white,' so tenuously balanced between the Southern and Northern wings of the Capitol, would represent—a joining of Northern and Southern whites, a confirmation of the freedom for those who already had it—than they were with the possibilities many in the culture were beginning to see in the figure of a manumitted slave on the apex of the nation's newly completed Capitol, summoning the United States to rethink itself in the dawning light of emancipation."]

Price, Kenneth M. "Walt Whitman and Civil War Washington." *Leviathan* 16 (March 2014): 121–34. [Examines how "the crisis of war remade both Whitman and Washington, DC," and analyzes the effects of the quickly changing capital city on the poet during the last two war years, showing how Whitman came "to admire both the wounded soldiers and the city now hosting them," while he focused his attention on "the war experiences of the common soldier, the stoicism and heroism of otherwise average individuals, and—above all—the suffering, dignity, and enormous courage he saw in his hospital visits."]

Arbour, Robert. "'Such Verses for My Body Let Us Write': Civil War Song, Sentimentalism, and Whitman's *Drum-Taps*." In Mary De Jong and Paula Bernat Bennett, eds., *Sentimentalism in Nineteenth-Century America: Literary and Cultural Practices* (Madison, NJ: Fairleigh Dickinson University Press, 2013), 161–80. [Explores the connections between popular Civil War songs and *Drum-Taps*, viewing *Drum-Taps* "as a response to popular American concerns about the security of the Union and the legitimacy of sentimental consensus during the Civil War"; argues that "Whitman weaves the broken bodies of soldiers into a musical tapestry, enfolding them into the corpus of a book in which the national family is displaced by the figure of the all-embracing poet."]

Coviello, Peter. "Whitman's Children." *PMLA* 128 (January 2013): 73–86. [Offers a close reading of Whitman's letter to the parents of Civil War soldier Erastus Haskell just after his death in order to focus on "the multiplicity of roles the poet inhabits in [his] war writing (mother, father, nurse, lover, confidant, scribe)" and to read "his acts of surrogacy as efforts to restore carnality, in its world-making force, to family and, in particular, to parenthood," calling this "Whitman's project of queer generation," a project "to enlarge the vision of sex and sexual possibility he had initiated in the 'Calamus' poems," and one at least partially realized when two of the soldiers he nursed named their sons after the poet.]

Gregerson, Linda. "The Self in the Poem." *Virginia Quarterly Review* 88 (Spring 2012): 17–21. [Comments on how "the central rhetorical vehicle of Whitman's art" ("the self so large, so exemplary, so all-encompassing that it empties itself of all specific content and becomes tautology") faces "a dramatic turning point" during the Civil War, when his "grandiosity and over-inflation" encounter "a terrific dose of reality," and his poems are "suddenly shocked into sobriety, plain denotation, and, utterly new to Whitman, understatement"; goes on to point out how deceptive the assumption is that Whitman's "life and work" were "intertwined."]

Plumly, Stanley. "Whitman's Compost." *Virginia Quarterly Review* 88 (Spring 2012): 13–16. [Portrays the Washington, D.C., that Whitman came to during the Civil War (its "massive muck and mess of hospitals and encampments"), comments on the *Drum-Taps* poems that they are "beautifully observed, accurately rendered, passionately felt," and suggests that "health juxtaposed in a slant rhyme with death has been a subtext in Whitman [since] early on in his writing," particularly in "This Compost."]

Duarte, Laura. "Addressing Wounds: Whitman Engaged." In Isabel Capeloa and Adriana Martins, eds., *Plots of War: Modern Narratives of Conflict* (Berlin: De Gruyter, 2012), 127–38. [Offers an overview of Whitman's Civil War experiences and examines how he felt a "renewed sense of perspective provided by the war" that released a "flow of words" as "despair drove Whitman to telling measures"; suggests that Whitman's prewar despondency was initially "reflected in the shattered bodies of the soldiers around him" but that ultimately the war "would lead to renewal."]

Conrad, Eric. "Whitman's Earliest Attempt to Absorb the Civil War into *Leaves of Grass*." *Walt Whitman Quarterly Review* 28 (Spring 2011): 209–10. [Reprints and analyzes a manuscript page from Amherst College that indicates "Whitman may have imagined fully integrating his Civil War verse within *Leaves of Grass* as early as 1865, much earlier than the appended *Drum-Taps* of 1867 suggests."]

Fuller, Randall. *From Battlefields Rising: How the Civil War Transformed American Literature*. New York: Oxford University Press, 2011. [Chapter 1, "Beat! Beat! Drums!," reviews Whitman's situation just before the Civil War began, examining the publication of his 1860 edition of *Leaves of Grass* by Thayer and Eldridge and the subsequent demise of their publishing firm as the war approached, and goes on to examine Whitman's early responses to the outbreak of the war; later chapters return to Whitman to recount his experiences at Fredericksburg during the war (136–40; featuring a reading of "A Sight in Camp in the Daybreak Gray and Dim"), his work in the Washington, D.C., hospitals (150–56; featuring a reading of "The Wound-Dresser"), and his reaction to the war's end (215–19; featuring readings of "O Captain! My Captain!" and "When Lilacs Last in the Dooryard Bloom'd").]

Turner, Frederick. "On Historical Art: Melville and the Poetry of the Civil War." *American Arts Quarterly* 28 (Summer 2011), nccsc.net/aaq/2011/summer. [Examines the visual and literary artistic responses to the Civil War and finds that "of the major poets only Melville and Whitman squarely faced up to the huge aesthetic challenge of the war"—Whitman by going "with his impressions, feelings and intuitions" and "largely evad[ing] the political, historical, philosophical and social issues that complicated the poet's task in this war"; argues that Whitman "does manage something that none of the other poets achieved: to create a verbal music that can encompass the large sprawling reality of a continental democratic war."]

Bradford, Adam. "Re-collecting Soldiers: Walt Whitman and the Appreciation of Human Value." *Walt Whitman Quarterly Review* 27 (Winter 2010): 127–52. [Argues that "drawing on his notebooks, Whitman went to work to generate a poetic project, *Drum-Taps*, which would not merely represent the war while arguing his broader social and political ideologies, but would create a textual means of reaching the dead—imaginatively recovering them and acknowledging their innate human value in contradistinction to the destructive processes of war"; examines the significance of Whitman's decision to record individual and specific soldiers in his Civil War prose but to offer "anonymous representations of actual Civil War soldiers" in his poetry, allowing "virtually any reader—Northerner or Southerner—[to] impress the text with his or her own soldier image in need of 'appreciation,'" and allowing Whitman "to democratize and universalize access to the lost Civil War soldiers while engendering a shared appreciation of human value."]

Price, Kenneth M. "Love, War, and Revision in Whitman's Blue Book." *Huntington Li-*

brary Quarterly 73 (2010): 679–92. [Examines how Whitman's Blue Book—his "copy of the 1860 edition of *Leaves of Grass* in blue paper covers that [he] heavily annotated and used as the basis for a never-published future edition"—"was a locus for Whitman's substantive and stylistic changes" and how it "illuminates Whitman's poetic practice, particularly as it changed during (and in response to) the Civil War," arguing that "the Blue Book is one of the most dramatic manifestations of Whitman editing himself," and analyzing his increasing use of the word *pensive* as "a useful barometer of his outlook" at this time.]

Wachtell, Cynthia. *War No More: The Antiwar Impulse in American Literature, 1861–1914*. Baton Rouge: Louisiana State University Press, 2010. [Chapter 6, "Walt Whitman: 'That Hell Unpent,'" examines how Whitman "struggled to come to terms with the Civil War," vacillating "between supporting and questioning the war," presenting "an uplifting and inspiring image of the war, and of wartime America, to his public readership," though engaging in "self-censorship and circumspection," since in his "personal writings" he recorded "some of the darkest observations and verses to spring from the Civil War," revealing that "he did not publicly acknowledge the extent of his dismay and ambivalence," leaving in his journals and notes "some of the most overtly antiwar lines of the entire Civil War generation"; suggests that Whitman decided to "censor his response to the war" in his Civil War poetry in order "to serve his patriotic purpose," to help "protect his readers, especially his female readers," and "to convince himself, and to convince posterity, that the war was not fought in vain."]

Miller, Cristanne. "*Drum-Taps*: Revisions and Reconciliation." *Walt Whitman Quarterly Review* 26 (Spring 2009): 171–96. [Examines the 1865 *Drum-Taps* and *Sequel to Drum-Taps* in comparison to the 1871 "Drum-Taps" sequence in *Leaves of Grass*, tracking Whitman's growing "participation in a Northern liberal turn toward nostalgia" in the aftermath of the Civil War, a "reflective rather than restorative" nostalgia that erases ideological difference between North and South in order to celebrate "reconciliatory nation-building," silencing the issues of slavery and sedition that generated the war.]

Cushman, Stephen B. "Walt Whitman's Real Wars." In John Waugh and Gary Gallagher, eds., *Wars Within a War: Controversy and Conflict over the American Civil War* (Chapel Hill: University of North Carolina Press, 2009): 137–56. [Examines Whitman's famous statement that "the real war will never get in the books" and suggests various ways the phrase could be interpreted, arguing that "in *Memoranda During the War* Walt Whitman carried out various prose experiments in writing Civil War history; that those experiments have as their common aim the production of an illusion or appearance of reality; that, despite several failures, at many moments in *Memoranda* his experiments are powerfully successful; that his statement about the real war not getting in the books is disingenuous when it comes to his own, in which he developed, if not pioneered, new verbal conventions for representing real war."]

Genoways, Ted. *Walt Whitman and the Civil War: America's Poet During the Lost Years of 1860–1862.* Berkeley: University of California Press, 2009. [Offers a close examination of Whitman's activities during the first two years of the Civil War, seeking "to fill in the gap of Whitman's years from 1860 to 1862 . . . [and] to debunk the myth that Whitman was uninvolved in and unaffected by the country's march to war"; contains many discoveries from newspaper and magazine archives about the publication of Whitman's work, newly discovered correspondence, and important new information on many figures in Whitman's life, including Ellen Eyre (who turns out, in actuality, to be a cross-dressing male con artist named William Kinney), Henry Clapp, William Thayer, James Redpath, and others.]

Keegan, John. *The American Civil War: A Military History.* New York: Random House, 2009. [Chapter 19, "Walt Whitman and Wounds," examines Civil War hospitals, the nature of battle wounds, and medicine when it was "very much at a point of transition"; summarizes Whitman's visits to Washington hospitals; and examines "Come Up from the Fields, Father" as "one of the finest war poems ever written."]

Salska, Agnieszka. "Dickinson, Whitman, and the Civil War: How Can Language Deal with Upheaval?" *Polish Journal for American Studies* 3 (2009): 23–34. [Reads two Civil War poems, one by Whitman ("A Sight in Camp in the Daybreak Gray and Dim") and one by Dickinson ("They dropped like Flakes"), "against the background of two Civil War photographs by Timothy O'Sullivan," with Whitman's poem demonstrating "the power of language and art to lift the sordid and horrible into the sphere of the sacred."]

Wry, Joan R. "Liminal Spaces: Literal and Conceptual Borderlines in Whitman's Civil War Poems." *Walt Whitman Quarterly Review* 26 (Spring 2009): 197–212. [Reads Whitman's Civil War poems "in the context of liminality, a cultural discourse that calls attention to margins and borderlines as transitional points but also focuses specifically on the 'limen' or the spaces between, as literal and conceptual sites of potential and illumination" and suggests that "in the more photographic poems, liminality provides Whitman with a framing technique, allowing him to sharpen his focus on the verisimilitude of a scene by delineating the outlines and interstices of the natural landscape," while another use of liminality "calls attention to hospital spaces as literal and figurative symbols of transition for wounded or dying soldiers," and yet another "mystical use of liminality allows Whitman to further define his role as an interpreting agent from the borderlines and margins of the war, the poet who gives meaning to the ultimate passage from life into death for all the nation's dead."]

Richards, Eliza. "Correspondent Lines: Poetry, Journalism, and the U.S. Civil War." *ESQ: A Journal of the American Renaissance* 54 (2008): 145–70. [Explores the ways in which poets during the Civil War, "influenced by developments in journalism, gave expression to the shifts in perception instigated by new mass-media networks," and examines how "Whitman's postbellum *Drum-Taps* gains legibility as a meditation on the wartime circulation of words as well as bodies, mediation as well as physical contact," as well as how Whitman probed "the transitive relations between lines of force and lines of poetry," while offering "a retrospective perspective that shifts the attention away from war's immediacies and toward its linguistic effects."]

Roper, Robert. *Now the Drum of War: Walt Whitman and His Brothers in the Civil War.* New York: Walker, 2008. [Examines Whitman's family life and his relationship with stage-driver Fred Vaughan, leading up to Whitman's departure for the war front to care for his brother George; effectively juxtaposes George's long experience in the war with Whitman's work in the hospitals and examines the close relationship between Whitman and his brothers, especially George.]

Warner, Michael. "Civil War Religion and Whitman's *Drum-Taps.*" In David Haven Blake and Michael Robertson, eds., *Walt Whitman: Where the Future Becomes Present* (Iowa City: University of Iowa Press, 2008), 81–90. [Examines the 1865 *Drum-Taps* as "an unusual piece of war discourse," noting that "much of the usual framework of war poetry is missing," leaving us with a book that "would not allow one to reconstruct the history of the war, or what was at stake in it politically, or who won"; argues that, instead, "its preoccupations—patient registration of collective history, a stare at mortality and fate, devotion of attention to the world, durative time—are given an implicitly and sometimes explicitly religious cast, though in the context of providential narrative they also carry an implication of critical worldliness"; concludes that "a reader of the book as a whole shuttles continually between a fatal immersion in temporal unknowing and, punctuating that sense of history, a higher time of nature, devoted to the unflinching staring at corpses."]

Genoways, Ted. "The Disorder of *Drum-Taps.*" *Walt Whitman Quarterly Review* 24 (Fall 2006 / Winter 2007): 98–116. [Examines the printing history of *Drum-Taps,* comparing "the March 1865 [advertising] placard to the final table of contents," establishing "the high cost of paper in the late Civil War and Whitman's financial concerns," identifying "the different type designs in *Drum-Taps,*" showing "how each change reveals a new stage in the production process," and reexamining "the surviving documentary evidence of the printing process to create a more complete chronology of the process of revision and publication"; concludes that the book was largely arranged to economize space and save paper and that *Drum-Taps* becomes a "poignant reflection of the war, embodying in its very arrangements the wounds and scars of April 1865."]

Genoways, Ted. "Civil War Poems in 'Drum-Taps' and 'Memories of President Lincoln.'" In Donald D. Kummings, ed., *A Companion to Walt Whitman* (Malden, MA: Blackwell, 2006), 522–38. [Examines Whitman's Civil War poems, dividing them into "Recruiting Poems," written in 1861 "to inspire young men, like his brother George, who were preparing for battle, and mobilize those men who were considering service"; "Journalistic Poems," "startlingly ahistorical" poems that were nonetheless sometimes "drawn directly from actual *New York Times* newspaper dispatches" and arranged in *Drum-Taps* according to "a personal, intuitive structure over a chronological narrative"; "Soldier Poems," including "The Artilleryman's Vision," which Whitman turned from "a straightforward description of the chaos of battle" into a "night-haunted memory"; "Hospital Poems," where Whitman gains "the intimate understanding of the common soldier that he so craved," building upon his volunteer work in the hospitals and focusing "our attention unflinchingly on the impact of the war"; and "Memories of President Lincoln," where "the reader is asked to permanently pair, as the poet does, the fallen soldiers . . . with the slain president."]

Luria, Sarah. *Capital Speculations: Writing and Building Washington, D.C.* (Lebanon: University of New Hampshire Press, 2006). [Chapter 2, "The Poetry of Internal Improvements: Abraham Lincoln and Walt Whitman in Civil War Washington," examines how Lincoln and Whitman were "in different ways both poets of internal improvements," as "Whitman's poetry celebrated the nation through circulation of all kinds" and "Lincoln and Whitman served as boosters for the Union as they sought to strengthen citizens' affective bonds to the nation by giving it poetic force," specifically through their promotion of "physical infrastructure" in Washington, D.C.; demonstrates how "Whitman's accounts of the Civil War hospitals . . . bring fantastic national domestic infrastructures to life," as he "circulates through the corridors lined with men from all parts of the Union."]

Mancuso, Luke. "Civil War." In Donald D. Kummings, ed., *A Companion to Walt Whitman* (Malden, MA: Blackwell, 2006), 290–310. [Examines Whitman's response to the Civil War, arguing that "Whitman moves from a libertarian antebellum confidence in confederate harmony among the states, to a more conservative recognition of the ghostly wounds that will always haunt the Union victory," leading to a "practice of memorialization [that] idealizes the social memory of heroic enlistments in home and nation, and largely ignores the excesses of patriotic nationalism"; deals with "the role of nostalgia and 'Brooklyniana'" and views "*Drum-Taps* and its *Sequel* as sites of nationalist and uncanny memory."]

Nabers, Deak. *Victory of Law: The Fourteenth Amendment, the Civil War, and American Literature, 1852–1867.* Baltimore: Johns Hopkins University Press, 2006. [Examines in detail the history of and debate over the Fourteenth Amendment to the U.S. Constitution, written by John Bingham; places Bingham's amendment in the context of Whitman's *Drum-Taps* and Melville's *Battle-Pieces,* and finds that "what Whitman's poetry observes and describes, Bingham's compendium of 'pleasant phrases' actually does."]

Trethewey, Natasha. "On Whitman, Civil War Memory, and My South." *Virginia Quarterly Review* 81 (Spring 2005): 50–57. [Suggests that "Whitman's take on the South is much like my own; it is a love/hate relationship," and examines how "the narratives of blacks" have been "relegated to the margins of public memory" in the South, another version of how "the real war will not get into the books," as Whitman said.]

Wardrop, Daneen. "Civil War Nursing Narratives: Whitman's *Memoranda During the*

War and Eroticism." *Walt Whitman Quarterly Review* 23 (Summer/Fall 2005): 26–47. [Demonstrates how Whitman's *Memoranda* "shares with the nursing narratives that preceded his work some important aspects of style and tone," and offers a "cultural assessment" of Whitman's book "within the context of those previous memoirs, utilizing themes of democracy, the typical American, motherhood, and . . . the eroticism that forms between nurse and patient."]

Feldman, Mark B. "Remembering a Convulsive War: Whitman's *Memoranda During the War* and the Therapeutics of Display." *Walt Whitman Quarterly Review* 23 (Summer/Fall 2005): 1–25. [Argues that "the war of disunion and the subsequent dismembering of bodies . . . convulsed and stalled Whitman's poetics, which depended upon a series of metaphoric relations between body, nation, and text," and that through a series of "gruesome narrative displays, Whitman struggled to find a way to represent the war therapeutically," inventing in *Memoranda* "a representational form that would preserve the convulsiveness of the period."]

Epstein, Daniel Mark. *Lincoln and Whitman: Parallel Lives in Civil War Washington.* New York: Ballantine, 2004. [Tracks the "parallel lives" of Lincoln and Whitman from the day that Lincoln first read *Leaves of Grass* to Whitman's delivering his Lincoln lecture, with a focus on their intersecting lives in Washington, D.C., during the Civil War.]

Herrington, Eldrid. "Fit Compositions: Whitman's Revisions to *Drum-Taps*." In Michael Hinds and Stephen Matterson, eds., *Rebound: The American Poetry Book* (Amsterdam: Rodopi, 2004), 29–43. [Examines Whitman's changes in the sequencing of poems in the 1865 *Drum-Taps*, the 1871 cluster "Drum-Taps," and the 1881 "Drum-Taps," arguing that "in shifting the 'intervals' between poems, Whitman recomposes them, and himself," and that, "for Whitman, re-sequencing his poetry is one continuous act of self-composition."]

Samuels, Shirley. *Facing America: Iconography and the Civil War.* New York: Oxford University Press, 2004. [Chapter 3, "The Face of the Nation," examines "the category of memory" by analyzing "visual accounts of the Civil War," including Whitman's "A March in the Ranks Hard-Prest, and the Road Unknown" and "Over the Carnage Rose Prophetic a Voice," arguing that the "faces that appear" in Whitman's writings "fluctuate between specificity and mass representativeness," and that "Whitman finds in such collections, and in his appreciation of the collectivity, a way to express longing and even desire"; Chapter 5, "Lincoln's Body," considers "the historical treatments of Lincoln's embalming and funeral train," and discusses "When Lilacs Last in the Dooryard Bloom'd."]

Nudelman, Franny. *John Brown's Body: Slavery, Violence, and the Culture of War.* Chapel Hill: University of North Carolina Press, 2004. [Chapter 3, "This Compost: Death and Regeneration in Civil War Poetry," investigates how Whitman's Civil War poetry develops his composting idea, and how he "describes (at the very least) two different ways of conceptualizing the dead and our relation to them: we can hold tightly to the relic, the material trace (however inscrutable) of a particular life; or we can take the absence of the corpse—most powerfully signified by the land's fertility and beauty—as an occasion to affirm the ongoing presence of the dead"; argues that *Drum-Taps* "represents the mourner's encounter with the dead as a necessary, if painful, step in the development of national community," and explains how Whitman structures his "narrative of war as a well-ordered procession that moves, in a simple, elegant rhythm, from past (innocence) to present (death) to future (unity)."]

Tang, Edward. "The Civil War as Revolutionary Reenactment: Walt Whitman's 'The Centenarian's Story.'" *Walt Whitman Quarterly Review* 21 (Winter/Spring 2004): 131–54. [Argues that Whitman's "poetic formalism" in "The Centenarian's Story" "stemmed from conventional themes deeply rooted in remembrances about the Revolution that pervaded the nation throughout the nineteenth century," and offers a reading of Whitman's poem against the backdrop of popular writings about Revolutionary War veterans, concluding that Whitman was "a participant in the trends of collective remembrance located in popular literature" as he "portrayed the Civil War . . . as a revolutionary reenactment—an intricate replaying with new variations—of challenges and heroics past."]

Hutchinson, George. "Race and the Family Romance: Whitman's Civil War." *Walt Whitman Quarterly Review* 20 (Winter/Spring 2003): 134–50. [Examines "the implications of Whitman's experience of the Civil War as a familial tragedy, remembering Whitman as a member of a white, New York working-class family that was experiencing continuous trauma throughout the war years," leading to Whitman's "striking transformation of the poetry of war into a poetry of primary relationships, attachment and loss," but also leaving "the relation of African Americans to the Civil War almost entirely unspoken, unrepresentable," because blacks did "not belong to the national 'family' Whitman imagined and addressed."]

Sychterz, Jeff. "'Silently Watch(ing) the Dead': The Modern Disillusioned War Poet and the Crisis of Representation in Whitman's *Drum-Taps*." *Discourse* 25 (Fall 2003): 9–29. [Offers "an analysis of the 1871 edition of *Drum-Taps*" in order to track Whitman's "compelling trajectory of poetic voice corrupted by the strange materiality of battlefield corpses," a trajectory that offers "the clearest statement of poetic voice shifting from idealistic nationalism to realistic horror" as Whitman becomes the first "modern War Poet."]

Dawes, James. *The Language of War: Literature and Culture in the U.S. from the Civil War Through World War II*. Cambridge, MA: Harvard University Press, 2002. [Chapter 1, "Counting on the Battlefield: Literature and Philosophy After the Civil War," has a section on "Alcott and Whitman" arguing that Louisa May Alcott and Whitman "represent the two opposed poles of war writing, and indeed of representation in general," as Alcott "risks exclusion" while Whitman "risks dehumanization," since "the contrast between Whitman and Alcott might be described as the contrast between the statistical and the narrative imagination."]

Blight, David W. *Race and Reunion: The Civil War in American Memory.* Cambridge, MA: Harvard University Press, 2001. [One section (18–25) discusses Whitman's "literary testament" to the Civil War and the ways he found in the war "authentic tragedy, as well as his own Homeric sense of self."]

Folsom, Ed. "Lucifer and Ethiopia: Whitman, Race, and Poetics Before the Civil War and After." In David S. Reynolds, ed., *A Historical Guide to Walt Whitman* (New York: Oxford University Press, 2000), 45–95. [Investigates how, "during his career, Whitman's attitudes toward African Americans altered significantly"; focuses on "two key figures in his poetry, the only two black characters to whom he gave voice in *Leaves of Grass*: 'Lucifer,' a young male slave who appears in Whitman's 1855 poem that he eventually named 'The Sleepers,' and 'Ethiopia,' an old female emancipated slave who appears in his 1870 poem 'Ethiopia Saluting the Colors'"; examines how "Ethiopia" relates to *Democratic Vistas*.]

Morris, Roy, Jr. *The Better Angel: Walt Whitman in the Civil War.* New York: Oxford University Press, 2000. [Detailed biography of Whitman during the Civil War years.]

Buell, Lawrence. "American Civil War Poetry and the Meaning of Literary Commodification: Whitman, Melville, and Others." In Steven Fink and Susan S. Williams, eds., *Reciprocal Influences: Literary Production, Distribution, and Consumption in America* (Columbus: Ohio State University Press, 1999), 123–38. [Looks at *Drum-Taps* in relation to the numerous other books of Civil War poetry that were available in the 1860s marketplace and argues that "although *Drum-Taps* probably earned Whitman nothing at the time, its carefully cultivated rebound effect yielded him a modest financial return, and . . . helped advance him to the threshold of canonicity"; reads "Come Up from the Fields, Father" as a successful melding of mass-market appeal and "avant-garde" aesthetics.]

Cushman, Stephen. *Bloody Promendade: Reflections on a Civil War Battle.* Charlottesville: University Press of Virginia, 1999. [Offers a "history of verbal and visual images" of the Battle of the Wilderness (May 5–6, 1864): Chapter 6, "Eyewitness," discusses Whitman's *Memoranda During the War* and his Civil War correspondence, and Chapter 13, "Poems," deals with *Drum-Taps* in relation to other Civil War poems.]

Mullins, Maire. "Stopping History in Walt Whitman's *Drum-Taps*." *Walt Whitman Quarterly Review* 17 (Summer/Fall 1999): 4–14. [Argues that the *Drum-Taps* poems tell two different histories, one the "larger story of the war" and the other—inserted in moments of "frozen" time—the story "of comradeship and homoerotic desire."]

Loving, Jerome. "Caresser of Life: Walt Whitman and the Civil War." *Walt Whitman Quarterly Review* 15 (Fall 1997 / Winter 1998): 67–86. [Excerpted from the opening chapter of Loving's *Walt Whitman: The Song of Himself*, this essay gathers extant information about the poet's life to provide a context for understanding Whitman's vacillating attitudes toward the Civil War.]

Thomas, M. Wynn. "Weathering the Storm: Whitman and the Civil War." *Walt Whit-*

man Quarterly Review 15 (Fall 1997 / Winter 1998): 87–109. [Uses a variety of sources including *Memoranda During the War, Specimen Days*, and *Drum-Taps* to examine Whitman's responses to the weather during the Civil War, investigating how weather worked as a trope for Whitman and how it carried meaning differently during the time of the Civil War than it does today.]

Ramsey, Julianne. "A British View to an American War: Whitman's 'Drum-Taps' Cluster and the Editorial Influence of William Michael Rossetti." *Walt Whitman Quarterly Review* 14 (Spring 1997): 166–75. [Examines William Michael Rossetti's editorial influence on the "Drum-Taps" cluster in *Leaves of Grass* and details arrangements of Whitman's Civil War poems by Whitman and Rossetti, arguing that the sequence, "as ultimately presented to the world by Whitman, owes its essential structure and meaning to Rossetti's editorial pioneering of 1868."]

Davis, Robert Leigh. *Whitman and the Romance of Medicine*. Berkeley: University of California Press, 1997. [Analyzes Whitman's Civil War hospital writings and related texts, including *Drum-Taps, Democratic Vistas*, and *Memoranda During the War*, viewing these works and Whitman's nursing experiences as central to his conceptions of democracy.]

Eiselein, Gregory. *Literature and Humanitarian Reform in the Civil War Era*. Bloomington: Indiana University Press, 1996. [Chapter 5, "Whitman and the Humanitarian Possibilities of Lilacs," focuses on the consolatory work of *Sequel to Drum-Taps*.]

Murray, Martin. "Traveling with the Wounded: Walt Whitman and Washington's Civil War Hospitals." *Washington History* 8 (Fall/Winter 1996–97), 58–73, 92–93. [Reviews Whitman's experiences in Washington hospitals, discusses the number and nature of the hospitals, gives information about some of Whitman's favorite patients, and reports the positive and negative responses of some doctors and nurses to Whitman's presence there.]

Thomas, M. Wynn. "Fratricide and Brotherly Love: Whitman and the Civil War." In Ezra Greenspan, ed., *The Cambridge Companion to Walt Whitman* (Cambridge: Cambridge University Press, 1995), 27–44. [Proposes that Whitman's Civil War soldier-brother George gave the poet key insights into and vicarious experiences of the war—"it was at least partly through George that Whitman was led to an intimate understanding of the real, hidden nature of the war"—and suggests that George was the source of "several of those imaginative configurations that articulated [Walt's] hopes and anxieties and that supplied the deep structure of his war poetry."]

Pollak, Vivian R. "Whitman Unperturbed: The Civil War and After." In Ed Folsom, ed., *Walt Whitman: The Centennial Essays* (Iowa City: University of Iowa Press, 1994), 30–47. [Pyschobiographical reading of "When Lilacs Last in the Dooryard Bloom'd," with an emphasis on Whitman's antipresidential sentiment and his subtle complicity in the act he condemns.]

Hutchinson, George. "Whitman's Confidence Game: The 'Good Gray Poet' and the Civil

War." *South Central Review* 7 (Spring 1990): 20–35. [Analyzes the ways that Whitman constructed, in the postwar years, a final stoic pose that allowed him to maintain an untarnished claim to his construction of the Civil War's meaning as the bloody initiation of American democracy.]

Sweet, Timothy. *Traces of War: Poetry, Photography, and the Crisis of the Union.* Baltimore: Johns Hopkins University Press, 1990. [Chapter 1, "Whitman's *Drum-Taps* and the Rhetoric of War," investigates how "*Drum-Taps* is important . . . for its revealing treatment of some of the common rhetorical structures that explained and justified the war": "the poems both reflect and reflect on the contemporary construction of the 'reality' of the war." Chapter 2, "'The Real War Will Never Get in the Books,'" argues that "in Whitman's poetics, as in Lincoln's politics, the pastoral provides a powerful, typifying structure of recuperation," as "both Whitman and Lincoln represent America as but one harmonious and undifferentiated landscape."]

Erkkila, Betsy. *Whitman the Political Poet.* New York: Oxford University Press, 1989. [Chapters 8 ("The Union War"), 9 ("Burying President Lincoln"), and 10 ("'Who Bridle Leviathan?'") rethink Whitman's relationship to the war by conceiving of it in a political context—how "the American political imagination" was "haunted" by "the specter of civil war as the just retribution for the sin of slavery"—and tracing how Whitman moves from the "poet-prophet" of the prewar years to the "poet-historian" during the war years, "preserving a record of the present moment for future generations."]

Shively, Charley, ed. *Drum Beats: Walt Whitman's Civil War Boy Lovers.* San Francisco: Gay Sunshine Press, 1989. [Collects and analyzes letters to Whitman from Civil War soldiers.]

Larson, Kerry C. *Whitman's Drama of Consensus.* Chicago: University of Chicago Press, 1988. [Chapter 9, "*Drum-Taps* and Beyond," examines how "the war had been foreshadowed in *Leaves of Grass* all along" and how *Drum-Taps* embodies "neither the overthrow nor a hardening of the poet's democratic idealism but a seemingly inevitable and in many respects brutal extension of its consequences," becoming a book that "strips names, places, and dates from the battle scenes it recounts, all the while implying that its essential mission is not to understand the war but survive it," as it becomes fixated on death and ultimately seeks to "negotiate some bridge between the slain and those surviving."]

Thomas, M. Wynn. *The Lunar Light of Whitman's Poetry.* Cambridge, MA: Harvard University Press, 1987. [Chapter 7, "The Other Civil War," examines how, for Whitman, "the war always seemed less an effort to free the slave than a struggle to liberate the common man, the average Northerner, the quintessential American," to conceive of it as "an artisanal revolution," a "fight of the people to secure authentic, popular democracy against its enemies both North and South"; Chapter 8, "The Pains and Obligations of Memory," tracks how Whitman dealt in the postwar years with the "brutal contrast between the dead or dying and the ruthlessly on-going society of the living," and how he took on the role of veteran who had never fought in the war.]

Cady, Joseph. "*Drum-Taps* and Nineteenth-Century Male Homosexual Literature." In Joann P. Krieg, ed., *Walt Whitman: Here and Now* (Westport, CT: Greenwood Press, 1985), 49–59. [Discusses "some of Whitman's *Drum-Taps* poems as documents of nineteenth-century male homosexual literature."]

Burrison, William. "Whitman's *Drum-Taps* Reviewed: The Good Gray, Tender Mother-Man and the Fierce, Red, Convulsive Rhythm of War." In Joann P. Krieg, ed., *Walt Whitman: Here and Now* (Westport, CT: Greenwood Press, 1985), 157–69. [Compares the 1865 *Drum-Taps* with the final 1881 cluster of poems "Drum-Taps," finding the latter more artfully constructed, with "three major movements."]

French, Roberts W. "Whitman on War: Four Poems from *Drum-Taps*." *Walt Whitman Quarterly Review* 3 (Summer 1985): 22–24. [Argues against previous critics' claims that the "order in which the poems appear in *Leaves of Grass* is of dubious significance" by demonstrating how four poems from *Drum-Taps*—"Cavalry Crossing a Ford," "Bivouac on a Mountain Side," "An Army Corps on the March," and "By the Bivouac's Fitful Flame"—form a coherent sequence.]

Thomas, M. Wynn. "Whitman and the American Democratic Identity Before and During the Civil War." *Journal of American Studies* 15 (April 1981): 73–93. [Examines Whitman's politics before and during the war; analyzes his changing attitudes toward Washington, D.C., in the war years; and reexamines the neglected poems at the beginning and end of *Drum-Taps*, finding them more complex and conflicted than previously thought.]

Askin, Denise T. "Retrievements Out of the Night: Prophetic and Private Voices in Whitman's 'Drum-Taps.'" *ATQ: The American Transcendental Quarterly*, no. 51 (Summer 1981): 211–23. [Argues that "two voices" emerge in *Drum-Taps*—"the prophetic and the private"—the first biblical, distant, and seeking "'Columbia's' grand destiny," the other finding "resolution only when the ghastly facts of warfare are faced in all their power."]

Ignoffo, Matthew F. *What the War Did to Whitman: A Brief Study of the Effects of the Civil War on the Mind of Walt Whitman*. New York: Vantage Press, 1975. [Argues that Whitman's metamorphosis from "hack" journalist to great poet was brought about by a successful struggle with the turmoil and doubt which afflicted America and the American Dream prior to and during the Civil War.]

Loving, Jerome M., ed. *Civil War Letters of George Washington Whitman*. Durham, NC: Duke University Press, 1975. [Contains an introduction on the Whitman family and the efforts to gain George Whitman's release from a Confederate prison; prints sixty-one letters by George, George Whitman's Civil War Diary, and other materials.]

Cannon, Agnes Dicken. "Fervid Atmosphere and Typical Events: Autobiography in *Drum-Taps*." *Walt Whitman Review* 20 (September 1974): 79–96. [Argues that we can identify many autobiographical elements in *Drum-Taps* and *Sequel to Drum-Taps*, with Whitman's poems divided into three groups: (1) "the reveille poems," (2) "the poems of camp and hospital," and (3) "the poems of victory and reconciliation which include the Lincoln poems"; and proposes that the quality of Whitman's Civil War poetry is dependent on the extent of his emotional involvement with his subject matter.]

Hudson, Vaughan. "Melville's *Battle-Pieces* and Whitman's *Drum-Taps*: A Comparison." *Walt Whitman Review* 19 (September 1973): 81–92. [Notes how, in *Battle-Pieces* and *Drum-Taps*, Melville and Whitman are alike in their dedication "to the preservation of the Union, victory for the Northern forces, the abolition of slavery, and compassion for the South," but that they differ in point of view and tone, with Melville cold, intellectual, sometimes cynical, and detached, and Whitman immediately involved, personal, reflective, and anguished.]

Snyder, John. "The Irony of National Union: Violence and Compassion in *Drum-Taps*." *Canadian Review of American Studies* 4 (Fall 1973): 169–83. [Argues that Whitman's Civil War poetry expresses a paradoxical relation between love for the ideal of union and the destruction that this commitment entails, so violence and compassion intermingle in *Drum-Taps*, echoing the combination of erotic force and comradely peace in "Calamus."]

Hibler, David J. "*Drum-Taps* and *Battle-Pieces*: Melville and Whitman on the Civil War." *Personalist* 50 (Winter 1969): 130–47. [Proposes that Whitman's *Drum-Taps* and Melville's *Battle-Pieces* do not contain great poetry but are candid reflections of the personalities and visions of their authors as well as valuable records of the expectations and frustrations of the Civil War era; concludes that Whitman emerged from the war with his fundamental optimism renewed and strengthened, while Melville looked toward the future with characteristic apprehensiveness and pessimism.]

Fredrickson, George M. *The Inner Civil War: Northern Intellectuals and the Crisis of the Union*. New York: Harper & Row, 1965. [Demonstrates how the Civil War profoundly affected Whitman and how he combined the role of compassionate comforter of the wounded and dying with the role of democratic imperialist; concludes that he eventually turned away from the particulars of suffering and death and dealt with his experience in terms of generalities and abstractions.]

Sullivan, Edward E., Jr. "Thematic Unfolding in Whitman's *Drum-Taps*." *Emerson Society Quarterly*, no. 31 (Second Quarter, 1963): pt. 2, 42–45. [Argues that *Drum-Taps* chronicles Whitman's developing and changing emotional response to the Civil War.]

Toperoff, Sam. "Reconciliation of Polarity in Whitman's *Drum-Taps*." *Emerson Society Quarterly*, no. 31 (Second Quarter, 1963): pt. 2, 45–47. [Notes that in *Drum-Taps* Whitman gives repeated expression to certain polarities—rural/urban, life/death, past/present, present/future, and most important, war/peace—and, in exploring the psychological, philosophical, and social conflicts that arise from these polar forces,

Whitman develops a philosophical view of unity through diversity, thus enabling a reconciliation of the dualisms.]

Cox, James M. "Walt Whitman, Mark Twain, and the Civil War." *Sewanee Review* 69 (April–June 1961): 185–204. [Demonstrates how Mark Twain fled from the chaos of the Civil War, creating years later "a past in which the issues that had torn a nation apart were reconstructed and played out in a child's world," while Whitman anticipated and prepared himself to confront the nation's political division and paralysis, and created in his poetry a personality that looked forward to the role that he himself would assume in the war, fashioning a future that could contain the dividing Union.]

Miller, F. DeWolfe, ed. Introduction to *Walt Whitman's "Drum-Taps" (1865) and "Sequel to Drum-Taps" (1865–6).* Gainesville, FL: Scholars' Facsimiles & Reprints, 1959. [Offers a detailed study of those "facts directly related to the composition and publication of the volume, set in an outline of data concerning [Whitman's] goings and comings."]

The Afterlives of Specimens: Science, Mourning, and Whitman's Civil War
by Lindsay Tuggle

Conserving Walt Whitman's Fame: Selections from Horace Traubel's "Conservator," 1890–1919
edited by Gary Schmidgall

Constructing the German Walt Whitman
by Walter Grünzweig

Democratic Vistas: The Original Edition in Facsimile
by Walt Whitman, edited by Ed Folsom

Every Hour, Every Atom: A Collection of Walt Whitman's Early Notebooks and Fragments
edited by Zachary Turpin and Matt Miller

The Evolution of Walt Whitman
by Roger Asselineau

Intimate with Walt: Selections from Whitman's Conversations with Horace Traubel, 1888–1892
edited by Gary Schmidgall

Leaves of Grass, 1860: The 150th Anniversary Facsimile Edition
by Walt Whitman, edited by Jason Stacy

Life and Adventures of Jack Engle
by Walt Whitman, introduction by Zachary Turpin

"The Million Dead, Too, Summ'd Up": Walt Whitman's Civil War Writings; A Selection with Commentary by Ed Folsom and Christopher Merrill
by Ed Folsom and Christopher Merrill

A Place for Humility: Whitman, Dickinson, and the Natural World
by Christine Gerhardt

The Pragmatic Whitman: Reimagining American Democracy
by Stephen John Mack

Selected Letters of Walt Whitman
edited by Edwin Haviland Miller

Song of Myself: With a Complete Commentary
by Walt Whitman, introduction and commentary by Ed Folsom and Christopher Merrill

Supplement to "Walt Whitman: A Descriptive Bibliography"
by Joel Myerson

"This Mighty Convulsion": Whitman and Melville Write the Civil War
edited by Christopher Sten and Tyler Hoffman

Transatlantic Connections: Whitman U.S., Whitman U.K.
by M. Wynn Thomas

Visiting Walt: Poems Inspired by the Life and Work of Walt Whitman
edited by Sheila Coghill and Thom Tammaro

Walt Whitman: The Centennial Essays
edited by Ed Folsom

Walt Whitman: The Correspondence, Volume VII
edited by Ted Genoways

Walt Whitman and the Class Struggle
by Andrew Lawson

Walt Whitman and the Earth: A Study in Ecopoetics
by M. Jimmie Killingsworth

Walt Whitman and the World
edited by Gay Wilson Allen and Ed Folsom

Walt Whitman, Where the Future Becomes Present
edited by David Haven Blake and Michael Robertson

Walt Whitman's Reconstruction: Poetry and Publishing Between Memory and History
by Martin T. Buinicki

Walt Whitman's Selected Journalism
edited by Douglas A. Noverr and Jason Stacy

Walt Whitman's "Song of Myself": A Mosaic of Interpretations
by Edwin Haviland Miller

Walt Whitman's Songs of Male Intimacy and Love: "Live Oak, with Moss" and "Calamus"
edited by Betsy Erkkila

Whitman & Dickinson: A Colloquy
edited by Éric Athenot and Cristanne Miller

Whitman Among the Bohemians
edited by Joanna Levin and Edward Whitley

Whitman and the Irish
by Joann P. Krieg

A Whitman Chronology
by Joann P. Krieg

Whitman East and West: New Contexts for Reading Walt Whitman
edited by Ed Folsom

Whitman Noir: Black America and the Good Gray Poet
edited by Ivy G. Wilson

The Whitman Revolution: Sex, Politics, and Democracy
by Betsy Erkkila

Whitman's Drift: Imagining Literary Distribution
by Matt Cohen